Other books by the author:

Longrider
The Ghost of Scootertrash Past
Hard Scrabble

The **L**onesome **L**owdown **L**ong-gone **O**utbound **S**cootertrash **B**lues

Mark K. Tiger Edmonds

Livingston Press
The University of West Alabama

Copyright © 2011 Mark K. Edmonds
All rights reserved, including electronic text
isbn 13: 978-1-60489-082-2 library binding
isbn 13: 978-1-60489-083-9 trade paper
Library of Congress Control Number 2011931227
Printed on acid-free paper.
Printed in the United States of America by
United Graphics
Hardcover binding by: Heckman Bindery
Typesetting and page layout: Joe Taylor
Proofreading: Joe Taylor, Stephanie Murray,
Connie James
Cover design: Jyn Brown
Cover photo: Ray "Shooter" Hale

Livingston Press is part of The University of West Alabama,
and thereby has non-profit status.
Donations are tax-deductible:
brothers and sisters, we need 'em.

first edition

6 5 4 3 3 2 1

The **L**onesome
Lowdown
Long-gone
Outbound
Scootertrash
Blues

PRERAMBLE, DISCLAIMERS, and DEDICATION

When my first book like this, *Longrider*, went into a third printing, the publisher called and asked me could I do it again. I told him if he'd let me do it two or three more times, I figured I might could get it right.

That resulted in a second book of motorcycle stories. They called that one *The Ghost Of Scootertrash Past*. I wanted to call the first one either *On The Road* or *War and Peace*, and the second one *More Scooterstories* or maybe *Roadkill Encounters*. I am not allowed to name my books. Everyone is real glad I never had children.

Since then I have rode a few more miles and had several more experiences worth telling about. Beyond new roads and tales, I've managed some introspection here in my dotage. So there are some ruminations and reflections and rants. And there have been a few breakthroughs in the ever-increasing senility that have permitted me to dredge up a few more memories from the long gone by, the distant past, and them bygone days of yore. And the statute of limitations has run out in a few instances.

Be a damn shame if these stories and perspectives were lost to history and censorship and neglect and a lack of bein' told.

Like the first books, this here one is total gospel truth. Except of course in the instances where I find myself confessing to crimes that are still pending in certain jurisdictions.

The moral of it all seems to be that The Ride Goes On Forever and The Highway Never Ends. Here we go again.

To quote further from the old song, The Lonesome Lowdown Long-gone Outbound Scootertrash Blues, We're all of us bound for Glory, and some of us have some stories about goin' at it the long way around and takin' the hard way out.

*

Prof. W. Joe Taylor sent the manuscript for this one back to me with more things to fix than he had on my previous three books, all together. Pissed me off. But I sat down and went to work on it. Took me a real long time. When I was done, it was a much better book. And that really pissed me off. Thanks again, Joe.

**

This has been a bad few years for losing old longtime goodfriends. This book is for my mom, Leila, and my Aunt Ruth, and for Nancy Pacey and Ken Johnson and Snake Yamka, and Pop Burney and Reb and Amtrak and Emma and Itty Bitty, and Floyde Nichols, for Dick McElroy, Mother T., Lorise Abraham, and Maura Snyder, and Dirk Budd and Judy Lawrence and Doug Simms, my cousin Tom Miron, for my dad, Gail Edmonds, and for my Uncle, Keith Edmonds. I miss you all.

***

My middle name is Keith. I was named for my uncle. I have always been real proud of that. He was one of the finest men I ever knew. He was my uncle and my big brother and an extra dad and my best friend. And with him gone, I am pretty much on my own now. Over the course of my life, my Grandpaw, Virgil, and my daddy, Gail, and my Uncle Keith all took a hand in raising me. They quite literally made me the man I am. And I'm grateful.

TABLE OF CONTENTS

chapter one
OLD COPS, NEW COPS, FAME (?),
and NEW TIME RELIGION

I over-tarried in Michigan a day longer than I had intended to. The TV weather conjecture folks had predicted rain all around the bottom end of Lake Erie. As I was headed to New England, and, as I am no longer willing to cross international borders, I decided to set it out and leave a day later in the dry.

It was a chilly, windy, overcast morning when I headed south down out of Michigan. It remained that kind of day until evening, when it got dark. I think I rode the whole day with my leather on. And for the most part, other than through the horror that is Cleveland, I ran most of the day on two-lanes and back roads.

The run around the south shore was really pretty uneventful. I wound up in some little Ohio lakeshore town for a late breakfast, and I got fed especially well. Then I got lost in Sandusky. That's easier than you might think. In my disoriented wanderings, I came upon the local police station there beside the lake.

There were two cops in a car in the parking lot, so I rode up beside their squad car. The one behind the wheel rolled his window down. It turned out to be an old cop and a young cop-in-training. The kiddie cop began to clumsily go for his gun before I could shut my bike off. The senior cop reached over and patted the boy on his gun hand, scowled and shook his head. He looked at me wearily and smiled.

I took my helmet off and commented, "Who says you can't ever find a cop when you need one?"

That made the old cop smile some more. It was obvious that my witticism was lost on his youthful colleague, who continued to frown and kept his hand near his gun. Then I told the old cop that I was lost and needed help. I called him sir and said please.

And he kept smiling as he looked at me real serious and said, real slow, in several long, well-articulated syllables, "You-are- in-San-dus-ky, O-hi-o." He pointed at me and then at the ground I was parked on.

The young cop-in-training was still sort of wiggling around, getting his hand nearer his gun. But when me and the old cop both busted up laughing over his clever repartee, even the over-eager lad had to give up on the pretext that I might be dangerous or up to something.

When the laughter had subsided, I told the old road cop that I knew I was in Sandusky, but I was real eager to find my way out of there and on to someplace else. He laughed and asked which way was I hoping to escape. I told him I was going east, and he peered at me a moment, trying to determine how dumb I really was, I presume. After all, I was lost in Sandusky.

Then he gave me some medium complex, but real explicit local directions. I repeated them back to him, and he nodded and smiled. I said my thank yous and rolled out of the parking lot eastbound. In my mirrors I could see the veteran highway cop, facing his youthful apprentice, administering what I assumed was a lesson in stereotypes, manners, respect, and old riders.

Later that day, after I had gotten on the superslab to fight my way through Cleveland, I found myself pulling into a rest area on I-90 up there where Ohio, and Pennsylvania, and New York all come together. There was a brand new BMW 1100 RT road bike with California plates at one end of the parking area. And there was an older BMW, a K-bike, about in the middle of the parking strip. It had New York plates. Both were loaded for long-distance travel.

I couldn't see either rider, so I rolled on down to the far end and parked my own ride in some thin shade. Got my Thermos and a road map out of a saddlebag and sat at a picnic table to study the map and drink a cup of coffee and eat an apple.

Having figured out my next couple logistical moves and finished my coffee, I headed for the bathroom. Coming out, I saw one of the riders at a nearby picnic table, the guy with the New York K-bike it turned out. He waved, so I wandered his way, and when I got up to him I said hello and asked him was he headed to the rally up in Massachusetts.

He smiled up at me from his bench at the picnic table, set his sandwich down, swallowed and said, "You rode all the way up here from Florida, didn't you?" He kept smiling, but it made me uneasy.

I knew he hadn't had a chance to see my license plate, and I wasn't wearing my Mouse ears. I knew I wasn't dropping orange peels or beach sand and suntan oil behind me. And I knew I didn't sound like a native Floridian. All I knew for sure was that he was younger and bigger than me. And he was smiling way too much. Confused and wary, I stepped back some.

He laughed and said, "And you write poetry, don't you?" By now I was cursing my senility as I tried to remember if I had brought a gun, and if I had, which pocket was it in. I backed away another step and looked foolish. After that poetry thing, I feared he would accuse me of being able to dance or maybe arrange flowers.

The rider finally got some control of his mirth and introduced himself between chuckles. Andy The Music Man. The folks running the Damn Yankee BMW Rally in Heath, Massachusetts had given him a copy of one of my poetry CDs in hopes that he would provide some live backup music for me when I told them a poem one night at the rally. And he had recognized my voice. We hugged one another like family. Beyond being relieved, I was real glad to find a highway brother, especially in the far north among Yankees and all.

I've had this happen a few times actually. People tend to recognize me. Usually it's my voice, typically from those poetry CDs. But sometimes they've seen my book covers or an article in a magazine or newspaper or something, and they identify me that way. That visual recognition thing is, of course, more difficult, as we all look alike.

Seems like most of the time it's a real big guy. Most of the time it seems to be a young, big guy, thereby eliminating the option of running. I had one big old boy awhile back, down to the local Flyin' J, who kept peering at me funny while I was gassing up my scooter. Finally he began to walk toward me, purposefully. The man was about six feet eight and weighed well over three hundred pounds. As he advanced, his shadow covered me long before he got close, and he said, "You're that boy they call Tiger, ain't you?"

I had several seconds as he lumbered toward and loomed over me to think about it. The best I came up with was to shower him with gasoline from the hose I had in my hand and then whip out my Zippo and threaten him with immolation. Turned out the guy and his wife had read my first two books, and he wanted to buy some more for his buddies. So instead of having to fight, I sold a couple copies of my books.

Women somehow seem to pick up on that voice thing more and sooner than most men. Several years back, I returned to the Great Northern University where I was once employed. I ran into a former colleague there and was standing talking to her in the hallway. Four secretaries heard and recognized my voice from twenty-some years ago and came out of their offices to join us.

One time, years ago, my voice made me some money. I've been variously told I sound like Johnny Cash, Don Williams, or Sam Elliott. Either way, I got hired to do the radio voice-over work for a bunch of boot commercials. Before it was over, I wound up writing the ads, too. It was great work with wonderful people, all professionals. The radio ads, I think there were six of them, played for a long time. Then the boot people decided to do some TV commercials as well. Again, I was hired to do the voice-over work and most of the writing.

By now I thought I knew what I was doing. That's almost always an error. But by now I was being treated well and put into a smoking-permitted sound booth and had people fetching coffee for me. I even had a shaded parking place for my scooter. By now I had a little clip-on ID card that identified me as "Talent" and permitted me to wander about the huge recording complex at will. The next error was believing that little ID card.

I was in the sound studio, in the sensory deprivation booth with the electronic earmuffs on and all, on a telephone conference call involving about half the Known World. The discussion centered on doing that series of television commercials.

There were boot manufacturing company executives and their lawyers, there were representatives of the FCC and several other radio policing groups and their lawyers, there were high-level advertising agency people and their lawyers, there were representatives of the major boot distributors and their lawyers, and there was the local producer and the sound engineer and the entire studio staff, and all their lawyers.

The lawyers had gotten into it earlier when I had written and recorded a couple lines which had been censored and labeled "politically incorrect," "potentially libelous," and "sure to piss people off." Oddly, one of the lines purged had referred to "slick lawyers." Apparently they found that redundant.

Anyway, in the middle of this multiple technological nine-way telephone conversation, I spoke up and suggested that I could do the TV work, appear on camera and all. Again, it was a combination of greed and thinking I knew what I was doing that got me into this. I figured it was a BOOT commercial, and from the knees down, who'd know? The signal was given to the sound engineer to throw the switch to cut me off so I couldn't hear or participate in the extended discussion which followed my inquiry. But he and I had become friends, and he just smiled and let me listen in. He did cut off the line that would have permitted me to respond to anything.

The various corporate boot people and their legal staffs on the long-distance phone began by asking those in the studio what I looked like. Everyone turned to observe me through the glass. I felt like an exhibit in a zoo, or maybe in a police line-up.

One of those in attendance peered at me through the glass of the recording booth and said I looked like every other burned out old biker he had ever seen. Another said I looked like Sam Elliott, only more beat up and run over. A third suggested an unattractive hybrid between Willie Nelson and Charles Bronson.

The local production guy and his wife who had played the pretty background guitar music, they went for "Really skinny, but kind of threatening and dangerous looking."

A little girl who was in charge of coffee and snacks and such, she said I looked sinister. Another one said she thought I was probably armed. The lawyers all used the words "felonious" and "liability" and "potential repercussions" and "culpability."

So I got excused from becoming a TV star. But with those six radio ads and the four TV commercials I did the vocal work for, my voice got played on the airwaves a whole lot. And on a few occasions, people, most of them telemarketers, would call me at home and recognize my voice and then forget to try to sell me some crap I didn't need. Often I would have to recall and recite a couple commercials to convince them it was really me.

That part about the TV commercials, that somehow put me in mind of a time thirty-some years back. I had ridden from Michigan down to Florida and was staying with old friends in Coconut Grove. One morning I rode to a nearby neighborhood store to get a six pack. It must have been near breakfast time. I parked my cycle out near the road, under a big tree for the shade. Then I walked across the parking lot and went in the store and got my beer and started back out to my machine in the shade in the parking lot.

As I opened the door to leave, a truly beautiful young woman clad in real short cut-off jeans and a tiny halter top was coming in the store. This girl was stone pretty. She was built like the proverbial brick structure and had long blonde hair and big blue eyes. I held the door open for her and stood aside. As she walked past me, she smiled and said thank you. Girl smiled pretty, too.

I spun around in the doorway in order to watch her walk away. Then I did one more full circle just so I could watch her walk some more. When I turned around again and got out the door, there was her friend, another beautiful young woman. This one was dressed in the same fashion as her companion, Miami Summer. She had long dark hair and pretty brown eyes, long legs and a world-class ass, and she was leaning on their car in the parking lot. She winked and smiled at me as I went by. And she said, "Hello, Pretty Boy."

I must have turned three more circles in two steps as I wheeled around to see who she was talking to and then to look at her some more. I felt like a damn merry-go-round. She kept smiling at me the whole while.

When I got straightened out and headed toward my bike again, I ran right slam into an iron sign post, face first. First and last time in my whole damn life anyone ever called me Pretty Boy. So you can imagine how it confused me greatly. Besides that, I was dizzy from all that turning around. I was glad I hadn't been on my scooter when she said it.

Yeah, I hurt myself some. Not as bad as I hurt my pride and my vanity. This was years ago, when I still had some pride and vanity. Fortunately, most of the injury was to my face. Worst part was I dropped the six pack and broke three of the beers.

By the time I had regained what was left of my composure and beer, both the pretty girls were beside their car laughing at me. Trying hard to recover some of my poise and dignity, I suggested that as long as I had three beers left, maybe they could join me in putting the survivors of the wounded six pack out of their misery. They each drank a beer with me there in the parking lot. And they both kept on laughing at me the entire time. Then, in the time-honored tradition of pretty women, they left me, alone.

And that reminded me of a portion of The Long-gone Outbound Scootertrash Blues: I knew she was bound to leave me. I knew that before she did, I believe. But she figured it out, and then she was gone. And all I was, was deceived.

Last time I had someone recognize me was awhile back at the local DMV while I was getting the papers and plate for my new bike straightened out. The woman behind the desk kept looking at me funny. I'm pretty used to this, so I just tried to be polite and all, kept my hands in plain sight and tried not make any quick moves or say anything unusually stupid.

Finally, she got up from her desk to get something and engaged one of her co-workers in conversation. They pointed and looked at me from across the room, and I became fearful that I had somehow popped up on the Local Ten Barely Wanted List or something such as that. Actually, I had just recently gotten some pretty good press on my second book in the St. Petersburg newspaper, and I suspected they had seen the article.

Eventually both women came back to where I waited and asked me if I had written a book. I confessed, and this seemed to set them at ease somehow. Apparently they had read my book or at least heard about me, as one of them said, "We're going to find you a real easy license plate number to remember."

But anymore, I've got to where when I answer the phone and someone says, "Tiger?" I ask who's lookin' for him.

Sometimes, in these situations, it's hard to recite the verse of The Lowdown Outbound Scootertrash Blues that goes, I have been abandoned and forsaken, and I have already taken my last chance and my best shot. I have been made to understand what it is that I'm worth. And I ain't worth a lot.

Anyway, this time up there in New York at the roadside rest

area, I sat and talked with Andy The Music Man at the picnic table for awhile. Andy was coming back from a Grateful Dead concert someplace in Wisconsin. He was going home to Albany before heading to the Massachusetts rally. And I was heading over into the Catskills to spend a couple days with an old friend and recently retired colleague before my own journey on to northwestern Massachusetts.

About then, the guy from California on the new 1100 RT came over and introduced himself. Pete was from someplace up north of San Francisco. He was headed to Long Island to see his brother. Andy and I convinced him to consider coming to the Massachusetts rally the next week.

For those who are looking for the irony here, Pete showed up at the Damn Yankee BMW Rally, and he won the high mileage award, having come all the way from California. Had he not accepted our invitation to join us there in Heath, I would have gotten the prize. I did, however, win a couple of attractive reflective cow decals to put on my saddlebags.

But what happened after that initial mysterious meeting at the rest area just got stranger. The three of us left back out on the highway separately, probably at ten minute intervals. Then, maybe a long hour down the line, the authorities in charge of confusing folks on the highway did themselves proud. I rode by what might have been my turnoff. The town indicated in that direction was correct, but the number on the highway was wrong. So I bailed off at the next opportunity and rolled into a gas station to get my map out and try to figure things out.

Andy The Music Man was setting on his ride in some shade there, concentrating hard on studying a map with a confused and perplexed look on his face. He was as lost as I was. I shut my bike off and rolled up beside him silently and snatched his map out of his hands and began examining it myself. Startled him. I was glad to have gotten some even.

But, a few days later, it came around again. A hundred miles or so from the rally, I had stopped for a late breakfast in Pittsfield or someplace like that. I ordered my food and then went to the bathroom to wash the highway off. When I came out of the can, old Andy The Music Man was sitting in my booth, grinning his face off and eating my breakfast. Yeah, he had seen my scooter in the parking lot on his way past and decided to mess with me some more. So I still kind of owe him one, even though he led me on to the rally after breakfast.

Actually I kind of owe him two. I told the Damn Yankees an old road poem called "Blue Moon" around a bonfire one evening at that rally. It's about a coast-to-coast run through the Summer Drought of 1988. The audience was perfect. I often find myself talking to a group of children, or a general audience of non-bikers, or a book club filled with elderly women. But this time I had a group of riders, most of them old ones with some miles.

That evening, I kept asking the President of the Damn Yankees who was running the rally when he wanted me to tell my poem. And he kept looking around and saying, "Not yet." He did that two or three times.

Finally, when he heard everyone opening their third beer, El Jefe, he smiled at me and said, "Now." Turns out Jeff Stein is a logistical genius.

Because, with Andy The Music Man and another guy playing beautiful guitar behind me, and a boy holding a flashlight over my shoulder so I could see to read, we made a whole bunch of grown-up, hard core riders near cry.

It all put me in mind of a verse from The Long-gone Lonesome Scootertrash Blues, Sometimes your hear someone bang the drum slowly. You hear a guitar play lowly, and someone speaks of the highway and other things holy, while we're just passin' through. This verse continues, Sometimes the talk is of old out and downers, of long-gone outward bounders, of times and places long ago, longriders and heartbroke rounders, and how we're all just passin' through.

Speaking of being owed something and karma and all, I was due for a wet ride sometime soon. I hadn't gotten a hundred miles from home when the deluge came upon on me. I was headed north up U.S. 98, and the storms came from the north. Luckily, I was near cover when it began. I set and watched it pour for a little while.

Then, when it finally let up some, I sucked it up and put on my rain gear and faceshield and headed out into the maelstrom. It continued to rain, on and off, mostly hard, mostly on me, from there to south of Dothan, Alabama, where it got torrential.

I mean we are talking duck strangling rain here. I couldn't see much other than the center line. Deep water was running down the road, and I was getting wet in spite of my rain gear.

I bailed off and sought shelter from the storm at the first opportunity. Rode up under an awning attached to a building that turned out to be a sort of a televangelist church of some kind. I guess it was actually the shipping building and loading dock that was attached to the television studio/chapel/videotape processing and copying lab/library complex. And while I don't know if that really counts as sanctified ground, it was dry. And that was my main concern at the moment.

The two burly gentlemen in nice haircuts, short-sleeved white shirts, and black neckties who came out to see what I was up to had other concerns, mainly barbarian pagan scootertrash on their hallowed property. But before they had a chance to tell me to leave or anything else, I ran right up and introduced myself to them both. Shook their hands and called them brother. Asked if I might continue to use their sanctuary in the tempest, spoke of weary travelers and damp pilgrims. Offered them some coffee from my Thermos. They declined the coffee, but they blessed me before they went back to sending videotapes out to true believers.

This was easily the most high-tech version of Christianity that I have ever sought shelter at. But it sure wasn't the first. I have found that churches often make pretty good places to hide from weather. Most modern churches are constructed so that there is a convenient overhang somewhere. Many rural churches have a covered pavilion area outdoors, often near the graveyard. And for the most part, other than Sunday and maybe Wednesday evenings, stray weddings and funerals, there isn't much going on at most churches most of the time.

And that reminded me of how that verse of The Outbound Long-gone Scootertrash Blues continues, Sometimes the rain gets to you. Othertimes it's the heat. Sometimes you just get beat by the stone cold concrete. And then to make it all complete, sometimes the highway cheats, and we're still just passin' through.

chapter two
YOUTHFUL AMISH ENTREPRENEURS,
WORK, and LEGENDARY LOVE

It was warm and partly sunny. It was a mid-day in mid-Summer. It was someplace in northern Indiana. I was headed north up to Michigan, and I was out there just poking along on local two-lane roads, bending north and east in a completely fanciful fashion. And I was having a real fine time, too, admiring the old farm houses and the little towns, the corn that was coming to ripe, the wildflowers, the hardwood forests.

That was when traffic came to an abrupt and complete stop. I got over left far enough to look down the road and see that it was stacked up for a long way in our lane. The other lane was empty for a real long way. The only thing I could see was an Amish restaurant and bakery up the way on the other side of the road a quarter mile.

Then I noticed two young men come out of the restaurant and walk into the road. One carried a big tray of assorted Styrofoam food containers, and the other managed the steel cash box. They approached each car and truck in the line in front of me, selling their goods to some of them. When they got close to me, I could see they were boys of thirteen or so. They wore traditional dark Amish clothing, white shirts buttoned at the collar and wrists, dress trousers, suspenders, brogan shoes, and straw hats. And they were both trying hard to grow a beard.

When they got close enough to talk to, I said to the one with the food, "Oh, wonderful, here you all are with something really good to eat, and I don't have no place at all to put it."

The kid handling the money didn't miss a beat. He smiled at me and said, "Don't worry, man. It ain't that good."

We were all three laughing as they moved on to the semi-truck behind me. And prior to this, I had no idea the Amish had a sense of humor. I knew they were solid folks, the kind who, unlike myself, tend to stay married for life, to the same woman.

In spite of my lousy marital record, I am a fortunate man for a whole lot of reasons. But one of the big ones is because it has been my luck to have been around several truly wonderful eternal love stories and great undying romances. Such a relationship is something to be revered and honored, like a look at the Shining Mountains in the morning, or riding a road through the desert in the Springtime, or crossing The River on a ferry boat. Eternal love should be venerated like watching the sun come up from the ocean.

My grandparents were married for over sixty years. My Grammaw was the only woman The Old Man ever loved. They had been married about half of that sixty years when I came on the scene. I got to watch them be happy with and because of one another. I never heard a cross word between them, but I sure heard a lot of laughter. Grampaw knew he would have been dead in his youth had it not been for my Grammaw. Me, too, probably.

My brother had a real happy twenty or so years with his wife before he got killed. He was around to see me through my first divorce and a half, and I kept asking him about his own marriage. He told me that even after all the years, everything just kept getting better, even the sex. I figured he was fucking with me and stopped listening to him. In retrospect, I wish I had taken notes.

I took my current job on the basis of such a legendary love story. The guy who hired me, who was my boss for ten or so of the best years I've known in higher education, he had a system. When interviewing someone, after he had decided to try to hire that person, he would take the applicant home with him to meet his wife. After a few minutes in his house, I figured anybody married to a woman that fine must be a pretty good man to work for. On the basis of that, I took the job. Several of my contemporary colleagues reported that he did the same thing when hiring them.

This job has worked out pretty good. I've been at it for twenty-some years now. After it became apparent that the man was going to hire me, I told him I intended to come to work on a motorcycle, wearing jeans and a black t-shirt. He had the perfect answer. He smiled and said, "Professor Edmonds, I hired an English teacher, not a fop."

After that, I got to spend some time with this couple. They were as well-matched and as devoted to one another as any two people I have ever known. The best part is that they both knew that. Some of the finest times I have ever known have been around couples like this. The other finest times in my life have, obviously, been out on the road.

As an English teacher, I get Summers off. After nine months of teaching The Legend of Literacy to contemporary post-literate, internet-dependent and -deceived students, I need to take a ride. When possible, I roll cross-country to California.

There is something about a coast-to-coast run, or a border-to-border ride, that makes you feel as if you have accomplished something. Watching the sun come up from the Atlantic and, then at the other end, watching it go down in a Pacific tide is a worthy exploit. There is something about the changes in the terrain from orange groves and swamps to bayous and hills to mountains and deserts to a whole different coast with different trees and earth that makes it a real fine ride. It provides you with, among other things, perspective. Then there is something about northern California that makes it worthwhile when you get there. And, when I get there, I am among friends, notably Captain Zero.

So there we were, me and The Captain, drifting through northern California. We had just put in a pretty weird day out there on the road. The weirdness began early that morning when we encountered a guy with an orange vest and a hard hat and a stop sign on a pole. It was a medium remote two-lane road out there in the mountains. There was nothing nor no one for miles. The man with the stop sign beckoned us near when we stopped a few yards short of him.

He smiled, one eye twitching hard in the sunlight. "You might just as well turn it off. You're going to be here for awhile."

He was smiling big by now. He was glad to have something to do, and he was elated to have some company. Zero named him CalTran Dan. Before we were let go, I was calling him other things.

We were there about forty minutes. During that time,

the highway stop sign man kept up a running monologue. He covered every topic from school reform (Drive a few school buses into every single neighborhood in America. Park them and knock the wheels off and turn them into classrooms with twenty kids, a blackboard, and a teacher), "Put a whole new slant on 'community education' "; to public transit (Hang gondola cars from the existing overhead wires all over America), "Whole country would look like Disneyland"; to punishment for rich men caught stealing corporate money, "Make them live in a crappy house in a crappy neighborhood with a crappy job and an unhappy woman and ungrateful children. Make them try to keep up the mortgage payments and grocery bills."

He confessed to several minor crimes (poaching, growing marijuana, borrowing state equipment), told us about his high school football heroics (three touchdowns one night), about working this job he was on (some days there was no traffic at all to hold his sign up for). He mentioned some time in the army ("They wouldn't let us win that fucking war, man").

He spoke about three ex-wives (the fat stupid one, the young disloyal one, and the one who needed to be in a city), four girl-friends (as these were all current relationships, I was unable to distinguish among them, but one had tattoos), two unappreciative children (the one in the cult and the one in re-hab), and minimal retirement (he had come to this job late in life) in a couple years.

CalTran Dan was bitter about the economy and inflation ("God damn price of gas and beer and cigarettes should never go over a dollar"), and he was unhappy about his own salary ("Between fertilizer and ammunition, a man can barely afford beer"). He proposed that any parent who had raised a kid to adulthood, and the kid was not in prison, a cult, or re-hab, those parents ought not to ever have to pay taxes again. He concluded with a suggestion that, "The rich white men who own this country want ALL the fucking money."

The Captain and I talked later on and agreed that the guy made for wonderful roadside entertainment; we regretted it when he got the call on his radio, turned his sign around, and sent us on our way. We could see him in our mirrors, still talking, as we rode off.

At the other end of the construction effort, which went almost all the way up to the brand new Mart-Mart Store, in whatever the next town big enough to warrant such a blessing was, there was another guy, a young man, with a stop sign on a pole. He confirmed everything CalTran Dan at the other end had told us. Then he bitched about having to drive all the damn way to Oregon in order to date a girl he wasn't related to. In spite of the Gala Grand Opening of the new Mart-Mart Store, we blew right through the town.

Next morning early, on the bank of the Trinity, Captain Zero said to me, "Tiger, next time I am in Florida, I want you to take me into the Everglades. In the meantime, what do you want to do in my part of the country?" The Captain has always been, among other things, the consummate host.

And I told him I wanted to see a whale. I explained that I had seen pilot whales and lots of dolphins and such, but I had never yet seen a real whale. He grinned and said he knew a place.

A couple hours later we were twenty miles south of the Oregon line on the north bank of the Klamath River along the Pacific Coast Highway. I was sure I had seen a Sasquatch in a little town along the way, but The Captain insisted it was a local wino.

The north shore of the Klamath is high over the river and the ocean both, several hundred feet in the air. There is a parking lot there at the official whale-watching station. There are signs identifying the various kinds of whales you are likely to see. They tell you about the whales' migration routes and so forth. We parked, and I joyfully scampered across the parking lot toward the edge of the high cliff that overlooked the Pacific Ocean so I could see my whale.

And the fog was so damn thick I couldn't even see my feet. The dense curtain of mist hung directly on the edge of the cliff. There might have been an ocean out there someplace, but I couldn't see it. Hell, there might have been a county fair with a Ferris wheel out there for all I was able to see. That coastal fog was so dense, I could barely hear the ocean breaking on the shore far below me. If it had been on the highway, that thick fog would have shut down the entire northern coast of the state.

It disappointed me and pissed me off. There I was, three thousand miles from home on the shore of the other ocean, and nature had conspired to prevent me from seeing a whale. I mean I was in tough shape over this.

When I was a young boy, about four, my Grandparents took me up to the St. Louis Zoo...on the day they had closed down the reptile house for repairs or something. Thirty years later I rode two hundred miles to a Johnny Cash concert specifically so Chinese 'Lizabeth could see Mother Maybelle Carter...on the night Mother Maybelle gave it up and stopped touring. Like finding out Plymouth Rock is about the size of a washtub, and it's busted. Like discovering that Niagara Falls was a bunch of water being dumped over a cliff. I was that kind of frustrated and exasperated over this current whale thing.

Crestfallen and forlorn, pissed off and heartbroken, I began to walk slowly back through the parking lot, kicking rocks as I went. I took my time, as I didn't want The Captain to see the tears of frustration in my eyes.

And before I had gotten back to Captain Zero, a great big white diesel GMC pickup truck pulled into the parking lot. Great big guy and a little tiny woman.

As we passed one another, the big guy rolled his window down to inquire, " 'Av ya sin da wahl yet, eh?" Before I responded, I stepped behind his truck to check it out. Quebec plates.

I returned to his open window and replied, "No sir, I have not yet seen a whale." I gestured toward the impenetrable curtain of fog and continued, "But I am fixin' to run into town and get a half dozen fans and a couple miles of extension cord and see if I might can blow this shit out of here so I can see something."

The man looked at me in confusion, one eyebrow raised in consternation. His wife, however, got it. She damn near choked, she got to laughing so hard. Frenchie finally caught on, and then he too began heartily guffawing. They were both good laughers.

When he had recovered from the mirth, Frenchie began telling me that I could cross back over the river, and via a complex route he outlined for me, we could get back out to the ocean on that side of the river. "I don' know will ya see da wahl, eh. But ya will be able ta see da ocean."

He delivered complicated instructions as to just how to accomplish the journey. Fortunately, Captain Zero had joined us, and he paid real close attention to the directions. Off we went, back across the bridge over the Klamath and then west along the south shore of the river to the much shorter cliffs.

We parked, and I walked over to the edge and looked off through the clear air to the ocean just beyond. And as I did, my whale surfaced. It was much closer than if I had been able to see it from the high cliffs along the fog-shrouded north shore. The whale, a California Gray, was huge and majestic.

I poked Zero and grinned and hollered, "Thar she blows!" or "Call me Ishmael," or something such as that. The whale came up a second time after that, just to make sure I knew how big and how noble she was.

About then, Frenchie drove up, specifically to make sure we had understood and followed his directions. He rolled his window down and asked again, " 'Av ya sin da wahl yet, eh?"

"Yes sir, I damn sure did. Just now." I was still delighted and still in awe of what I had just seen. "And I sure do want to thank you for the directions."

He parked his truck, and he and his woman got out to join us looking westward for more whales. They were both still smiling. Big Frenchie towered over his tiny wife. She looked like a child beside him.

There were no more whales, so Frenchie began delivering a spontaneous Canadian Retirement Economics Lesson to us there on the short cliff on the south bank of the Klamath overlooking the Pacific Ocean. He began by putting his arm around his wife and explaining, "Da main ting ya got ta 'av is yer little buddy wit' ya, eh."

His little buddy rolled her eyes and smiled. It was obvious they were happy in what they were doing and that they were happy with one another.

But the main point of his oration was that for fifteen thousand dollars a year, American money, you could stay out gone gypsying around with your pickup truck and travel trailer.

There were details, "Now ya need ta figure out which states down 'ere got da best places to stay, da best parks. And den ya got to find da places where ya can use da coupons and get da discounts fer memberships."

He went on to suggest stocking up on diesel fuel, wine, and cigarettes in states with minimal taxes. He continued, "An' ya got to find da places to stay what got da cable. Udderwise ya just can't get da 'ockey down 'ere on da damn TV, eh."

He was about to go on with his lecture when the Captain interrupted him. Zero said he was sure this was all good and valuable information, but, unfortunately and sadly, he and I had jobs to return to.

Frenchie looked like someone had punched him in the stomach. He made a face and backed off a step or two. Finally he shook his massive head and proclaimed, "Oh, work. Work is a...a...." Here he frowned and paused. We could see he was trying hard to come up with the correct word in English. He screwed his face up in hard concentration. It was an arduous struggle.

Finally he looked up in victory and announced, "Work is a hindrance! It's a damn hardship!" He banged a big fist on the hood of his truck in emphasis.

I was so overcome with the weight of the wisdom, with the enormous and overwhelming truth of his words, that I just had to take a knee there on the short cliff beside the Pacific Ocean. But the Captain maintained his composure and ran back to where we had parked to get a pencil so he could get it down on paper.

The epilogue here is that, even though I gave Frenchie and his little buddy a copy of my first book, they have never showed up to visit me, as I hoped they would. The other epilogue is that Captain Zero, scholar and well-educated man that he is, he paid better attention to the Canadian Economics Lesson, especially that last part, than I did. He retired about a year later.

When we got back to San Francisco a few days later, he showed me why he should retire. Captain Zero worked for the Municipal Transit Authority for way too long. He's driven everything from diesel buses to electric trolleys, but the main portion of his career was in the cable car division. He was a conductor, the guy in charge of collecting money and ringing the bell. That bell ringing thing it turns out is more than just colorful local noise for the tourists. The conductor is signaling orders to the gripman who stops and starts the car.

Anyway, the problem with all those jobs was that he had to deal with the dreaded, loathsome General Public. Worse yet, because it was San Francisco, he had to deal with tourists, or as he called them, "The Amusement Park Impaired." It turns out that the General Public is cheap, rude, ignorant, inconsiderate, and often angry. And the tourists are all these things, as well as truly impaired.

The Captain took me to work with him a few days after our Canadian Economics Lesson. He positioned me in a corner of the car. It was out of the way of things and a good vantage point. He spent much time explaining to people from New Jersey and Iowa that, NO, the cable car is not free. Just like everything else, it costs money to ride. I spent most of my time getting glimpses and vistas of San Francisco. For a city, it sure is a pretty place.

Then, within a few minutes of beginning our shift, a small, elderly woman got on the cable car. She had about a metric ton of tourist brochures and maps in her hands. This was April in San Francisco, and I have never been over-warm in that city, even in July. But, as most tourists figure that it's California, so it must be warm, she was wearing a t-shirt with a local logo of some kind and Bermuda shorts and a floppy straw sun hat. And like most American tourists, she was unprepared to walk much, so she was shod in flimsy sandals. Her thick bi-focals were shrouded in the city's hilltop mist and fog.

As the cable car crested a hill, the cold wet wind near blew her out of the doorway. She grabbed her hat and maps and looked out at the cold water of San Francisco Bay. She tried to wipe her glasses off. Then she turned on Captain Zero. All San Francisco municipal workers, including police and sanitation employees, are considered tour guides by most out-of-town tourists. The Amusement Park Impaired will seek help from anyone in a uniform.

She pointed out at the churning waters of The Bay as she peered through her damp glasses at the fluttering map in her hand and asked the Captain, "Young man, is that Alcatraz Island?"

Zero smiled, winked at me, and replied, "Yes Ma'am, that's the famous prison you have read so much about." Ding ding.

The old lady squinted at her map a moment, then she looked back out at the famous prison on an island. Then she had a follow-up question for the Captain. She demanded of him, "Well, why on earth did they put it so far out in the water?"

Captain Zero shook his head sadly and didn't miss a beat, ringing the cable car bell as he explained to her, "Lady, it's lots closer at low tide." Ding ding ding.

Less than a half-hour later, he was again called upon to administer a local lesson. An old boy with a big hat and belt buckle and cowboy boots (to walk around the city in, presumably) got on the cable car. His tourist map was in his shirt pocket.

After just a few minutes, he turned on the Captain and asked, "Hey Boy, when you all get these here cable trolley cars to the end of the line, what do you do, somehow turn 'em around and bring 'em on back?"

Zero rang his bell and, again, not missing a beat, told the guy, "No sir, we burn them. You get a fresh car every time." Ding ding.

I bailed off the cable car at the next opportunity. I was on sabbatical, so I didn't have to deal with idiots. As I walked the several miles back to Zero's Pentshack, uphill and downhill, wearing a pair of boots appropriate to such a hike, I pondered my friend's job. In addition to the Amusement Park Impaired, he has to deal with the local folks trying to get to work and back in the midst of all the tourists. And I should also point out that fewer and fewer, of both the locals and the tourists, speak English.

And, like most of us anymore, he also had to work for bottom line (bottom feeder?) boys in business suits who have no concept of what his job was, but who issue orders telling him how to do it, nonetheless. He had to deal with a union that had abandoned its members in favor of making more money for the boys in business suits who now run the union.

That night, when the Captain got home from his shift, we compared jobs. Sitting on the deck of The Pentshack, we determined that both of us have to put up with the same sort of crap from the same sort of people. As we watched the lights of the Golden Gate Bridge twinkle in the fog, we calculated that we were about equally underpaid for what we do. And, as we listened to the foghorns and the seals on Fisherman's Wharf, we determined that he has a better union and retirement plan than I do. That's how and when he decided he could retire some early.

chapter three
TEXAS, THE BOOK OF JOB,
and OLD FRIENDS

I have a friend who lives in Texas. She was a student in one of my classes thirty-some years back. She's a nurse, and she was there, as a nurse and as a friend, when both my grandparents went down. Both those old folks died easier because of this girl, and I will always love her for that.

In spite of the fact that she is a well-bred gentlelady, and I am old burned-out scootertrash, we have somehow maintained a bond and a friendship and a correspondence over the years between of then and now. And, as I was headed to the far left coast in April one time, I took the middle southern route, going through Dallas and Fort Worth. This girl lives some north of there.

Before this tale of stopping in Texas, I should spend some time telling about that ride. I have mentioned that as a school teacher, I seldom get to go anywhere except when school is out for the Summer vacation. I have always resented that. I became a school teacher so I would have my Summers off to ride, but after thirty-five years of that, I would dearly love to travel during another season. And, this particular year, due to sabbatical circumstances, I had more than a Summer off, and I found myself westbound in April.

The sabbatical itself is a long short story. It was like everything I touched turned to shit. The local, regional ongoing drought had about ruined freshwater fishing. Many of my favorite local lakes were literally gone. And the scarcity of rain had also made a mess of saltwater fishing by increasing the salinity as a result of a lack of freshwater run-off being added to the Bay and the Gulf. The hunting was even worse, and I have never been a man to try to kill a good dog in 90 degree heat.

That had all been compounded by vehicular problems. I had made plans to drive up to Michigan to hunt, but my truck came apart on me before I had left the state. A month later I tried to go out to Kansas to hunt some, and a different truck broke down on me again. That second time, I blew a tire and threw a fanbelt and used up a fuel pump within about forty miles of one another. The dogs had begun to question climbing in a truck with me and a shotgun. When I tried to hunt locally on Christmas Day, we saw no game at all, but the dogs picked up around a hundred ticks each.

When, a few days later, I headed to Alabama with both dogs, and quail still on my mind, I blew another tire and had a water pump go to hell before I had cleared the county line. I spent New Year's Eve under my kitchen table hiding from the forces of failure and evil.

This was all intensified by a couple real bad, but luckily brief, romances with darkly neurotic women. And then I got so desperate lowdown physically sick that I figured I must be dying, and I stopped buying groceries and began putting little Post-it notes on my stuff so everyone would know who got what. I was sure it had all finally caught up with me. When I pondered things, I had to admit that I had it coming. I determined it had been a good life and settled in to see where it went next.

But my doctor, Todd LaRue, said the only thing he could see wrong was that I was committing slow suicide eating my own cooking. One of the few breaks I have caught in my life is this doctor. Man's a tribute to the people who raised and educated him. I have always understood everything he has ever said to me, and most of it made sense. I don't get to see him but about every couple years when I drop a scooter or catch a cold that won't go away, but I always look forward to it. Always come away feeling better and laughing.

Captain Zero, my religious and spiritual advisory staff, had begun referring to this all as my Jobian Sabbatical. He quoted Scripture and even speculated that I got ticks instead of locusts. My health eventually improved, but the weather, my luck, and my despondency did not.

That Spring was when I started west on my scooter. It was

not a real good frame of mind to take out on the road. Over the years and miles, I have learned that you need a clear head and a worry-free mind on the highway. You can't ride easy when you are concerned about leaving your woman home alone, or when you are worried about having not kept up the maintenance on your bike, or you've just buried a good friend, or when you are distressed by the nature of your debt and your current lack of employment and cash funds. A bad head will ruin a ride as fast as bad weather or police.

This time I was in constant fear of a relapse and recurrence of my illness while on the road. I was apprehensive that the motorcycle would follow in the manner of the trucks and break down on me. Hell, I was anxious about the weather and the road, and uneasy about highway food, and afraid of getting lost or busted.

Wasn't much of a first day out to begin with, and then before I had crossed a state line, the weather went to hell suddenly. There were a pair of great big overloaded Goldwings on the highway in front of me when the storm first hit. It blew them both clean off the road. Both guys managed to keep it all upright. But as they sat there on the roadside while I went by, I was pretty sure they were discussing going home.

I suspect they were reflecting on that first line of the Scootertrash Blues which goes, The Highway it is said never gives up her dead, but sometimes she abandons her wounded.

I rode most of a short three hundred miles in a cold hard steady rain that day. Next couple days were pretty much more of the same. Damn shame, too, because I found some really nice roads in southern Alabama and Mississippi. There were gentle curves through pastures and easy hills through forests. But the whole thing was in black and white, and I had to run easy because of the rain and wet roads, and the wind. And it was still April and damn chilly.

When I finally rolled into my old friend's place in Texas, I was cold and wet and tired of fighting a bad wind. I needed to change my oil and wash my machine. I was out of clean, dry clothes. I hadn't had a decent meal or a good night's sleep since leaving home. She took care of all that within a day or so.

One of the best parts of this visit was meeting my friend's new husband. He was just who I wanted him to be. The second good part was being put up in the absent teenage daughter's bedroom, among the frills and doilies and dollies and dainty furniture and stuffed animals. The third best thing was being able to change my oil in their garage while it poured rain outside. Two of the other finest parts were being taken back toward Ft. Worth for some real good Mexican food and to a place north of there up by Denton for one of the best steaks I've ever eaten. The Mexican place had a mariachi quartet that insisted on standing nearby and playing and singing "Guantanamara." And at that steak restaurant, they were still, honest-to-god, line dancing. But my homegirl, she washed my clothes and fed me.

No, I lied about the parts. The best part was spending some time with my old friend, listening to her laugh, reminiscing and catching up and talking with her. Besides being a good friend, this girl has a world-class laugh. One of those laughs where you just want to keep on trying to be funny so you can listen some more.

The second or third day there, she loaded me in her car and headed toward Ft. Worth. This is one of them women who, when she tells you to get up and put your boots on and get ready to go, you don't question or demure or ask. You just do what you're told.

Once we were on the road, I inquired about our destination. She smiled and said she was taking me on the tourist excursion route. I begged her not to, but she persisted. She already had her mind made up anyway.

And I had a truly fine day. I wasn't all that impressed with what I was told was the largest indoor country music dance club in the entire Free World. But it was kind of fun watching the people look at us and wonder why the pretty girl was with the old burnout.

And the Stockyards and Museum were flat out wonderful. When I was done staring and grinning at old pictures of cowboys and antique saddles and such, we got back in her car. I thought we were going back to her house, but she blew right on by that exit. When I asked, she said we were going to Dallas. Again, I begged her not to take me there. I been to Dallas. Hell, I been to Paris. Dallas is a city. Sort of Detroit with better weather.

But, again she persisted, as she is wont to do. And I got to see some really pretty, bigger-than-life, bronze sculptures of horses and cattle. And then I was taken to Deally Plaza where they killed John Kennedy and most of the hopes for a better America. She knew I would want to see it, even though I didn't know that. Place is a lot smaller than I figured it would be. I believe I could have made that shot. One of them, anyway.

By the time I left Fort Worth, I felt better. I had clean socks and had been dry and well fed for several days. And I'd been taken on the tourist tour. I had a fresh oil and filter change on my machine. It was clean again, and it was running just fine. The Jobian Sabbatical evil juju was over. I could sense it had lifted somehow.

Then the weather went from bad to real bad that first day out of Ft. Worth. It got more overcast and colder and windier. I fought a hard headwind from the moment I turned north toward Lubbock. And the sky up that way looked dark and ominous, so I gave up on riding through the Palo Verde Canyon and headed west instead.

Those of you have rode this road will understand my decision; a northwind blows the stench of the nearby oilfields and propane gas and such right at you, right up your nose. Not what you could call a real scenic road even if it smelled good. And it don't. I saw a roadrunner, but that was the only bird out in that wind.

It was still cold in New Mexico, but at least now I had a side wind and the stench of petroleum was dissipating as I rode west. I stopped in Clovis around sundown and got a room and some damn good burritos and tamales. The cold sky was a beautiful, magnificent, dark purple color that night. It looked soft, like plush velvet.

As I stood under that purple western sky, I was reminded of a verse of The Scootertrash Blues that explains, If it wasn't for the middle, there'd be no cause to run for the borders. If it wasn't for the mountains in between, there'd be no reason to ride to the oceans. And if it wasn't for used-up longriders, there'd be no one to celebrate the motion.

Next morning, it was twenty-eight degrees in Clovis. I drifted on through Ft. Sumner, visited Billy The Kid's Grave and got some gas there. I thought about rolling through the Painted Desert and Petrified Forest in Arizona, but the admission fee was ten bucks, and the Winnebagos had the entrance clogged up. Instead, I looked, in vain, for that girl in the flatbed Ford there in Winslow. I believe I stayed in Kingman that evening.

I do recall that it was that evening that I began trying to figure out when the last time I had rode this road had been. I was unable to do the math. But I did determine that now the traffic was twice as bad, all the cities were twice as big, the prices were double, and there were five times as many cops along the way.

Next day, it was 106 out there between Needles and Barstow. And then after that, northbound up The Valley toward The Bay, there was the Tehachapi Wind. There is always the Tehachapi Wind.

Somewhere that night, the Chinese kid at the motel I stopped at counted my change back to me. Most cashiers and clerks, anymore, have them damn scanners and computers and such, and their tendency is to hand you back a wad of money. Most of the computers have little pictures of the products on the cash register keys, so they don't have to deal with numbers at all. Most prefer you use a credit/charge/AM&T/debit card so they don't get their hands dirty on cash money coming or going.

I thanked the kid for doing that and asked him who had taught him to count a customer's change back like that. He said his dad insisted he do it that way. I told him to thank his father.

Some time and miles up the road after that, I made it to San Francisco and Captain Zero's Pentshack up there on Russian Hill. He had found shelter for my scooter in Davey The Driver's garage.

That night Linda The Hawk came by with a Municipal Transit Fast Pass for me. She also brought groceries and fed me, as she has always done. When you die and go to heaven, if you have been really good, Linda cooks for you.

About a week later, me and Captain Zero and Linda The Hawk took off from San Francisco back inland into the foothills. And in a town called Murphy's, in a cold rain, the kid running the desk at the hotel greeted us with, "Welcome to Murphy's. We sure are glad you came. Please enjoy your stay, and please try to be gone by the weekend when the goddamn jumping frog contest people are going to fuck things up beyond understanding."

We all laughed, and we thoroughly enjoyed our stay there in

Murphy's. And we got the fuck gone by the weekend. Later, on that run, I administered a lesson about getting asphalt off our boot soles by using gasoline. The Hawk had seen a sign proclaiming the nearby Old Timers Museum, and she made and me and Captain Zero stand in front of it so she could take a picture. That's where we all got the asphalt on our boots. I explained that gas removal thing worked equally good with tar, creosote, and chewing gum. Linda The Hawk proclaimed me a Truckstop Martha Stewart. She suggested I could write my next book about such Helpful Highway Housekeeping Hints. I might.

A few years back, I had made enough money selling my books and tapes at a rally that I could take an extra day or two coming home. So I headed toward The Blue Ridge, as I have done many times before. I got on The Skyline Drive, north of the Ridge, real early in the morning. The ranger lady who took my money reminded me that the speed limit on that portion of the road was thirty-five. She told me that four times. It was a good thing, as there were a half dozen cops in the first thirty miles or so. Seems like they could find a better place to look for a crime.

But after that, there was hardly any other traffic at all. It was late August, so a few of the trees up at the higher elevations were beginning to show some of their Fall colors. It was a truly beautiful day. I started the morning in my leather jacket, had it off by mid-day, and then had to put it back on again a couple hours before the sun went down. And, it was Tuesday, so the road was as close to empty as a road can be in modern America.

I wish I had counted, because I don't think I saw more than thirty cars on the whole Parkway that day. I did see some bad traffic in the two or three places they detoured me off the Parkway, apparently around some repair work. But The Ridge itself was nearly devoid of vehicles. It was the kind of day and kind of ride that caused me to not resent that forty-five mile-an-hour speed limit on the Blue Ridge like I usually do.

This is one of those deals that confirm that irony is the only humor in my life. The only time of the year that Florida is even remotely empty is in the Summer. The Damn Yankee Tourists (woops, I mean Valued Winter Visitors) and the Drunk Spring Breakers (woops, I mean Welcome Scholars on Vacation) and the Senile Elderly (I mean Senior Snowbirds) have mostly gone home.

Florida is really a pleasant place when half the people leave.

You are able to ride the highways pretty much unassaulted by idiots in rent-a-cars, and old people in a prescription drug-induced stupor, and inept clowns trying to drive Winnebagos. In the Summers, you can go to town without fear of being run over in a parking lot by the ancient shoppers looking for a parking place on the sidewalk. In the Summertime, you can get on the interstate down to Tampa without being molested by hordes of Winnebagos pulling small SUVs. Few foreigners (woops, I mean Exotic Visitors) pull out in front of you with their white rent-a-cars in the Summertime. If a person were, for some reason, to want to do such a thing, he could probably get into Mouse World, or Whale World, or Movie World without being trampled and deafened by the swarm of nasty, noisy, pre-civilized children (I mean Visiting Youngsters With More Money Than God). Hell, in the Summer, you can cross the road at will.

But, it is just godawful hot most of the Summer here. Not only are the sun and heat relentless, but there is a pretty regular chance of late afternoon thunderstorms. And, while these tropical torrents cool things down some, they ain't much fun to ride in.

chapter four
MOTORCYCLE RALLIES, BOOK FAIRS,
and MODERN FARMING

In the first two books of this nature, I made some pretty disparaging remarks about motorcycle rallies. It still seems to me that one of the main reasons for having a motorcycle is to get away from other people and to be alone. Gathering in huge groups pretty much ruins the solitude. If I had wanted to be in a crowd, I'd have gone to an airport or got on a bus or took the train.

But since having written those two former books, I have been invited to motorcycle rallies and dealerships and bookstores and libraries in locations from Franklin, Nebraska to Columbus, Ohio to Okeechobee, Florida to Heath, Massachusetts, and some other places in between. It's always flattering to be invited, almost anyplace. And most of the time even the franchise bookstore and dealership folks treat me real good.

Past couple years, I have become The Pet Author In Residence at the bookstore in Daytona across from the speedway for Bike Week and Biketoberfest both. And I have been to the weekly Bike Night down to Tampa in Ybor City a few times. And, even though I did sell some books, I still don't get it.

Way too many way too clean machines with inexperienced, often drunk, riders. I listened to one guy bitching about having to wipe the dust off his machine because it scratched the chrome. Way too many trucks and vans with motorcycle trailers, some of which match the bikes. But, I did sell some books. And I am a good whore, and I always change my underwear and put on my party dress and show up on time whenever and wherever I have to to sell some books.

In addition to the bookstores and motorcycle festivities, I

have been invited to several book fairs and festivals. For the most part, these folks treated me especially well. I got to meet some famous authors. And usually I get to read some of my stuff to a group, tell them a poem, or give a lecture or something, and sell some books.

Typically, they put me up in a nearby big deal whoopie-do expensive hotel. It's become routinely pretty funny when I wander into the lobby with my helmet in my hand. Right away, the desk staff begins shuffling to try to not be the one who has to deal with me. One place, I got up to the check-in desk, and the kid running the computer looked at me like I was vermin, and in a real haughty voice said, "Is there some way I might possibly help you?" He sounded like he was pretty sure there wasn't.

I sucked it up and told the boy my name, said I was pretty sure the book festival folks had arranged a room for me there. He frowned like he couldn't imagine such a thing and pecked away at his little computer awhile. Then the expression on his face changed from disdain to disbelief to astonishment. He damn near came to attention as he spun back to face me and announce, "Oh no, Dr. Tiger, they've arranged a suite for you, sir."

They had, too. I had a bedroom and a bathroom and a parlor and a kitchen and a balcony, all nicely appointed. Damn thing was on the eighth floor overlooking the Gulf of Mexico and the setting sun. Got another one like that in Panama City Beach a few months later.

Then there is always a couple obligatory cocktail parties for the authors. Someone ought to write a book about these author cocktail parties. Turns out most writers are a bad bunch of rowdy drunks, just for openers. Most of the time, these events are limited to a specific time period. I think someone researched this one and ascertained that ninety minutes is how long it takes a bunch of book writers to get drunk enough to become obnoxious.

I am always quite popular at these open bar events. One of the other authors figures out that I don't drink and that I have two hands. My instructions are usually, "Here, Tiger, hold these."

Often, these galas are hosted by wealthy folks who are patrons of the arts or the local library or something. I was at one such event awhile back. This one was at a rich people's mansion, and someone, the hostess I presume, got fucked up and walked one of their horses, a polo pony I presume, through the house. Horse was really cool. You could tell he had done it before. He glanced longingly at the relish tray, but he behaved himself better than some of the guests. Told you these parties were good times.

Later that night, a drunk rich lawyer patron of the arts cornered me and engaged me in motorcycle conversation. He had recently bought himself the obligatory mid-life crisis Harley-Davidson, and he wanted to tell me about it. He got to the part about how he bought it because he fell in love with the way it sounded before I excused myself. Told him I had to go hold drinks for another writer.

Besides these events, I have been to some regional motorcycle rallies. I was enticed. One of them had to do with a woman, and they have all provided me an opportunity to sell some of my books and CDs. And I need to say right outfront that I had a real good time at these motorcycle rallies, especially the one that involved the woman.

And I took a lesson. A lot of folks make a Summer or a career out of just gypsying around the country attending these events. They'll ride from rally to rally, setting up their tents and hanging out with the people they were hanging out with at the last rally, and the one before that. Way things are going, I will probably wind up on The Rally Circuit trying to peddle my books and CDs.

But that'll be OK because I always eat real good at all these festivities. One of the book fairs fed us at the local college, where the culinary school put on a damn feast. Most of the rallies, they are in rural areas, and the Ladies of The Grange or the nearby church ladies or the volunteer firemen cook up some fine vittles. One of the rallies had fresh coffee twenty-four hours a day. That's my idea of a good place to be. Besides the food and coffee, most rallies have organized local rides, tours of nearby points of interest and such.

But beyond that, I met some real fine people. One example occurred out in the middle of the country at the BMW Nightriders Cornhusker Rally in Franklin, Nebraska. I got there some late, having wasted a whole lot of time trying and failing to find a new battery on my way there. Mine was about done. And it died at the rally.

As the festivity was breaking up on Sunday morning, someone drove a truck over near enough for me to jumpstart my ride, but I knew I was screwed the next time I turned it off. However, a man and his wife and kid who I had met and hung out with at the rally, they came to my rescue. They made it a mission to find me a battery, in south-central Nebraska, of a Sunday. I kept my machine running while we got some gas, and he outlined his strategy.

When we arrived at the first and second places where he hoped to locate a battery, I stayed in the parking lot and kept my bike running while he ran in to see if they had what I needed. They didn't. But the third place, a giant lawn mower and garden store of some kind, did. The battery was much smaller than any I had ever put or even seen in a road bike, but it fit. And it was about twenty-five bucks instead of the usual hundred and change.

I followed my new friends back to their house where we installed my new battery, had a snack and refreshments, before I headed back east to home. I asked my savior what he would have done if he had been unable to find a battery for me at his fourth and fifth options. He smiled and explained that he would have taken the one out of his bike and given it to me.

I remember saying to him in reply, "Mike, I ain't sure I would have done the same for you."

And he smiled at me again and said, "Well, yeah. But you would now, wouldn't you?"

Damn right. Anytime he needs it.

Along the way to that rally in Nebraska, I kept noticing a recurring phenomenon with which I was previously unfamiliar. My tendency is to try to stop to conduct my limited human interaction and business during the slack hours of the day. I will ride a hundred miles or so before seeking breakfast, just to avoid the crush. I even try to avoid buying gas during rush hour, especially the morning rush. If my intention is to get a motel that night, I try to loosely plan the ride so I can stop either late or early, when everyone else isn't.

Anyway, I found myself out there in The Heartland in little diners and cafes in small towns on the two-lanes at ten in the morning a lot. These local restaurants not only usually have good food, but they are typically cheaper and are often populated by some pretty colorful local characters. The waitresses treat longriders better out on the two-lanes, too.

This trip, I kept encountering whole gatherings of local farmers who should not have been screwing around dawdling over their coffee at mid-morning. But there they were in their double hammer hanger bib overalls, brogan shoes, flannel shirts, and John Deere and Massey Ferguson caps, yappering at one another about all kinds of things while Emma Lee Kathy Jean kept pouring coffee.

And occasionally, from my vantage point across the room, I would hear a cellular telephone ring. Actually cell phones don't ring; they make a horrible obnoxious noise like a robot throwing up. One of the farmers would pull the phone out of a pocket and listen to it a minute, maybe take some notes. Sometimes they would punch numbers into the cell phone and not talk to anyone.

Other times they would dig a GPS out of another pocket and punch numbers into it. Occasionally a laptop would be involved. Then they'd go back to their coffee and conversation.

I watched this occurrence several times before I became curious enough to interrupt and ask what the hell was going on. I think I was in Kansas, or maybe Oklahoma, at the time. The good ol' boys all smiled at me and asked me to join them. Then they explained and showed me what was going on. In response to what the hell were they doing, I was told they were turning their remote-controlled tractors, and lifting plows and harrows, and opening sluice ditches, and increasing the amount of fertilizer going on a poor section of land. All of it with computers.

Once they understood how computer-stupid I am, they began using small words and basic concepts. But I got it. And so did one of the older techno-agrarian engineers at the table. He shook his head and looked around the table to make sure all his buddies were listening. Then he leaned forward on his elbows, looked at me sadly and said, "You probably think we should still be doing it with teams of mules, don't you?"

I didn't even offer an opinion on that one. I just thanked them for the lesson, bought their coffee for them, tipped April May June Edith, the waitress who had been giggling the whole time, and went back out on the road where I belong. I spent much of the next several hours looking for remote-controlled robot tractors without drivers.

Years ago, like thirty or more, I can recall riding through this same area out in The Heartland and having the local farmers gather around my bike when I stopped at the local cafe. They were all curious about the machine, about the boxer-twin design and the driveshaft. Anymore, I expect I would have to have a laptop on my tank and a handlebar-mounted GPS and a palm pilot on the other handlebar to get their attention.

Some things change; others don't. Mostly, technology changes, and people tend not to. He was old. Not as old as he looked, but damn old. He wore his dusty ancient leathers and the lines on his face with a sort of insane dignity. His thin, unkempt hair was the color of dirty ice in the Winter, and he had a two or three day grizzled beard going. His glasses, repaired with wire and duct tape, sat crooked on his face. He looked unhappy, displeased, and angry with everything going on around him. I didn't know him. I'd never seen him before. But it was apparent from the way the folks around him who did know him were acting that he was a giant pain in the ass.

I was at a rally selling my books and CDs. They had me set up at the registration table near the entrance. I had spent the past couple hours sitting around with some real nice folks, members of the host club working the registration paperwork and all. The rally folks had provided me a boom box to play my CDs on for advertising purposes, and the nice folks at the registration desk were listening to them.

This old man joined us, took a chair and frowned at everyone individually and then collectively. My new friends all looked at one another with apprehension. Then they checked the time. Turned out this old guy was their replacement at the registration table, and he had showed up early, as he was prone to do. He began talking, but no one really paid him much mind. So he reached over and shut the boom box off and continued muttering about bad traffic on his way to the rally.

Conversation somehow turned to gasoline, specifically running out of it in inconvenient places. We discussed the bad time in the middle seventies when Richard M. (Tricky) Nixon had hidden all the gas and created lines and skyrocketing prices. We reviewed the current president and current gas prices. We talked about places in the West where it was a hundred or more miles between gas stations, and the gas was even higher. We spoke of how far you could get after you had spun the petcock over to the reserve part of the tank. Someone said that he used to carry a half-gallon in his saddlebag, but that was dangerous and made everything in the bag smell of gasoline.

This was when the unhappy, scowling old man rejoined the conversation. He cleared his throat in preparation for his declaration. He once again made eye contact with each of us, no mean feat, as he now had one eye kind of rollin' crazy in his head.

He said he, too, used to carry gasoline with him. "But the trouble with that was that it screwed up my gas mileage..."

Here he paused meaningfully and at length. He frowned hatefully over his glasses and again made eye-contact with each person at the table. There was malice and threat as well as madness in his eyes. Then he reached into his jacket and from an inner pocket extracted and displayed a thick notebook. It was old and dog-eared and weatherbeaten. He waved it about in the air like a weapon or maybe a Bible.

Then he finished his sentence, "...records!"

He continued, but no one heard. People leapt from their chairs, handed over the registration paperwork, and fled off into the middle distance. I abandoned my book sales and joined them. One of them mentioned that the old guy had a similar record book that logged his maintenance. Another said he also had a third record book that detailed his routes. The question was asked, Does he keep track of the brand of gas? Then another guy suggested that he could keep better records on the laptop computer mounted on his tank. That was when I fled again. Two days later, miles from the rally, the old man blew by me at well over a hundred. And that was, to my delight, the last I've ever seen of him.

One day, at the rally, a boy with Ohio plates came to a halt in a cloud of dust and a group of people. He climbed off his machine, beat some of the dust off himself, took his helmet off, and looked around at the small crowd and announced, in a still shaky and confused tone of voice, "I was out across the double yellow lines before I realized it was the chief of police that I was passing."

He was given the award for the Best Line of the Rally. And he was not given a ticket. Turned out the chief of police rode a BMW cop motorcycle, with very little subtle indication that it was a cop bike. He was also one of the main sponsors of the rally. The Chief took us on a couple truly wonderful tours, one of them by wagon pulled by tractor, to a mysterious mountaintop, where we were told to stay out of the blueberries. Seems a local bear was doing enough damage without us helping.

Turns out no one really knows about that mountaintop, but speculation is that Vikings or maybe Celts of some kind were there a thousand years ago. And this mountain is a hundred miles inland, among other mountains, far from navigable water. But someone, and the local Indians claim it wasn't them, set up some kind of weird Stonehenge-looking affair. Damn thing lined up with the sun and stars at certain times of the year.

It was a week of black bears, both during and after the Damn Yankee Rally. The first one was during the rally on a side-trip up in Vermont, and it was huge. At least by Florida bear standards it was. I only got to see the back end as it crossed the road in front of me. But its bear butt was about the size of a semi-truck tire. And it made a path through the thick forest that you could have driven a car through.

The next three were all on the far north end of The Skyline Drive in Virginia as I headed back home a few days later, all of them on the same day. And, bears aside, that was an especially fine day on the road. It was of a Thursday, and most of the day I was the only one on the road. Little in the way of Winnebago traffic to fight my way by, less in the way of cops to be paranoid about.

The first bear was smaller than the one in Vermont a week earlier. I saw it over on the left shoulder of the road from about a hundred yards. As the speed limit is thirty-five on The Skyline Drive, I had ample time to slow down. By the time the bear was on the center line, I had closed the distance to around ten yards. I stopped, and so did the bear. He looked at me a minute, like he was trying to figure out what I might be. I recognized the look, as I have been getting it from humans, especially women, for years.

Then the bear continued on to the far side of the road.

The next bear happened another twenty miles south down The Skyline Drive. It was a big cub, maybe a yearling. At first I mis-identified it as a real big dog. Then, from maybe fifteen or so yards away, this bear stopped right on the center line. Then he stood up on his back legs. He brought his paws up in front of his face as he peered at me in a kind of near-sighted squint. It was very cute.

We stayed like that, me stopped with my feet on the ground and one hand on the throttle and my other hand on the horn. And the young bear stayed like that, standing up on two legs, for a full minute or two. Then, he apparently got bored, dropped back down on all four feet and slowly ambled off into the woods on the far side of the road, occasionally looking back over his shoulder at me.

The final bear was near the middle of The Skyline, on my way south to The Blue Ridge Parkway. And this one refused to cross the road. And I wasn't real eager to ride by her. I feared she had a cub with her there in the underbrush beside the road. Whatever the reason, she just stood her ground and glared at me. It took me a minute or two to figure out that she wasn't going to move. Took me another couple minutes to get my courage up to ride on by her. I got way over to the far side of the road, and I hurried. She stayed where she was, her head down and swaying from side to side, and she frowned at me the whole way by her.

Between the last two bears I got to see a coyote. Most of the eastern coyotes I have seen have been cross-bred coydogs of some kind, but this one looked purebred. Like the bears, he was crossing the road as I came around a curve. He stopped in mid-road, checked me out, and then hurriedly turned around and beat it back to where he had come from.

On this same ride, I also got to hang out with a herd of deer for quite awhile. I was at a picnic table, and they were grazing in a nearby meadow that was screened off from the highway, The Blue Ridge Parkway, by a line of trees. Might have been a dozen of them. Occasionally one of the deer would lift its head and look my way, but they didn't seem bothered by my presence. I had a cup of coffee and smoked a cigarette while I watched them graze. The coffee steam and cigarette smoke drifted away from the deer, as I was, luckily, downwind of them.

About then a giant SUV roared into the picnic area, and two or three screeching children erupted from the back seat. An adult came out of each front door, both of them yappering on cell phones. When I looked back to the meadow, the deer had fled. By the time the kids had gotten up to full-scale screaming, I had too. Down the road, a few hours later, I stopped again. And as I had a cup of coffee there, I recalled some of the other rides up and down The Blue Ridge. I remembered a time when motorcycles from a nearby national rally had literally clogged the road. I thought about the time Bosco had raced the Devil to The Highside at the Peaks of Otter. It turned out to be a draw. I recalled the time the hail and thunderstorm came upon us at The Fences. And then I reminisced some about the time the federal tree-trimming crew had dropped a tree on me down at the south end of this road. I also remembered the time I had snapped a throttle cable on a downhill curve. I thought about the very first time I had ever ridden this road, thirty-some years ago. I recalled a bad fog on one occasion. And I thought about sundown and wildflowers in bloom and the leaves turning to autumn colors and the haze in the mountains, like the smoke from many fires.

But this day was going into the memory banks as one of the best. The weather was fine, the road was empty, the police and wildlife were cooperative, and the scenery was magnificent. But the day and the road came to an end as they always do.

In spite of the fineness of the day, as I sought shelter for the evening, I recalled a sad verse from The Lonesome Lowdown Outbound Scootertrash Blues. I have ridden out beyond The Highside, I have been on a Magic Carpet Ride. And I have rode The Lost Highway, too. I have ridden in The Lonesome Valley and along beside The Blue Bayou. I have ridden through rainbows in the full moon light, back then when the road was brand new.

chapter five
THE DAILY HIGHWAY, SCHOOLS,
UNREQUITED LOVE, and LAWS

In the last couple volumes like this, I wrote about the evolution of the American highway and the things around it. But in those books, I discussed the changes over the past forty years. Need to get into the daily and seasonal changes here a minute.

At dawn, most days, the road is near empty. Oh, there are always a few long-haul or local delivery truckers running late or trying to get the jump on it all with a real early start. And there are the inevitable few poor bastards who are on a real early first shift, and a couple tardy drunks going home. But mostly, if you get out there with the first sunlight, you can have it to yourself for awhile. You can almost hear your tires heat up on the cold concrete. This has become one of my favorite parts of the day on the road.

Then the catastrophe begins, rush hour. And anymore, rush hour happens everywhere. They'll get out there and thrash at it on the outskirts of Andalusia just as hard as they do in Chicago. The traffic jams are smaller in Valdosta than they are in Atlanta, but they're still there. Ain't no place to be on a cycle.

A year or so back, I wound up teaching an evening class. Ran from six to nine o'clock. As a split-shift worker that semester, I went home in the middle of most days and then back to campus for my six o'clock class. And damned if there wasn't a local rush hour and consequent traffic jam here locally. Used to be cows, now there is traffic. Used to be tractors, now there are Lincolns pulling golf carts. It doesn't take as long to get through Dade City as it does Seattle, but the swarming intensity is still there.

Anyway, as those of you who ride to work know, rush hour ain't no place to be on a bike. It's even less fun on an unfamiliar road in foreign surroundings. You don't know the traffic patterns or local customs, or the cops, and you ain't kin to nobody around there. If you get involved, you will get punished for your inattention and ignorance.

Then by mid-morning, the crush lets up some. The mid-morning highway is mostly truckers and delivery route guys. Anymore there is a whole lot of minivans with overwrought mothers and too many small undisciplined children in them. In the Summer you get the vacation folks, and they are near as intense as the rush-hour commuters. Anymore, both the distressed mothers and the fanatic vacationers are all on their cell phones as they make a mess of the highway.

Recently, the middle of the day has become lunch hour. And, as lunch is the most important meal of the corporate day, it's another rush hour episode. And because of the crowds and the fervor and competition of the short hour for the meal, you can pretty much forget about having lunch yourself.

And then the post-lunch afternoon hours are when folks shop. Sportshopping is near as important as that corporate lunch thing. And anymore I see a lot of boys in suits yammering on their cellular telephones with a laptop on the seat beside them doing a lot of things besides driving. But other than that, mid-afternoon can provide some pretty safe and easy riding. There are still a lot of trucks, but most of those boys are professionals and are paying attention.

By late afternoon, we're back to the early commuter thrash. It seems to me that the rush hour, like the Christmas Holiday, has gotten longer and longer as time has gone by. And the Commuter Chaos is usually followed by the Happy Hour Mess.

Nights are best, because the highway is less crowded. But nights are dark and perilous. There are all sorts of things on the road that you would easily see and avoid in the daylight. And night is when the drunks come out.

Sometimes, especially out away from cities and suburbs and plazamalls, the evening highway can clear out and calm down enough to be a pleasant ride. My tendency at the end of the day, at the end of a ride, is try to find some elevated ground with some perspective and turn the bike off to admire sundown and review and reflect on the miles and the day. Usually I have some tepid coffee left in my Thermos, so I finish it and have a cigarette while I ponder things. If I'm lucky, I get a couple lines for a new poem or part of a chapter for a new book come to me. If I'm clever enough, I write it down. Sometimes I just review a few stanzas of the Lowdown Long-gone Scootertrash Blues. I might check a map to see where I am, where I should quit for the night, where I am going to head the next day.

Other things I need to bitch about here are the fact that Friday has somehow become National Fuck Off At Work Day, normal weekends are no time to be on a scooter, the number of three- and four-day weekends has escalated, and most of the folks out there driving around just ought not be. They ain't much good at it.

One of the weirdest experiences resulting from publishing books has been being invited to schools. No, it doesn't happen a whole lot, but I have been asked to several. Sometimes I get lucky and wind up in a class full of high school or college kids who are serious about writing. And sometimes the overworked, underpaid, weary teachers just want me to entertain their kids for them awhile.

While I am on this subject, I should note that contemporary high schools are containment facilities. The primary purpose of modern American Public Education is to keep the kids off the streets and out of the plazamalls during the hours between mid-morning and mid-afternoon. Their function, distinctly, is not to teach the youth to be literate or questioning or thinking people. The current system fails at both.

I spend much time with recent high school graduates, many of the better ones. Most of them don't read much anymore; it's too hard. Beyond their truly frighteningly limited attention and literacy skills, they have been taught that the U.S. won the Vietnam War. They know nothing of the protests and unrest of the 1960s or the civil rights movement. Chicago and Kent State mean nothing to them. They know less about the American Revolution than I know about computers. Many have been to Europe but are unable to point to it on a map. Most just kind of instinctively believe everything they are shown on a TV or computer screen. They think being well-educated means knowing which button to push.

Once in awhile a kid comes up with something so bizarre, so utterly grotesque, it just kills teachers a little. Couple years ago one of my freshmen wrote, "Just because we don't know the meaning of very many words and have a small vocabulary does not mean we are inarticulate." I handed her a dictionary and wept.

Next semester, thanks to "research" on the damn internet, I read that Daniel Boone led the Spanish forces at the Alamo, Bob Dylan was married to Joan Baez, and President Martin Luther King, Jr. emancipated the slaves. I was also given to understand that the Magna Carta ended the Futile System and freed the English Surfs.

But the best school invitation I had was being asked to the SUNY campus at Potsdam. They teach a Literature of The American Road class there, and they were using my book. I was treated like royalty in that cold northern town in the St. Lawrence Valley.

The invitation was for mid-March. There might have been a time I would have tried that ride up the road on a cycle in the early Spring, but that was a long time ago, and probably only in my fantasy memories. As I am unwilling to fly on the airplane, the nice folks at SUNY offered to provide me with a rent-a-car.

It was a real slow Sunday at the rent-a-car place, and the part-time weekend kids running the outfit thought an old burned out rounder renting an automobile to go north to an academic gathering was about the funniest thing they'd ever heard. We talked about it. I showed them my book. They somehow took both great pity and pride in me, and I wound up driving a brand new, bigass, money-green colored Cadillac up the highway to New York. Every cop on I-95 spun his head around in wonder as I drove by.

The first day up there in Potsdam, I lost the rent-a-car Cadillac in a parking lot in a blizzard. Couple days later, after being on the local NPR radio, I found myself back on campus outside a classroom building in a snowstorm smoking a cigarette with the other freezing pariahs. One young man kept looking at me kind of funny. As I have become used to this, I was pretty much ignoring him. Finally, recognition came upon him. He grinned and walked over to me, and as he shook my hand, he said, "Oh wow, man! You're the assignment." I figured I had arrived at the pinnacle of my literary and academic career.

The funniest one was local. A former student of mine graduated and went to work nearby as a junior high school teacher. She asked me would I come and talk to her seventh grade class. And I said, "Hell no!"

I told her I didn't have much to say to thirteen-year-old kids to begin with, and after that I couldn't imagine that contemporary thirteen-year-old children would want to listen to anything I had to say. She persisted. Told me she hoped I could somehow inspire the children to read, maybe even to write, to pursue an education. As she pressed her case, I finally caught on. She works in a less than affluent school, and she wanted me to come do a Poor Boy Makes Good Via An Education talk.

Well, this girl was a real fine student, and she married a friend of mine. In fact they asked me to come tell a poem at their wedding reception. And pretty women have always made me stupid, so I eventually agreed to address her class. She gave me real good directions to the school and named a specific day and time. Told me to set on my scooter out front until she came and got me.

I arrived punctually, as is my habit. I set out front on my bike smoking a cigarette, but she did not show up to take me into the school. No, the cop assigned to the school came and got me.

And, as I don't get out much, I didn't even know that cops were assigned to schools in America. Hell, I didn't even know that junior high schools are now called middle schools and that the schoolyard is now referred to as a campus. I was completely unaware of mandatory school uniforms in public schools. And I was totally ignorant of the fact that it is illegal to smoke a cigarette on a middle school campus, maybe even upwind of one.

This cop, who was young and overzealous and apparently bored with bullying small children, made me aware of all this. He kept his right hand on his gun during our entire confrontation. I kept my own hands in plain sight the whole while. The school cop used his left hand to point and gesture forcefully. He began by telling me that there had been reports that "An old guy on a motorcycle was out front of the building...looking at the children."

I looked around to see if my friend and hostess, the teacher, was going to rescue me. The cop must have thought I was looking for an old guy on a motorcycle. One eye began to twitch, and he tightened his grip on his pistol. He continued to use his other hand to gesture to where he wanted me to park my cycle. Then he walked beside me to the designated place, one hand on his gun, the other on my tailrack. I spent the time trying to explain to him who I was, and why I was there, and who I was supposed to meet. The campus cop didn't hear a word. I suspect he was already planning where to hang his citation for apprehending me or where to mount my head or something. I wondered if he would collect a bounty.

He escorted me, one hand still on his gun, the other hand on my arm, into the nearby administration building and turned me over to educational authorities in business suits. The young officer remained there to guard me. These folks in suits, they finally summoned my friend the teacher. She thought it was all pretty funny. Not only did I fail to see the humor in the situation, but I also failed to see any humor at all as I was frisked, and made to go through the metal detector, get photographed, finger-printed, sign the loyalty oath, issued a parking permit, and given the anti-smoking-on-the-campus lecture.

My inability to see the mirth in this mess continued as I was taken to, not my friend's classroom, but to the auditorium. The campus cop, still suspicious and hopeful, came with us. Yup, my former student had suckered me good; I was to address a hundred and fifty adolescent children.

They were hungry, it being the hour before lunch. They were rowdy, noisy, and unruly, without manners or much sense of public deportment, them being contemporary kids. They were already bored, as they had figured out there would be no partial nudity, blood, discordant but loud music, no special effects, no pyrotechnics or melting or morphing of anyone, in the presentation. And being thirteen, they were like hundred-pound hormones with feet.

I have never been one to duck a challenge. And I realized I had no hope of escape, especially as the campus cop, still suspicious and hopeful, had remained, hand still on his gun, in the auditorium. I rose to the occasion. The acoustics in the auditorium sounded pretty good, so I quickly asked for a cassette tape player to plug into the system. One of the poems on my first tape of epic motorcycle poetry is called "Dialog in a Rainstorm." It's about a conversation I once had with the Devil. And, as it was very near Hallowe'en, and this is a pretty creepy poem, I figured this one might somehow get some of their attention.

This might be another one of them lines from the Lowdown Lonesome Scootertrash Blues, the one about, Whenever you find your back to the wall, you need to take big bites, but swallow small. And that reminded me of another line about how, Sometimes you have to bite the bullet before it all goes to hell. And other times you are required to smile about it and chew and swallow, as well.

My friend introduced me. As I had suspected, she leaned hard on the part about me having an education, a doctorate, and a pretty decent straight job. She mentioned that poor boy kidhood thing. She went on to tell them I was the hardest teacher she had ever had at college or anywhere else. Then she mentioned the tape, told them that these were epic poems in the tradition of *The Iliad* and *The Odyssey*, of *Beowulf* and the *Canterbury Tales*. Finally, she told them about my book, *Longrider*, and then she motioned me out on the stage. Some of my audience was asleep already, but most were involved in animated conversations with friends several rows away. I received a squatting ovation.

I did a real brief introduction of the poem I had keyed up to play for them. Told them it was a true story, just like all my poetry and prose both. Explained that I had no need to make anything up; all I had to do was write it down. I asked someone to lower the lights for effect, then I poked the play button and went to stand by my friend, offstage.

And damned if it didn't work. Within a short minute, they were nearly silent, something thirteen year olds seldom accomplish. I didn't get a hundred percent attention, but I had most of those young people focused on the poem. Like all epic poems, this one lasts fifteen or twenty minutes. As the average attention span of young teenagers is about three minutes, I considered their rapt concentration high praise.

While the poem was playing, I whispered to my former student, asked what she thought I should do next. It turned out that instead of the half hour I had planned for, she needed me to hold these children in the auditorium for an hour and fifteen minutes. If it hadn't been for my new little buddy, the campus cop, standing in the back of the auditorium, hand still on his pistol, I believe I would have choked her to death right there.

She marveled at the kids' attention a moment, and then she asked about stories in my book about wrecks in the rain, blood and eyeballs on the concrete, the dying rider's lament. She whispered, "These kids just love gore."

Well, there is such a portion in that *Longrider* book, so when the poem about the dialog with the Devil was done, I got back up on stage and regaled the children with gory stories about scooter wrecks and getting busted up and bleeding all over the concrete. I told them about the Lowdown Lonesome Blues stanza which goes on about, One headlight in the dark of the night, of the stress and the steady strain. I continued quoting the part about, Losing your place and putting it all sideways in the rain. I disclosed some of the details of the dying rider's lament. Their teacher was right; those kids do love carnage.

By now I was forty-five minutes into it, and still had a long half hour to go. I found a couple stories in that book that I thought might amuse them, mostly tales about the olden times of yore, of back in the day, of things long ago.

This went medium well, but it didn't entertain them near as good as creepy poems about the Devil or gory tales of blood all over the whitelines. I was sort of shuffling and stalling, trying to figure a way out, when my friend walked back on stage and said I would now entertain questions for the remaining fifteen or so minutes.

I damn near killed that girl in front of a hundred and fifty small witnesses and an armed campus patrolman. Last thing in the world I wanted to do was deal with these kids on a personal level. And question-answer sessions are usually pretty goofy to begin with. People often have no question at all; they just want to tell you something or make a general announcement to the crowd. And that's OK if they have something interesting to tell you. Most don't.

Other times, especially at motorcycle rallies and such, the "questioner" wants to share stories of his own, tales of his own rides. Again, fine idea if they're good stories. They usually aren't. As often as not, they will tell a tale of a ride that begins, "Day

One..."

And, usually, the people with real questions have some damn strange inquiries. I have been asked if I believed in God, what kind of oil I used in my scooter, what I was doing on the Ides of March, 1974, have I ever been to Upper Southwest Mabou, Nova Scotia, what did I think of the new Honda model, have I ever run across an old rider named "Weasel," and to name a good restaurant in Texas.

First kid I called on asked me how many miles did I ride on an average day. We discussed weather and roads and averages. Next boy asked about gas mileage on a road bike. Another one inquired about weight and distribution of the luggage and gear on a scooter. One boy asked if I carried a gun with me. Then he referred to the poem he had just heard and questioned me on what kind of motorcycle did the Devil ride. Had another one, a girl, wanted to know did I camp or stay at motels. Then she asked about did I ever take a woman with me out on the road. Another asked about riding alone.

So, there I was, talking with thirteen-year-old kids, and they were asking some of the best questions I have ever fielded. Perceptive, inquisitive children have always been one of my very favorite things. I was mightily impressed. They asked me about riding in the rain; they inquired about mountains; they wanted to know about the changes over the years and along the way. They even asked about getting back up and onto your bike after a bad wreck.

That was when it went all to hell. An incredibly beautiful little girl stood in the back of the room. She looked like Athena rising from the mist and parting the waves. Girl walked down the aisle from her place in the back and took a seat in the front row. She did that with grace and style and presence beyond her years. She was, with her pretty smile, long blonde hair, huge blue eyes, and her brand new woman's figure, a distracting sight. Yeah, it made me feel old and dirty, but I couldn't help but look at her. Then when she raised her hand, I just had to call on her, even though I knew better. I got a hunch I had a silly grin on my funny looking face when I called on this child.

She stood to ask her question. She smiled at me and became even prettier. Then she looked at me right in my good eye, like a grown woman, and asked, "Do you ever fall in love out there?"

I damn near had to take a knee there on the stage. Finally, as my friend, the teacher, raced on stage to rescue me and announce that the assembly was over and lunch was served, I managed to compose myself enough to ask the little girl, "You mean like right now?"

Yeah, it happens. There are a couple stories of this nature in my second book, *The Ghost of Scootertrash Past*. The legendary Love At First Sight. The kind of Immediate Attraction that demands to be paid attention to. But more often than not, it's unrequited love.

One time up around Saddle Mountain in West Virginia, I drifted into a cafe to have some coffee. Wasn't nobody there but me and the little girl working the counter. She was about fifteen or sixteen, and stone damn pretty. And the bond, the spark, the attraction was so sudden and so intense that it kind of frightened me. Not her. When you're fifteen, you ain't scared of much.

She got my coffee, and herself a soda pop, and then she sat right down with me, across from me in the booth. Looked at me right in my eye and smiled at me. I told her that would be a foolish and dangerous thing to do with a lot of men. She smiled some more, and the dimples were disarming. She told me her name was Emmy Mae. And I had already named her Melba Minnie Maudie Mariah.

I told her my name and repeated my warning, said something to her about flirting with old men and strangers. She giggled and said she really knew better, but that she also knew it was OK with me, that she was safe. It was a good thing she knew that, as I was beginning to wonder myself.

Then we talked awhile. Eventually we moved outside and drank our drinks at a picnic table with a breeze and a view of Saddle Mountain off to the east in front of us. There were no other customers, and the traffic on Highway 50 was minimal. We continued talking. And we agreed it was a cryin' damn shame that she was only fifteen and that there was twenty or thirty years between us. I maintained my avuncular attitude in spite of my elemental feelings.

She said if she was a few years older, she would lock the door of the cafe and climb on behind me. And I allowed as how if she was a few years older, I'd let her. We talked for maybe an hour, and she held my hand briefly as I saddled up to leave. Like Jesus, I wept as she got littler in my mirrors.

I've had similar, if maybe less intense and intelligent, situations and conversations with young girls coast to coast and border to border over the years and along the way. I don't mean to imply this happens often. As a general rule, I am not especially attractive to women. And I have lately been required to understand that old and ugly is even less attractive than young and ugly. But in the forty or so years I have been out there on the highway, it's happened a dozen times or so. Might be it's because I am the guy their mothers warned them about.

Sometimes it goes the other way, and I fall in love with a woman too old for me. There used to be an old girl who ran the tourist facility on the Natchez Trace. We had a bad crush on one another for a good while in spite of the fact that she had twenty or more years on me. It was thirty years back that I met this woman. It's been ten or more since I saw her. Now that I think about it, I realize she is in her eighties or probably her nineties now. And I still think of her fondly and with some regret.

In fact, there was a woman at one of those book festival things awhile back, I think she was 83. And we damn near ran off together right there. Same kind of sudden, intense attraction. We held hands and laughed about it some. We spent a lot of time with one another, and we still write and keep in touch real regular.

And sometimes, the woman is married, or I am. I got a real firm rule about not messing with a girl named Mrs., and most of the time these women sense that. They wind up introducing me to their husbands and kids, or anymore, their grandchildren.

Maybe it's all summed up in a profound verse of The Lonesome Scootertrash Blues that goes, The asphalt screams, the concrete cries, the wind never sounds the same. Sometimes it wails a warning, sometimes it tells you lies, sometimes it calls you by your name. Some women will tell you things you didn't need to hear, show you things you were never intended to see. Some women will shake your rattle and rock your ride and take you places you were never meant to be.

The first two books like this were full of stories about waitresses and restaurants. That may be over. Florida, following

California's fascist lead, recently passed an anti-smoking law in restaurants. I suspect other states, many at least, will follow suit. So far I have been able to avoid such places, but from now on I got a hunch I am doomed to take-out food.

It isn't so much that I feel I need to smoke a cigarette as it is that this used to be America, land of the free and home of the brave. And we have become the land of the accommodated and home of the surveillance camera. I'm just real tired of being pushed around.

And anyone who thinks such laws are about public health needs to review. These laws are about power, about pushing people around. Seems like to me that the people who own the restaurants ought to be the ones to make such decisions. Kind of like it seems to me that the parents should be the ones deciding what their kids wear to school and what they ought not read. No, this is all about power.

If it were about anything else, they would have enacted an anti-shrieking children in restaurants law. If it were about anything other than power, we would have anti-yammering hollering cellular telephone users in restaurant laws. If it were about discomfort or health and allergies, we'd have anti-heavily over perfumed women and overly cologned men in restaurants laws. If it were about fitness and well-being, we would ban the hugely fat from restaurants. No, like the current laws concerning the "disabled," including the obese and the mad, these mandates are about accommodation and about pushing people around. They're about power.

One of my few heroes, the jurist Oliver Wendell Holmes, once commented that the only way to get rid of a bad, oppressive, or silly law was to enforce it to the fullest. That solved that idiotic statute involving the prohibition of alcohol. It has also helped do away with some helmet laws.

It's like with smoking; I just can't imagine why folks who don't smoke or ride a scooter would care whether I light a cigarette or wear a helmet. It's none of their business to begin with, but after that, they aren't qualified to have an opinion on those matters. You know, sort of like, as a non-breeder, I should keep my mouth shut about the rearing and behavior of children.

I have developed a system. Anymore, when most people

welcome me into their house, they feel the need to announce loudly and often that theirs is an anti-smoking home, and I am not allowed to light a cigarette. Great. It's their house; they should make the rules. And then I explain that I will certainly honor their wishes and not smoke a cigarette in their house. I continue that when they come to my house, they have to smoke.

The whole general state of contemporary America makes me pretty sad. Causes me to recall the verse in The Lowdown Long-gone Blues that goes, Lonesome as two wheels out on the highway, sad as a young widow's prayer. Like findin' out that it don't mean nothin', and don't nobody care. Like children in graveyards talkin' to the dead in unknown tongues. Like finally findin' a reason to believe, and then ridin' by it before it's even begun.

It's America. We don't need repressive laws or surveillance or accommodations or political correctness or legislated morality. We just need smart people, citizens who read and write well, and then vote.

chapter six
THE SOUTHERN ROUTE,
INTERSTATE HIGHWAYS, and EL NINO

There are several advantages to having time off other than in the Summer. One of them is that there are far fewer intense vacationing, recreating people out there on holiday, even fewer with their children. And those who are out there seem far less fervent in their pursuit of entertainment, amusement, and relaxation.

As I have mentioned often, one of the great parts about teaching school is having my Summers off. That's also the curse. But one year I found myself headed back east out of California in May, some before the schools let out and everyone had taken to the highways and shorelines and mountains and rivers and lakes and parks in pursuit of recreation in a crowd.

As the pass at Donner had been recently closed down by a late Spring snowstorm, and as the pass there at Yosemite was still clogged up hard with snow, and probably early tourists, I took the southern route outbound east to home from northern California. As with all things, living in contemporary America and teaching school for example, this has both advantages and drawbacks.

The southern route has no high, snow-capped mountain peaks. Well, I guess there is one. But there are comparatively few winding, serpentine, up and down mountain roads along the southern highways. Isn't as much in the way of towering forests or majestic views between the coasts down out along the southern border either.

But the weather, especially in May, is bound to be better. Fewer skiers, the roads aren't near as tore up with Winter frost heave. There is little chance of being shut down by an avalanche or a flood. And, if you pay attention, and maybe take a local lesson or two, you can see some stuff.

Coming south out of San Francisco, you can get bad windburned and near baked to death between San Jose and Needles on anything but the coast road. And the coast road is a much better ride to the north of there rather than to the south. Even the stretch between Monterey and Morro Bay has been developed and crowded. In spite of that, it's still a beautiful road with some magnificent views, but now it's crowded. And down at the bottom end of it, there is a motorcycle rider's worst nightmare, Southern California, and Los Angeles.

And inland, there is the fast route south, down I-5 through The Valley. This road is nearly always full of sporadic bad traffic, construction, and constant wind. On this particular ride, the wind had my windshield bent back at a bad angle into my face most of the day. There is no way to get out of it, few places to stop and hide and rest. Not much in the way to get in the lee of. And, as we all know, a bad wind in your helmet will eventually cause madness.

Sometimes you can get lucky here, and the traffic thins out. But that damn wind is incessant all the way south to Buttonwillow. There aren't many options down in this part of the state. Oh, you can get off the superslabs pretty easy, but the big roads are the only direct routes. After that turn east out of Buttonwillow, the wind may let up some, but the heat seldom does. From Bakersfield to Needles is hot, it being a desert and all. And there is little to break the monotony. You can drop farther south and get on I-10 so you can take the ride around the Joshua Tree National Park. But after that, there are few alternatives eastbound other than going up to Las Vegas.

But once you get into Arizona and New Mexico, there are some pretty good roads going more or less where you need get to. Few of them are direct, and you wind up going north when you kind of need to go east. And most of these roads are intent on taking you to whatever is the closest city.

But there are some wondrous things to see out there on the two-lanes in southern Arizona and New Mexico and even on in to Texas some. There are lots of little towns full of real nice people. There is some damn fine regional food. And there is some truly magnificent scenery. If you get lucky, there is some pretty neat wildlife, too.

On this run east in May, I got to see the desert come to bloom. The ocatillo and prickly pear were blossoming. There were patches of wild flowers everywhere. Few things I know of that pretty. And I got some tamales along the way that I still dream about. There were antelope and birds I don't know the names of. I saw some javelinas and a snake or two. And, if you're of a mind to, you can check out the aliens, both the wetback kind and the outer space kind.

Besides the scenery, there is some powerful quiet in this part of the country. You can get off by yourself, out on a backroad in the wilderness, and pull over and shut the bike off, and nearly be overwhelmed by the silence. You can set there for a long time and hear nothing but the ticking of your machine as it cools down, and maybe the wind. And, blowing across mostly rock and sand and through real sparse vegetation, the wind, it whispers.

As an easterner, my whole life has been filled with the sounds of traffic and trains and airplanes in the air. As a rural southerner, my world is permeated with the sounds of cows and tree frogs and birds singing. As a man who spends as much time as he can outdoors, my life is filled with the sounds of the wind in the trees and underbrush, water running in rivers, with rainstorms and waves on the beach. As a Floridian, the air around me is filled with the sounds of growth and development, of traffic and loud, rude, inconsiderate conversations, and screaming children.

Sometimes I think all the noise that isn't in New Mexico is in Florida. Sort of like I suspect all the parking spots in New York City are in Wyoming. All the pretty women in Georgia are in Atlanta, all the old people in Michigan are in Florida, and all the money in Oklahoma is in Tulsa.

Before I had crossed the Clear Fork of the Brazos eastbound on that trip, it had all turned into a rainstorm. I mean it poured for days. My tendency in bad weather is to just suck it up and take to the interstate highways. There are few surprises on the expressways, and there are plenty of places to get off and seek cover and shelter if it gets to that.

And the scenery sure isn't going to cause inattention to the road. The interstate highways were built for efficiency, not for scenic beauty or local interests. They are boring but practical, at least in some situations. As a general rule, I avoid the superslabs, but they are often the best roads and have the best refuge in bad weather. And I had real bad weather from west Texas all the way to Georgia.

So I sucked it up and ducked north through the rain and got on I-40 along with everyone else. And, while I am sure Amarillo is a nice city, I'd sooner look at scenery. After awhile I got bored and dropped back south hoping to get out of the weather and off the interstate. But, alas and crap, the weather either came with me, or it was waiting there for me all along.

I wound up eastbound on I-20. And, while I am not all that sure that Dallas and Shreveport and Jackson are nice cities, I had to ride through them all eastbound. It was raining too hard to see the Mississippi River, much less any southern scenery. Hell, it was raining too hard to see what was about to come past me, and throw water all over me, in my mirrors.

I dropped one more notch south, ever the optimist, still trying to find a dry two-lane highway. Nope, instead I wound up on I-10. By the time I made the turn south off I-10 to home on this trip, the weather had finally recovered, so I was able to complete my mission.

I have no idea why I did such a thing, but on my way out of Florida westbound weeks before this, I had stopped along the way and filled a water bottle from the Gulf of Mexico. Then I carried the damn thing all the way west with me.

And then, somewhere along the northern California coast, me and Zero stopped long enough for me to walk down to the beach and pour the contents into the Pacific Ocean. I recall it was Captain Zero's brother's birthday, the one they killed in Vietnam for no apparent reason. But I disremember how old he would have been.

The Captain, he waited up on the highway while I walked down to the Pacific shoreline with my bottle of water from the Gulf of Mexico. I stood there a minute, looking west. I thought about my own brother, who a drunk killed with a car, and Zero's brother, who they killed with insane foreign policy. I may have made a dramatic gesture. I mentioned both their names to the western waves, to the sundown shoreline, to the distance beyond.

Then I poured the water into the surf there. And then I

waited. I have no idea what I thought was going to happen. About the time I gave up on mystic phenomena, the next breaker came in, and I got my feet wet. Later that trip I filled a bottle with water from San Francisco Bay and took it back east with me.

When the weather had finally cleared on my inbound ride, I turned toward the Gulf of Mexico. Found an empty, shady, quiet place to park my ride by the shoreline. Got into my saddlebag and walked down to the beach with my bottle of Pacific Ocean water and poured it in. As there is seldom any surf in the Gulf of Mexico, I kept my feet dry this time. Once again nothing happened. But my suspicion is that my actions will eventually have some sort of weird and mysterious irreversible global environmental impact. Maybe I ought to take credit for El Nino.

I recall I did a similar thing many years ago. Me and Bosco The Bandit were westbound. I don't remember when or why or where to. But we wound up outside Douglas, Arizona at the Geronimo monument there. It commemorates the place where that tough old Indian finally surrendered. I left a feather there that I had picked up along the way. And I picked a flower there and put it on my handlebars. Weeks and miles later, I put the flower on Chief Joseph's grave up in Montana.

Nothing mystical happened that time either, but I felt as if I had paid tribute to two old longriders. Sort of like the memorial gesture for my brother and for Zero's.

Over the years and along the way, I have run across some old riders who should be commemorated, too. Anymore it has become real fashionable to have your mileage certified and verified so you can get a long-mileage patch to put on your motorclothing or an award of some kind to hang on the wall of your den or office. Considering that most of these current awards are passed out to folks with brand new, multi-thousand dollar scooters, many of them on tours with groups and a parts truck, there just don't seem much point to being awarded anything. Kind of like Tee-Ball.

When I talk to non-riders, when they read about my million miles on motorcycles, they often ask in awe and wonder, "How did you do it?" And I tell them there wasn't no trick to it. All you got to do is set on the damn things. Ain't like I pushed them a million miles.

And when I talk to bikers who are new to it, they usually ask questions about the olden days, before computer operated cycles and gps machines. About back when you had to be able to at least read a damn roadmap and start your machine manually. They ask about the high mile days back before the superslabs. Some of them ask about the breakdowns and the turn arounds, about the price we had to pay. Sometimes they inquire about wrecks and downfalls.

But when I talk to other old riders, the conversation differs. We seldom speak of the breakdowns and wrecks and puttin' it all sideways in the rain. Most of us are too stove up and lame to deny we never went down. We do talk about the one headlight in the dark of the night, about livin' out of a saddlebag, and of particular roads. We talk of the Mexican Wind and goin' again.

Real old riders, along toward the late Fall of the year, they begin to speak of a place they know to hole-up, to winter in, a place to set still awhile and work on the bike and eat and sleep regular. See can you lay over somewhere and heal up some.

The talk also always turns to old machines and The Ghostriders. And that nearly always leads to a discussion about The High Side and The Lost Highway. We recall verses from the Lowdown Scootertrash Blues about, Legendary highway cops, and real bad breaks and a few heartaches and the crap we had to take back in them bygone days of yore. We speak of the old and the true ways and the good old days. There are exchanges of tales of coast to coast runs and all the fun and how There Was A Time.

We talk of how it's over.

chapter seven

STATISTICS, HISTORY, ECONOMICS, SOCIOLOGY, and CHANGES

I recently read a bunch of statistics about riders. Actually it was a bunch of statistics about BMW riders; and, it was compiled and reported by the *BMW Owners News* magazine. No, I don't recall any of the exact numbers.

As a man who has spent his entire professional career in higher education, I already know what can be done with statistics. Most corporate entities now have a second double under associate to the assistant vice president in charge of spin, data deceit, statistical obfuscation, and outright lies. A semi-literate friend of mine refers to statistics as "sadistics."

One time years ago, I was taken to task at work and somehow got a target on my skinny butt. Before the purge was over, I had been held responsible for declining enrollment, lower standardized test scores, a losing basketball season, inadequate parking, and poor food in the cafeteria. The corporate suits did it with chicanery, duplicity, treachery, data, statistics, and bar graphs.

It was a ruse, a damn hoax. When I was able to make my defensive rebuttal, I presented pie charts. I drew little rats in little business suits eating the pies out from the bottom.

But basically what this biker survey indicated is that BMW riders are better educated than owners and riders of other makes of motorcycles. I immediately took mild umbrage. Most of the folks I know riding monstrously expensive new Harleys are businessmen, doctors, and lawyers, all kinds of professional folks with lots of education and even more money. Politicians, TV and movie stars, and their ilk.

And most of the people I know who ride big Honda and Kawasaki road bikes are similarly pretty well-educated people, many of them retired one way or another. While I have no statistical data of my own on any of this, my anecdotal observations indicate that new motorcycles are real expensive. That statistic cuts right across all the various demographic lines. It's true of Japanese and German and American and English and Italian scooters. And most poor folks just can't afford the damn things.

I am confident of this next statistic: as a general rule, people with some education make more money than high school drop-outs. Just to real quick test this out, try to name a poor doctor or a destitute dentist or a needy lawyer, or, for that matter, a penniless architect.

The obvious exception to this is, of course, school teachers. But that can be expected of a society which pays its professional sport-entertainment athlete performers in the millions and its teachers near nothing. One of the results is, of course, illiterate children. The other is badly behaving children; they have, after all, taken their examples from the role models that professional competitors, both athletes and politicians, provide. Statistics indicate there are currently often as many as a dozen convicted felons participating in any given professional football game or Congressional committee. So the kids are glorifying and emulating wife beaters, tax cheaters, girl hitters, child support skippers, drunk drivers, drug abusers, and other losers. And it ain't just O.J. and Representative Gary Condit (Rep., Calif.).

And at any level of education, when the coaches make more money than those who are trying to teach the kids to read and write, the result is good football teams.

Anyway, the statistics in the BMW magazine also indicated that BMW riders were a pretty old bunch as well. That one made way more sense to me than the one about education. And that set me to thinking about it all. Got me to reflecting on old times, and current prices, and demographics generally.

Used to was, back in them bygone days of yore, that the boys with motorcycles were poor boys. Rich boys had new convertible sports cars and girls. And we had cycles. That money thing, that's a main reason why we were on scooters to begin with. Cars and insurance and gas and upkeep and all were just too damn expensive.

But contemporary motorcycles are just way too costly for

most kids anymore. Even the used bikes are beyond the range of regular working at the McFood Mart-Mart Store kids. Oh, some of them manage to afford one of those throw-away Ninja bikes, but they simply can't pay for most other cycles. And that leaves rich kids riding motorcycles, as well as wealthy adults.

And, in all fairness to history, back in them olden days of yesteryear, we were the guys mothers warned their daughters about. We were the boys the police followed out of town as we were passing through. We were the ones the local cops followed around the town where we lived. In the bygone days of yore, there was a distinct motorcycle rider sub-culture. And it didn't include many insurance agents, doctors, money managers, lawyers, architects, real estate brokers, or CEOs with temporary tattoos.

Back forty or so years ago, boots and a leather, didn't matter what you were riding or if you were wearing colors, were just automatically and universally associated with a lot of things, most of them bad. Anymore, there are way more grown-up, educated, rich lawyers on bikes than there are poor boys. Talk about your weirdly shifting statistics and warping demography.

I recently became aware of an even weirder trend, that of separating, labeling, and classifying of riders. I mean I knew that the sport bike folks and the racers and the road riders and so forth were all sort of segregated. But there is division beyond this, and I suspect it is corporate greed inspired. They are fragmenting us like the damn Balkans.

BMW folks have been broken into air-head and oil-head riders, for no apparent reason other than parts availability. Although I see a whole lot of poor old boys on old BMW air-heads anymore. And as a further division, there is the Chain Gang, folks whose bikes have a chain instead of a driveshaft.

Other brands are doing much the same thing. Seems like the Harley folks are the only ones who remain connected and unified. I learned about all this during a recent conversation with a publisher who was unable to determine if I was a "biker" or a "motorcycle enthusiast." Yeah, we need to partition ourselves up like we need more restrictive laws or a return to the days of yesteryear when there was a bounty on us. Unity, as usual, is our only hope.

Motorcycles have become a hobby, mostly for the wealthy,

not unlike sailing or golf. These hobby bikers, I think they are the ones who like to refer to themselves as "motorcycle enthusiasts." A friend of mine, an old boy with as many miles as I got, he once commented, "They might call themselves bikers, but they damn sure ain't riders."

Over the years and along the way, I have stopped and talked to a whole bunch of other riders. In rest areas and campgrounds and motels and gas stations and scooter shops and restaurants and picnic areas, if one biker comes upon another, we usually talk to each other about it all. Anymore, I'm as likely to encounter people named F. Geoffrey and Buffy as I am folks called Snake and Lydia Lou.

Last summer I met three architects, four lawyers, two musicians, a couple engineers, an interior designer, several many insurance and real estate brokers and agents, two medical doctors, a chiropractor, three librarians, a couple cops and firemen and parole officers, two veterinarians, a guy who owned a big car dealership, numerous high level computer geeks, some social workers, a half dozen school teachers of various sorts and levels, a couple tooth doctors, a few CEOs, and several just independently wealthy people.

Never talked to anyone named Bubba who worked at the gas station. Not a single encounter with someone called Crazy LeRoy or Screwy Louie. Nary a single stray chance meeting with an out of work truck driver or unemployed former factory worker. No, the folks I met on motorcycles were all handing one another their business cards and calling on their portable wireless cellular telephones and exchanging e-faxes on the interweb. Many took their laptops out on the road with them. Cell phones abounded. A couple had their laptop and GPS computer mounted on their bikes. Told you it was like golf and sailing.

While I have been called a social critic and a pundit, I really don't know what to conclude on this one. I should further point out here that I have also been called a dinosaur and generally resistant to change. As I have said before, I see little point in change for the sake of different or for the purpose of fashion or fad or trend. But things have changed.

As an example of my personal resistance to it all, at a faculty meeting a couple years back, the Academic Vice President proudly announced that we now had a "paperless" campus. I had done my homework, and I understood that trick. It was typical of technological jargon. Paperless means secretary-less. Much like "virtual" means fake. The computer people are right fond of romantic adventurous sounding jargon: firewall, webmaster, search engine, virus, etc. Anyway, the V.P. continued for some time, pointing out proudly that the whole campus was now wired, and everyone had a computer, many a laptop. He was quite smug.

Then he turned to me and explained to the academic assembly that the next phase would involve trying to upgrade me to a ballpoint pen. I smiled and declined as I held up my user-friendly number two pencil. The fewer moving parts, the better.

Other things, over which I have no control, or even a vote (not unlike the 2000 presidential election), have changed. On the one hand, riders are generally being treated better anymore, thanks to the multitude of hobby bikers and mid-life crisis and too much money riders, and motorcycle enthusiasts. I have been told the term for such folks is R(ich) U(rban) B(ikers), or RUBS or RUBBIES.

But it's been years since I've been run out of town, or roughed and cuffed and hurt and robbed by a guy with a badge and a gun. Now that some of us are doctors and lawyers and such, that wouldn't be police prudent. But, on the other hand, I kind of miss Snake and Lydia Lou and the old sub-culture. Oh, I still get frowned at and treated badly and ostracized sometimes, but that happens whether I am on a scooter or afoot. Good to have some constants in life with all this change going on around us.

So there I was with a 1984 BMW R80/RT with some over four hundred thousand miles on it. Karl The Kraut BMW Mechanic, who is as responsible for those miles as I am, he suggested it was going to get harder and harder to find parts. He said maybe I should look around for another ride. Jimmy G., down there on Dirty Street by Karl The Kraut's Afterhours Scooter Shop and Social Club, he concurred. So I began a search. In fact, Jimmy advised I should maybe look at older bikes, but I ignored his wisdom at first.

First two dealerships I went to made me wish I rode a different brand of bike or that I had stayed with that robbing liquor stores career. I don't recall the exact price I was quoted for a new machine, but I do remember that my first house didn't cost that much. I finally figured out that the new BMW models were running about eight or nine times as much money as the first new one I bought back in 1971. And, thanks to the nature of my chosen profession and the insatiable greed of the corporate weasels I work for, I am not making eight times as much money as I was back in '70.

Beyond that, these new machines had all kinds of things that I either didn't want or didn't understand. Or both. They were all computer-infested, for example. And, although I am confident automatic anti-lock brakes are a good safety feature, I feel pretty secure without them. Same deal with running without a GPS and a cell phone and a laptop. Similarly, I was unimpressed with the low profile tires and multiple digital gauges. I think I saw one with a hydraulic center stand.

One of the bikes I looked at had more damn gauges and meters than early rocket ships. And I can't image why one might need three different means of determining one's oil pressure. I actually saw a couple models that had gas gauges. Seems like you would hardly have time to mind the road with all that digitalized computer information coming at you.

Some models had a bar-b-que pit in one saddlebag and a swimming pool in the other. When I found one that had an electric windshield, a computer that told you your gas consumption and mileage, a heated seat and handlegrips, and a radio and CD changer and player, I finally remembered Jimmy G.'s counsel and began looking at older, used bikes.

And the same damn problem came up. They, both dealerships and private individuals, wanted way too much money for a used machine. I looked at several two- and three-year old models with modest mileage on them, and none of them was under five figures. And these somewhat older motorcycles were similarly heavily into computer-dependency and unnecessary gadgets. Confused and angry, I looked at several Japanese models. Same problems.

One of the big problems with all the newer bikes I looked at and test rode and read about is that the damn things don't have no soul. The motorcycles in my life, especially the good ones, are in the same category with my dogs and horses. They are family members with rights and obligations appertaining thereto.

I am closer to my dogs and horse and scooters than I am to any humans. My dogs and my horse and my scooters, they are my friends. They take me hunting and riding, two of my favorite things in this life. I feed them and take care of them and talk to them, discuss important things with them.

Most of my meaningful decisions have been made on a bike or a horse, or behind a good dog or two. I write stories and poems about them. Hell, I write stories and poems because of them. I bury them nearby and honor their names and accomplishments. Motorcycles, like dogs and horses, are what have kept me sane and even and out of prison.

And these new scooters, with all the computer stuff and conveniences and accommodations and emphasis on ease and comfort, well, the damn things just don't have no soul at all. You can't talk to a computer like you can to a machine. You just can't get close to a computer-infested, digitalized, accommodation/fashion/ aftermarket-calculated, convenience-engineered, rocket-ship lookin', mostly plastic motorcycle. No spirit to them. And that was one of my main reasons for rejecting any of the newer models I encountered. Right behind money.

Somewhere in here, I called my dad, of whom I have written before. And, he came to my rescue, as he has done before. During the phone call, I mentioned to him that the cost of contemporary scooters had gone the way of the price of vehicles, real estate, live bait, gasoline, cigarettes, hay, shotgun shells, and breakfast cereal. Told him all the damn things were full of computerized nonsense that I didn't need or want.

Much like my current pickup truck has three electric buttons to mess with the position of the seat. So far I have discovered seventy-one different but equally uncomfortable positions. It also has a goddamn automatic transmission; I snatched the ashtray into second gear for months, and there is now a dent in the floorboard. It also has electric windows and a radio that I still haven't figured out and am afraid to turn off. And I have already had several serious problems related to all the computer technology. There are few things on that truck that a man could fix with a wrench and a screwdriver.

Dad laughed at my motorcycle problems, as he is prone to do with me. Then a couple days later he called me back to tell me his neighbor had just put a For Sale sign on his cycle. I knew that man, and I knew that bike. So I told my dad to hang up the phone and go take the sign down.

What I wound up with was a really well maintained 1983 BMW R80/RT just exactly like my '84, only with 400,000 fewer miles on it. Yeah, both my bikes are old enough to vote and drink legal. Karl The Kraut stepped up and found an outfit that trucked the bike down to Florida from Michigan. And I put it on the road down here with tags and paperwork and all for some less than three thousand dollars.

The only problem is that the damn thing is red. I have no idea what designation the Little Elves in The Black Forest have for that shade of red, but I personally think it is mid-way between Freudian red and Yoo Hoo Cop! red. My other bike, the one I think of as my old bike, even though it is a year newer than the red one, it's black. I have, over the years, ridden mostly black scooters.

That one, my '84, is named simply RT, and it started out as a real pretty blue color. Eventually, after miles and years and a couple encounters with the pavement, and mismatched color fairing replacement parts, that went to hell. And I decided flat primer black was just fine. I have to repaint it every year or so, but that's no real problem as I can find matching paint lots of places.

One of the local dealerships, in the portion of the work order for color, they wrote in "ugly." Must be it is, because Karl The Kraut and Jimmy G., they both threatened to hurt me if they saw me near the new Red Ride with a can of black primer paint.

When people ask me why I bought such an old machine, I smile and point and tell them, "Carburetors." Then they begin to lookin' at me funny and frowning. They'd look at me even funnier if I tried to explain that motorcycles having souls thing.

A whole lot of other things besides motorcycle prices and technology have changed since I started back in them bygone days of yore. Used to was, if you rode, you wore a pair of jeans and boots and a black t-shirt, and, when it was cold enough, a leather jacket. If you had some money and a sense of fashion, you might have had a denim or a leather vest as well. Maybe a helmet, depending on the law and your own feelings on such things.

Awhile back, I was introduced to the contemporary concept

of "motorclothing." Someone should reward the corporate genius who came up with this one. What a great marketing ploy. It's right up there with convincing folks that what the fast chainfood franchise places sell is actually food. So now, just like with so many other rich people's hobbies, sailing and golf for example, they've got appropriate expensive clothing to indicate their enthusiasm.

Many of these people, I've noticed, have ear plugs. Even the folks riding the quieter machines tend to sport ear plugs along with their body armor and all. Makes me wonder how they can hear the machine, or for that matter, their CD players.

The couple I encountered had matching motorclothing. I mean everything from helmets (with walkie talkies) to boots matched. Even their doo-rag/skull caps matched. Sunglasses, too. Gloves with zippers but no fingers in them, and real colorful rhinohide-endurolast-gortex-monsterfab-eternosubstance jumpsuits with body armor and more zippers. Hell, even their haircuts matched.

Now pay good attention here, because I don't mean that just their costumes matched one another. No, their outfits matched their matched bikes, as well. The girl, Jennifer Buffy Heather Amber, she began explaining to me that their double motorcycle trailer also matched everything else. Her old man, the barrister J. Winslow Pierpoint Geoffrey, Esq., he was smiling and eagerly nodding his agreement as I made my swift departure. I saw a bumper sticker awhile back that I wanted to send to them. It said "I rode my bike to Trailer Week."

There was a time when outlaw bikers and pretenders to it all seemed to think they were supposed to have tattoos and ear rings and dress like gypsies and pirates. And that was weird and scary enough.

But now that most of the outlaws have faded off into organized crime and historical obscurity, we've got this new breed of wealthy enthusiasts out there who seem to favor trying to look like deep sea divers or astronauts or maybe space knights of some kind. Jennifer Buffy Heather Amber and old F. Geoffrey, they had on more protective body armor than most professional racers. Looked like they were fixin' to joust. And a lot of the enthusiasts on Harleys, they look and sound like they are mounting a cavalry charge.

For all these reasons, anymore I tend to make a lot of swift departures. Find myself bolting for the door more than I used to. I do that at a lot of meetings of late. Mostly it is because I have got old and just no longer give a damn about offending idiots. Where I used to think I should be polite and remain in pointless interaction with a fool, lately I've got to where I think I've listened to enough fools for one lifetime.

That somehow reminded me of a verse from the Lowdown Outbound Scootertrash Blues that goes on about how, Most of us are slow learners, a few are slow to finish, and some of us were just slow starters. And we could have all of us amounted to something, if we'd been just a little bit smarter. Hell, if it hadn't been for Billy and Captain America, all us old longriders would've been martyrs.

As a result of listening to too many fools, I have finally come to a conclusion on the whole abortion issue. I think it is a woman's issue and that women should decide it. First time a man opens his mouth on the topic, a couple girls should just bitchslap him to his knees and make him quit it. Especially men in judicial and religious robes.

Same deal with kids. I think folks named Mom and Dad should be in charge of determining what the kids should eat, drink, smoke, wear, read, and watch. Seems like this might work best if someone were to stay home and raise the kids to accomplish it. I just can't understand how such things became the function of government, not in America.

Smoking rules for restaurants, like the menu and daily special, should be determined by the guy who owns the restaurant. Unfortunately, anymore we're dealing with giant huge franchise chainfood emporiums; the owners are a multi-national corporate entity headquartered in Brussels and Singapore. But, ideally, the guy who owns or runs the restaurant should decide. A real good guy would let his employees voice their opinions on these matters.

Similarly, or so it seems to me, individual businesses should be allowed to decide if they want to put in a wheelchair ramp and Braille menus and such as that. If they want to piss off the crippled, that should be their American prerogative. Same deal with language. If the owner figures his customers ought to have to get along in English, it being America and all, then he ought not be required to put up signs in foreign languages.

After that I think the real problem is overpopulation, and overdevelopment, and overcrowding. Beginning with the planet and coming right on down to where I live. Wouldn't be so bad if folks weren't so senselessly inconsiderate and pointlessly rude. But crowding brings out the worst in people. My new neighbors bought twenty acres across the road from me. Then they subdivided. Used to was, I could walk across the road and shoot enough quail for supper just near any time I wanted to.

But not now. These new folks all set their houses very near the road, facing mine. Then they put in gates directly across from mine. They got a couple hundred feet of frontage, but they put their gates directly across the damn road from mine.

And they carry on all their noisy activities, from cutting their screaming children loose to shouting on their cell telephones and honking at their gate to playing their car radios loud to screeching at their barking dogs and screaming children, in the short space between their house and the road. They also all put in lots of real bright lights way up on telephone poles out in their yards. Made sure they shined in my windows. Damn birds were so confused they were singing at midnight the other night. City people love their noise and light, and they seem to want to bring it on out here with them.

There was little to do to my new Red Ride when I got it. I changed the oil and filter and put a tube in one of the tires. All that was left to do was to ride it. So I did. I rode it down to Dirty Street to Karl The Kraut's Afterhours Scootershop and Social Club to show it to him and Jimmy G. They were both impressed. Karl replaced the wheel bearings and adjusted the valves and put some crash bars on it for me. Then I rode it to work every day for a month or so. Evenings and weekends, I rode it locally to wherever I was going. Two things happened as a result of that. That new Red Ride, she told me her name. It's Omega.

That brings us back once again to that old motorcycles having souls thing. I don't think the current computer dependent, convenience based, accommodation and ease infested plastic scooters tell you their names.

And the other thing is that the old Black Bike, RT, is the one with 460,000 miles on it. The old Black Bike is, as I said, a year newer than the red one. And the second thing that happened was that the old Black Bike got bitchy from all the settin' still. It refused to start or run the next time I got on it. I have since worked out a time-mile share plan in which both get rode.

Then when I took the new Red Ride out on the road for the Summer, I changed the custom saddle off the black one and onto the red one. Then I unhooked the battery of the Black Bike on my way out. See could I avoid some of that bitchiness.

The main difference between the way you set and ride the two bikes is that seat. Oddly, the Red Ride came with a stock seat that is the only real comfortable stock BMW seat I've ever sat on. And the Dunlop tires on the red one make some difference. But it was a good choice, buying a machine just like the one I been riding for fifteen years. I'm too damn old to try to be retrained. I am still trying to master that number two pencil, for example.

I mentioned that I had to be retrained relative to car radios awhile back. The radio in my new, computer-infested pickup truck went all to hell. So I drove down to the local car radio place. Told them let's pull the radio out and see which tube to replace. They laughed. No, you don't do such as that anymore. Now the scheme is to replace the whole radio. And, while I was some upset at the cost of such an endeavor, the real problem is that the new radio has no knobs. Nothing but tiny little buttons of various shapes to push. Some appear to be color-coded. I really was scared to turn the damn thing off.

When you turn it on, there is a little screen lights up on the front panel that says, "Hello." Then it tells me the brand of my new radio and a few other things I don't need to review. Takes awhile. When you turn it off, which also takes awhile, the screen reads, "See You." That of course makes me wonder if it is some kind of contemporary American citizen surveillance device.

Between those events, I am given all manner of information on that screen, most of which I don't need or want or understand. I have finally mastered that turning it off thing; you have to mash on the tiny little button extra long. Most of the functions require a time lag before they kick in, and I am often startled by what happens.

But I am still unable to determine how loud "seventeen" is.

And when the digital read-out clock tells me it is 8:17, I have to translate and figure out which way Mickey is pointing with which hand. Unlike contemporary children, I do not believe everything I see on a TV screen or a lighted digital display.

Several Summers ago, I had a woman invite me to ride with her awhile. She had her own scooter and was out there at it in the Summertime. Before it was done, I had followed that girl about three thousand miles down the highways and backroads. She did a lot for me in terms of bringing me up to date with the present.

I was introduced to all manner of after-market accessories of which I had been previously ignorant. I been doing it the same way for the past forty-some years. That Summer was when I found out about motorclothing and body armor and such as that. The corporate greed-based bountiful motorcycle aftermarket.

This girl had a jacket that matched her scooter, with about eleven pockets and assorted other zippers that were air vents. She had gloves without no fingers in them. She had a full-face helmet with some kind of special face shield and vents and such in it. She had some kind of trick boots that had a hidden zipper behind the laces.

She also had a load that weighed way more than she did piled up behind her. And she was doing all this on a mid-sized sport bike. I knew I was way past ever being able to do such a thing, so I didn't have much in the way of sarcastic commentary or snide remarks. No, I just set back silent and took a few lessons.

One of the lessons was Motorcycle Rallies. As I got on a motorcycle in the beginning expressly to get away from other people, the concept of rallies had pretty much evaded me. But this girl was on her way to a few, and I was invited. And now, I get it. Hell, I even get it from a woman's point of view.

I'm not an especially social person; I seldom seek the company of other humans. Although I have been married repeatedly, and sometimes for long periods, I have also enjoyed many years of solitude between those matrimonial events. I like the isolation. I fully savor time alone. I'm not a bit bothered by eating alone or sitting quiet in a room by myself reading a book. I thoroughly enjoy the company of my dogs and my horse. Hell, I've even got to where I kind of like that cat. But I'm just fine by myself without other people.

Used to was, most longriders were of the same breed. We would run into one another out there on the edges, at rest areas, at scenic overlooks, and remote campgrounds and distant picnic pavilions out on the periphery, beyond The Forbidden Zone. We'd find one another on lonely beaches and beside rivers and on back roads and tell one another our old highway tales and more recent road stories. We would discuss places and roads more than we ever talked about the mechanics of motorcycles. We would speak of the sky and the wind. Then we'd pass through.

I have one more statistic that needs sharing. As I have mentioned, the past several years I have been invited to a number of motorcycle rallies, mostly to promote and sell my books and CDs. Up until a short while ago, I did pretty well, too. It's always flattering just to be asked to appear. And I have met some fine people, made a few good friends, some of whom still write to me and come to visit here at The Redoubt.

Couple Summers back, at the Nightriders Cornhusker Rally, there were about two hundred people, and I sold around twenty books and half that many tapes. Same deal with the Damn Yankee Rally, and with a recent Central Florida Rally. A couple hundred people, a couple dozen books and ten tapes and CDs got sold.

Usually the event organizers set me up at a table with a pile of my books and tapes. Sometimes they provide me with a CD player so folks can listen to a sample of the epic motorcycle poetry and the pretty music. And then, beyond this, I am often asked to do a presentation, a reading from one of the books or a poem told live with some musical accompaniment.

Awhile back I got invited to the ABATE of Florida Spooks and Scoots Rally. It was around Hallowe'en, and it was nearby. I have been a loyal member of ABATE for some time, and I was promised a table between the Security/First Aid tent and the CMA booth. Figuring location was everything, I readily accepted.

This was a much larger gathering than the local and regional rallies I have become accustomed to. There were in excess of two thousand people there, or so I was told. It looked like to me that many of those in attendance had arrived in vehicles, but there were easily a thousand motorcycles. It was loud, and it was colorful. It was warm and dry and dusty. Chrome glittered in the sunlight, exhaust smoke and noise filled the air. Beer was a buck and a half, and there were all kinds of shopping opportunities.

And I sold two books and one CD, all to the nice folks in the nearby Christian Motorcycle Association booth. Beyond that, someone stole a CD. Yeah, the ratio of bikers to books sold was frighteningly inverse. Turned out there weren't that many readers in this group. In fact, on the second day, just before I packed it up and headed home, I finally realized that the only ink these folks were looking at was on one another. As I rode off, I regretted that I hadn't taken tattooing lessons instead of going off to book writin' and poem tellin' school.

chapter eight
WOMEN, IRONY, and REFLECTIONS
ON A WAY OF LIFE

Just recent here, I went and wound up with a Full-Time Good Woman. In that last book, I claimed I had learned my lesson and was done with it. But somehow romance loomed its funny lookin', emotional head, and I went and fell in love with a girl I have known for twenty years or more. Working out real well so far, too. Oddly, or so it seems to me, most people who know us both seem to think it was inevitable that we get together.

This has happened, even though I have memorized the verse of the Scootertrash Blues that goes, The highway is like a beautiful woman who keeps you distrustful and gives you no peace. Like a young girl who smiles at you and gives you false hope, when all you needed was sweet relief.

This New Full-Time Woman, she has known me long enough to understand that I ain't goin' to tame down, or clean up, or ever amount to much. Girl has known me way too long to put up with any of my crap. She has been a good friend. And she has fed and tended to my animals and watched my house every time I was gone out on the road for most of those twenty years. You have to trust someone a lot to give your house and dogs and horse and cat over to her care. This woman was the one who heard all my old highway stories and poems when they were new, at least the ones from the last twenty years.

Hard to even try to lie to a woman who knows you that well. For example, I didn't even attempt to tell her that thing about me coming from royalty, on my daddy's side. She's met my dad, too.

I don't understand it of course. I mean she could do better than me by feeling around in the dark, one-handed. And, if nothing else, she has known me long enough to know better.

Maybe I've finally got old enough to be able to identify and appreciate a good woman and to try to treat her well. Perhaps all the practice and experience over the years and along the way is paying off here. Possibly I have gotten into a good situation, where all I have to do is not fuck it up, and I finally understand that.

Those of you all who have read my other books understand that if it weren't for irony, there would be no humor in my life. Yeah, I got me a truefine goodwoman here, but I lost an exceptional house and animal sitter.

She is another one of those women who, when she tells you to get up and put on your boots and do something, expects you not to argue or defer. I tried once. She just smiled and patted me on my head, and said, "Darlin', that is just so cute, the way you think you have a say in it like that."

Anyway, she's been up behind me a few times on the scooter here recent. So far she is real good at it. Tall, pretty girl, with legs to her neck. She's spent a lot of her life with and on horses, so there is that extra advantage. That benefit is when a potential mess occurs in motion on the scooter. She doesn't tighten up and try to help like most passengers. No, she just relaxes and settles in to let the horse sort it out. We've only been on some real short local rides. I doubt she's got three hundred miles on her butt so far.

We were going to ride over to Daytona for Bike Week. I am the Pet Author In Residence at the Barnes and Noble store across from the Speedway there every Bike Week and Biketoberfest. And, because they always treat me better than kin over there, I always go.

Besides that, pretty Tina, who runs the place, is in large part responsible for the title of my second book. Several of us were sitting around her bookstore one rainy Biketoberfest, and talk turned to my upcoming book. I said I expected it would be called Longrider II. And Tina straightened me out on Roman numerals in book titles. A discussion ensued, and somehow *The Ghost of Scootertrash Past* got voted the top title. Everyone agreed it was honest.

Awhile later, I sent that title idea to a friend up in Maryland who runs an ad agency I used to do some radio commercial voice-over work for. He said it was the worst book name he had ever heard of, and that I might just as well call it Springtime For Hitler. He suggested Whiteline Dancer. But I thought that just sounded way too 1970s Cocaine-Disco Dancin' for anyone to buy and read.

But back to this new woman, the Tallgirl, and not riding in the rain. It was storming bad that first weekend of Bike Week this year, so we took my truck the hundred and thirty or forty miles across the state. And with every downpour and deluge we passed through, she thanked me for not getting her wet. Both ways.

Sometime after that, I got invited down to Fort Myers to the Lee County Reading Festival. We made plans to ride down there, but the weather reports warned me off at the last minute. As usual, the weather reading TV newspuppets were wrong, and we didn't see but about nine drops of rain the whole time. And she frowned at me and chided me for not taking the bike. Both ways.

Anyway, that all got me to thinking about other women who have got up behind me one way or another. The first one I recalled was new to it. She claimed she used to ride behind her daddy or brother or ex-husband or someone like that, but I doubted it. She was a determined novice, however. We had taken a couple short day rides before we started out on the big one. She might have had a hundred miles on her when we took off on what she began referring to as The Long Journey. We rode between five and six hundred miles that first day out. It was mostly two lanes through the heat of August in the Southeast.

And she was a brave girl the entire while. I didn't hear a complaint or a whine or a bitch or whimper the whole day. And it was godawful hot. Whenever I saw her in my mirrors, she was smiling. But when we quit for the day, she looked wounded and weary. Fatigue was in her eyes. She didn't quite fall off the bike, but she nearly collapsed once she got off. I had stopped at a motel, one somewhat nicer than I would have chosen if I had been solo or with a highway brother.

When I saw that she was exhausted, I hurriedly opened the motel door and walked her in and sat her down with a cold drink. Turned on the air-conditioner for her. Then I went back out to unpack and unload the bike. By the time I had most of the gear in the motel room, she was up again.

Her first move was to go into the bathroom and grab a wash cloth and turn on the hot water to wash her face. Even though I kind of knew what was coming, her scream when she saw what had come off her face and onto the washrag kind of startled me. Louder than I had anticipated I guess. Apparently the white washcloth had come away even blacker and grimier than I had figured.

I gave it a minute to let her recover, and then I stepped to the door of the bathroom and said to her, "Darlin', blow your nose, too." I'd given her this advice two or three times during that day's ride, but she had just looked at me funny and ignored my counsel.

Her reaction to seeing what had blown up her nose in five hundred miles was even more dramatic than discovering what was on her face. She gave it a little lady-like toot, and then there was silence. Then there were a couple giant huge honking nose blows. When she examined the Kleenex, she said in a loud, yet resigned voice that reverberated around the motel bathroom, "Jesus Fucking Yuck!" Then she began running water for a bath. I had to come pull her boots and jeans off, as she was too sore and lame to do either one.

Normally, there are few things in this life that I would rather do than take a girl's clothes off, but this was different. This woman kept looking at me with an accusatory eye. Yeah, I was the prick who had gotten her into this. I helped her into her hot bath, and then I got the hell out of there to check my oil and tires and such.

It was another girl one time who didn't last that long. Young girl, hard into appearances, make-up and fashionable clothes, and looking good and all. Florida had recently repealed the fascist helmet law, and she decided that she would avoid helmet-hair. I think mandatory helmet laws and similar statutes are unjust and un-American. And I have fought such repressive, tyrannical inequities all my life. I have also always worn a helmet. I promised my Grammaw I would fifty years ago.

But, despite being a young girl, she was a grown woman, quite capable of making such decisions on her own. So I told her to go ahead on and leave the extra helmet to home. I suggested maybe she might want to don a skullcap or some kind, maybe a bandanna over her head, at least a braid or a ponytail. But, no, she wanted the breeze blowing in her long pretty hair. And the wind did blow through her long hair for a hundred long miles.

The problem with that is that the breeze tangles long hair just about like if you'd put it in a blender. I learned this one years ago, personally, the hard way, as all important lessons are gathered. Over the years and along the way I have learned to put my own long hair in a pony tail, tie it with about a half dozen of those elastic pony tail things, and then tuck it in a shirt pocket. But I have also learned along the way not to try to debate with a woman who has her mind made up. No, once they've got to that point, there is no use in trying to confuse them with reason. Same rule applies to men in suits. Dogma wins out over logic every single time.

We ran that long hundred miles before she figured out she looked like the Bride of Frankenstein in an electric hurricane. It was made even more problematic because her hair had also become somewhat entangled and ensnarled in the preposterous long fringe of her cool looking leather jacket with the roses tooled into the yoke. She had chaps that matched. I had prudently said nothing about the fringe either. Guess I was just glad she hadn't donned spurs.

Besides that bird nest leather fringe and long hair thing, there was the high speed and make-up problem. Seems the fringe and long hair had sort of beaten her mascara and eye-liner and lash volumizer off and near blinded her in the process. She looked like a near-sighted raccoon having a truly bad hair day. It took near an hour to repair the damaged make-up.

But first, she made me help remove the fringe from her hair and then help her comb and brush the tangles out of her hair. I had to cut a few fringes and one snarl of hair with my pocket knife. Then she put her hair in a braid and put a bandanna over it. She took my jacket away from me; the fringed jacket was tied on behind her, fringe side in. Then she took my helmet away from me for the ride home. Helmet hair, like most things, it turns out, is relative. And then, as you might expect, she never got back on the bike ever again.

As the Long-gone Scootertrash Blues indicates, Sometimes they hold your hand and walk into your arms and give you a reason to believe. Sometimes they ease your pain until things go to hell, and then it all turns into grief. And the best you can hope for either way, is that she gets right to it, and makes it blessedly brief.

Back to that current Full-Time Woman here a minute. This past weekend was the book store gig in Sarasota, about a long hundred miles away. I was hoping for the opportunity to put the Tallgirl up behind me and let her look at a hundred miles of stone abject interstate highway boredom on the way down. Then I was going to bring her back home on some backroads to let her observe the contrast.

Instead I got to bore her to death in a pickup truck in a rainstorm on the expressway for two hours in both directions. West Central Florida doesn't get a lot of rain in the Winter and early Spring, but what we do get happens on the weekends. Check the precipitation totals for Bike Week weekends sometime. And you ought to review someplace in here for comments about vehicle drivers in the rain.

On the way back from Sarasota, the Tallgirl got kind of cocky and decided that instead of thanking me for keeping her dry, she would mess with me for being a weenie and not riding in the rain. Next chance I get, we're going riding in the rain.

And I had another passenger just recent here. Old Captain Zero (ret'd.), now that he is done with the hindrance that is work, he came to visit. One day we took off locally, mostly because I wanted him to set on my new Red Ride awhile. First place we went was over to the Waffle House so Tammy Kay LeTara Amy could feed us a hearty breakfast.

We got gone north from there and rode up into the hinterlands of the Pasco-Hernando Alps. The moon was full the night previous to this, and me and the Tallgirl had taken a ride out under it. It was a windy and ragged night. We wore our leathers. A cold front had come through earlier in the day, and it was still borderline chilly. In fact, I had already gotten real wet coming home from work that evening.

The wind was still pushing the weather. The bike kept getting bounced around in the cross-wind. So I headed up onto a road that runs through the Green Swamp, through the tall pine and cypress trees that block the wind. And that road was stone empty in the moonlit night. Shadows of the taller trees stretched across the two lanes and the centerline.

That wind put me in mind of a line from that old song about how We have heard The Bad Wind rising, and we have seen wild birds in the air flying.

Was a hell of a moon in that wind. It was big and full, and jagged clouds were blowing across it in the wind. Then a big circle, an aureole of pink light, formed around that full moon. Irregular, tattered clouds continued to streak across the yellow moon and the pink circle around it. Pretty night.

This ride with Zero was a pretty day, too. Mid-seventies with mostly sunshine. The perfect day for a t-shirt and a denim jacket. And there was still a little wind.

The wind was a good thing though. It was blowing high, thin clouds all over the early April sky. And somehow that created a couple huge sundogs. And there was plenty else to demand our attention. Fortuitously, there was little traffic to make a mess out of the passin' through as we watched the sky and the roadside.

An old and dear friend of mine, girl named Carol, tells a story about sundogs. She was with her niece one time, on the east coast of Florida when a sundog appeared in the sky. She explained to her niece and later to me that the bright shiny sundog is the sun reflecting on the ice crystals in a cirrus cloud.

Zero, like he tends to do, got right into it. "Tiger, this is THE way to travel, at least on days like this in places like this."

"What you talkin' 'bout, Captain?" I knew exactly what he was talking about, but I wanted to hear his take on it.

"You can FEEL the contours of the land on a motorcycle. Everything seems closer, more intense. The highway, the trees, the livestock, the sky. This is real intimate." He pointed up and smiled. That sundog was stretched through a wispy cloud that was near horizontal across a large portion of the southeastern sky. Below the green segment of the spectrum, the purple was real faint, as the cloud was thinnest there.

We admired the sky as we rode on. There was the occasional bird to distract us from the colorful sundog. Again, as there was little traffic, and a medium straight road, all that was possible. I happened to glance off to the side of the road to a huge, dead, ancient, solitary oak tree in an empty pasture. And damned if there wasn't an eagle on one of the bare branches.

So we drifted over to the side of the backroad and turned the machine off and admired the bald eagle for ten minutes or so. Zero continued his observations as he took a long, deep breath. I followed suit and encountered the aromas of dust, and cattle, and the wild flowers in bloom all around us, and the odor of water a long way upwind.

Captain Zero, he continued, "You know, Tiger, you can smell things when you are out on a bike, too." Yeah, I knew. I have always known. But it sure was reassuring to hear it again. The Captain, he claimed he could discern a half dozen different kinds of flowers in bloom.

I recalled that a few weeks previous, me and the New Full-Time Woman had taken a ride out among the orange blossoms. Although a native Florida girl, she had marveled at the perfume of the citrus blooms as we blew down the roads between them.

Me and Zero sat there some time, but our presence didn't bother the eagle a damn bit. We saddled back up and pressed on. About a half mile down the road, there was a small swamp on the south side. That explained the smell of water up the road. Then I saw a wild hog out in the open on a small cypress head. I pointed him out to the Captain, and we rode parallel to the pig for a slow hundred yards or so. We weren't bothering that little piney woods porker any more than we had the eagle.

"I'm telling you, Tiger. You should hock everything you own, call in all your markers, take out a big loan, and put an ad in rich people magazines and newspapers. You market this right, and you'll have them thinking they're on an adventure. This involves all the senses.

"Old Weird Tiger's Cross-Country Setting Behind Him Motorcycle Tours. Hell, man, they would even think the restaurants you take them to are adventures." Captain Zero was getting hard into this new idea.

The hog went one way, and the road went another, so we rode on and re-directed our attention to the still-shifting sundog in the Spring sky. And Zero proceeded with his soliloquy on motorcycle travel.

"Listen to me, Tiger. Rich people would love riding around the country like this. They're paying big money for lots less. This would really give them something to talk about at the country club and on the links. You could turn one saddlebag into a cooler for the martinis and fine wine, put a few little watercress finger sandwiches up for the picnic. I think you have to cut the crusts off for rich people." He wasn't letting this plan for my new career go.

Now that he is retired, he has way too much time on his hands. He paused to watch a flock of birds, probably bobolinks, go over our ride. Then he continued. He nodded toward the road, "This is so much more personal than the airplane."

I pointed out that I didn't think rich folks were much into feeling the bumps and contours of the road. My limited experience is that rich people think camping is someplace without a rheostat on the light switch. The few real rich folks I know, their idea of roughing it involves places without room service.

I said so to Zero. I also opined that there is little to recommend flying on the airplane, other than speed.

Captain Zero, who is setting a fine example for those of us who hope to retire someday, somehow, he just smiled at me. When he first came to visit, I would sometimes say something like, "Hey, Pard, I could use some help patching that piece of fence in the corral later on."

About the second time I did such a thing, he held up a small sign he had made. It's about the size of a playing card. It has the word "WORK" printed on it. There is a circle around the word and a red slash through it. Then he got a dictionary and slowly read the definition of the word "retired" to me.

From behind me on the scooter now, he continued by saying, "Or on the train."

The Captain had arrived at the Orlando Train Station in Florida on the wheels of Amtrak's Sunset Limited. Rode that train all the way from Los Angeles. Rode a different one, the Coast Starlight, from San Francisco to L.A. He's been on lots of trains, in lots of places, many of them in other continents. And as the cable car conductor for the San Francisco Municipal Railway for many years, he has on the job experience as well. So, the Captain, he knows about trains.

"Or even in a car." We had already discussed how one advantage of a BMW motorcycle is that you can have conversations of this sort, even with helmets and no walkie-talkies. You can talk more easily in a car of course, but you really can have serious intelligent conversations on a BMW cycle. Maybe, because of this limitation, they become more serious dialogues because you have to think more carefully about what you say.

And Zero's next comment addressed that, "Damned cars are all sealed up. There is little opportunity to get truly personal and intimate with the countryside in an automobile. You can't see around you like this from a car." He gestured grandly. "Or as far, somehow." He paused and frowned off into the distance as he considered this aspect. "And we sure wouldn't be having this conversation in a car." He pointed to the sky as he said it.

"What you reckon we'd be talkin' about, Pardner?" There was a long, easy curve downhill. The Captain waited until we had got straightened back out to answer me.

"Something else. Women. Books. Hunting. Old Times. Guitars. Women. Fishing. Old Friends." That slowed him down some. We had each of us buried a couple of our real good longtime oldfriends just recent, one on each coast.

He shook it off and smiled, "You'd be bitching about the hindrance that is your job. And I would not." The Captain chuckled and took another short break as he looked back up at the sky. "You know, the kind of conversations that air-conditioning, a CD player, and a sealed environment bring on."

"Don't be goin' esoteric and existential on me, now, Captain."

"I'm serious. The beauty and..." Here my old pardner paused and searched his mind for the appropriate word. Finally he continued, "...the perfection. The total cosmic, Zen orientation in the moment. Being here now. It's priceless, Tiger."

Again, I have known all this all my life, but it was good to have it reconfirmed. We were in hilly country now. There were grapefruit groves on both sides of the sweeping, curving old two-lane road. The blooms had mostly become tiny fruit. But a few fragrant blossoms remained in the trees. Small lakes appeared between the hills in the near distance. Insects rattled against the windshield, and wooden planks clattered beneath the tires as we crossed an old bridge over a small stream. An armadillo scampered for cover beside the road. We went into the shadows under a canopy of trees, and several kinds of birds were singing in the branches.

The Captain reached around me and into my shirt pocket for a cigarette. I could feel him bunch up behind me as he got out of the wind to light it. "Thanks, man. I think the rich people will demand that you light their cigarettes for them."

The pavement went to hell for a few miles, and I was too busy with that to pay much mind to the scenery or the wildlife. Zero narrated some of it for me as we passed through. I recall he took notice of the bee boxes out in the blossoming orange groves.

And he also continued his recent fantasy about how I was going to make money. "You could make a fortune. Wealthy people could spend a couple days with you doing this. Feed them at the Waffle House a couple times and at The Redoubt a time or two. I'd suggest that marinaded duck dish we had the other night."

A late stray flock of mallards had gone over our quail hunt awhile back, and The Captain had been complimenting my marksmanship and culinary skills ever since. He said the same thing about the venison chili.

"Tiger, trust me. I'm your test case here. Now, if you could just arrange to have a chocolate put on my pillow each evening. And someone needs to talk to the staff about making less noise when they go off to work early in the morning. I'd give it at least three and a half stars."

"I already got a job." That was as close as I was coming to a clever rejoinder. The road required my attention.

The Captain, smiling at the bird songs, went on, "Seriously, man, you really experience the country this way. You encounter it. I mean, I saw four busted bolts, two pieces of ripped off chrome, part of a spring, a dog collar, and a piece of a tail light lens at that last stop sign. You don't see that stuff in a car, or on expressways."

We were briefly interrupted as I slowed down and rode around several chickens in the road.

"Don't get to see much of that, neither." I gestured toward a nearby pasture. There were a couple dozen longhorn cattle, most of them spotted brown and white. Some had horns five and six feet across. They were pretty impressive, so we pulled over to smoke a cigarette and admire the bovines.

Across the road from the pasture was a flooded field. The shallow water was festooned with birds. I recognized two kinds of egrets, snipe, wood storks, ibis, herons, and a bunch of coots. There were two or three others that remained unidentified. A turkey buzzard landed nearby and chased another one off some piece of carrion. Other vultures wheeled high overhead. A red tailed hawk swooped past, the sun behind it setting its tail on fire.

The Captain had earlier bought a fieldguide book to help him distinguish the flora and fauna and fish of this area. He got it out now and identified the unknown species of birds as a least bittern, a rail, and an immature sandhill crane. Then he went to work on the nearby flowers.

"You could supply the rich people with these reference books. Turn this part into a nature hunt and give them badges or patches or framed certificates to put up in their offices and dens. Rich people love certificates." He went on to identify more trees, shrubs, and wildwood flowers.

We rode on. That sundog diminished as we continued to admire it. Then it just finally disappeared from the sky. I was sad to see it go.

The Captain, he resumed, "I'm serious, Tiger. You ought to somehow set up a business of taking rich people on the back of your bike like this. They'd truly love it. And think of the stories you'd have for your next book."

"I don't think so, Pard. I like it too much myself to mess it up with rich folks."

The Captain came at it from another angle, a retired one. "Yeah, you're right. Then it would all turn into a job."

We sang a short verse of the Lowdown Lonesome Scootertrash Blues as we rode on. The road forever reminds us that we may not have a future, but we damn sure got a past. The highway tells us we can never ride away from where we been and what we've done, no matter how hard or fast. The only thing left after figuring that out is how to make some of it last.

chapter nine
RIDING IN THE RAIN (or not),
YOUTHFUL MEMORIES, and MORE IRONY

I have never enjoyed riding in the rain. Even alone in a good rain suit and all, I have never ever had an especially fun time on a motorcycle in the rain. And I have ridden in some storms, some of them with names. I once came within two hundred miles of riding in the rain coast to coast. And I have managed that damp feat from border to border. My rides in the rain have been solo, and with a passenger, alone and with other riders. Once in awhile I will run into a rider who claims he likes riding in the rain. But then I know some guys who apparently enjoy hanging out with sociopathic women and working for fascists in business suits.

No matter what you do or wear, you are going to get wet if you try to ride in the rain. Hard rain will find a gap in your brand new modern expensive rain suit. Usually, if it's raining hard, the inside of your helmet gets wet early. And then it will seep in around that gap in the collar of the jacket, and it will soak through the break in the elastic cuff, or it will start up your pantleg. Or, probably worse, it will get in your boots.

And that's just the unpleasant part. After that it gets hazardous and dangerous. You just flat out can't see very well in a hard rain. It's much worse than trying to see through a vehicle windshield with the wipers going.

And then there is the road surface. I can't think of a road that improves in the rain. And some of them get downright slimy. Slipping a few inches or so sideways in a vehicle is pretty scary; the same move on a scooter can be fatal. And your brakes get wet and grabby. And it's dark.

And, as every longrider eventually finds out, rain turns vehicle drivers into raving idiots, less attentive and careful than is their usual habit even. I have no statistics on this, but I am confident more riders are hit in the rain than on sunny days. So now you have bad weather, disabled sight, a bad road surface, personal discomfort, and poor drivers to contend with.

Awhile back, I was rolling down a two-lane backroad someplace in either east Indiana or west Ohio. It was a brisk and breezy late Summer morning out there in the hardwood hills, and then it began raining. I dropped into a gas station and put on my rainsuit and Tote boots and face shield, tried to wrap and cover my gear so it would stay dry behind me. Then I got back to it.

Down the wet road a few miles, I noticed a pair of bikes behind me. They made no effort to catch up or pass or join me, but they were in my mirrors for about a half hour. And the wicked rain intensified the whole time. It got windier and colder too.

When it began raining hard enough that I felt it unwise to continue, I found an abandoned used car lot with a convenient overhang. I bailed off the road and into the roadside shelter. Lightning provided me some extra illumination on my way in. Thunder accompanied shutting off my bike. I parked so that there would be room for the riders behind me if they also sought shelter from the weather.

But the two other bikes blew right on by me. I could see they were boys. They really didn't turn and sneer and laugh at me as they rode by, but I felt like it. There I was, hiding from the storm. And I had a big, overdressed road bike and a rain suit and all. And these kids were on mid-sized scooters with nothing even remotely like rainsuits. I felt like an elderly sissy as I poured a cup of coffee from my Thermos and unwrapped a dry package of Oreo cookies.

Then, as I watched their tail lights disappear into the damp distance, I thought about forty-some years ago. As one of the early verses to the Outbound Scootertrash Blues says, We were runnin' a hundred miles an hour, and the whole world was on fire. We had a full tank of gas and nothin' else but desire. There was still a thrill in crossin' a state line, leavin' what little you had and knew behind.

I reflected on those times, back when my idea of rain gear was a face shield and a towel. As I pondered all this, I began laughing when I remembered that face shield was heavily tinted and badly scratched. Ah, youth.

Back then we were all poor boys, and the idea of a big and/ or dressed bike was only a dream in a dim future sometime. We rode used, often abused, hand-me-down second and third-hand motorcycles. And, because of that lack of money thing, they were all pretty much naked, stock bikes with nothing like a fairing or a windshield or saddlebags. If we had any extra money, it went into buying oil and new chains and occasionally a tire.

And we would take off in boots and a leather, with a change of socks and an army surplus pup tent tied on the back of the seat or across the handlebars. Sometimes we took a sleeping bag, often decorated with cowboys and Indians. As bunji cords, along with rain suits and frame-mount fairings, tail racks, tank bags, pullover rubber boots, and interstate highways had not yet been invented, the socks and sleeping bag and tent were tied on with rope. As the Lonesome Lowdown Outbound Scootertrash Blues explains, We picked up some mud and some local color, too, in them early days as we passed through.

These trips were customarily taken at Summer's end, with the vestiges of the last Summer-job-paycheck in our pocket. There were three constants on these rides. We always ran out of money, we always broke down, and it always rained. No, I lied. There were four. We always had a good time.

As I watched the two kids ride off down the rainy midwestern highway, I clearly recalled one such ride. It must have been about 1961, or '62, or '63. I had spent my Summer, as I always spent my Summers and weekends, all holiday vacations, and a few evenings during the week, working at a meat packing plant. My dad worked there, so I always had a ready-made, whether I wanted it or not, part-time kid job. During a twenty-year period, I did every job there was to be done there.

As a tiny child, my dad took me on his truck route with him. I was in a blood- and grease-stained diminutive white meatcoat carrying loaves of lunch meat and roll sausage and slabs of bacon into little neighborhood Mom and Pop stores. I got a nickel an hour for my efforts. A nickel was quite a bit of money back in '50. And I learned how to tell time and count money as a bonus.

When I was a little older, my job was washing pickled bologna jars. Later, when I was tall enough to stand on a box to work on the bench, I got to pickle the bologna. Both these tasks were taken on a piecemeal basis. And later, on an hourly basis, I swept coolers and scrubbed freezers and shoveled snow from driveways. Eventually, I graduated to loading semi-trucks, and then on to driving them. My nickel an hour wages and my math skills improved as I learned how to count the spots on dice and cards on paydays.

One of the advantages of the job was that there was a huge garage to park my motorcycle in. It was the kind of neighborhood in which it would have been imprudent to leave a scooter unattended outside. And sometimes I was able to work on my bikes in the garage, too. By the time I had started college, I was still parking my cycle in the garage there. And I was doing office work and sales jobs during the regular employees' vacations.

But that Summer of 1961 or '62, or '63, I took a long week before school started, loaded up my 250 Bultaco, and hit the road into the wilds of northern Michigan. The children who had ridden by me in the rainstorm were riding a 500 and a 650. That set me to thinking about the Olden Days of Yore when we thought nothing of heading out cross-country on a 150cc machine. Peter Beagle wrote a hell of a book about traveling across the U.S. on a Cushman Eagle in the 1960s. Times and motorcycles have changed. But youth has not. Aw, youth.

These kids were in jeans and tennis shoes. Each had a bundle and a fishing rod strapped on behind him. Neither had a fairing or even a pretense of a windshield. They were soaked, and they had to be cold; one just wore a t-shirt, the other had a nylon jacket on. I couldn't see them well enough to tell for sure, but I bet they were both of them smiling and having a fine time.

I took some consolation in thinking that they would have arthritis as bad as mine in forty years. I thought this as I fought with the knot in the drawstring of my rainsuit with my crippled old fingers and aging teeth.

On this ride into northern Michigan forty years ago, there were no rainsuits or drawstrings. But there were fish to be caught and then badly cooked that night over a campfire in a cast iron skillet. There was no rainsuit. But there was a snapped chain on a dirt road in a rainstorm miles from civilization and help. There was nothing remotely like shelter as I pushed my disabled ride down the road. But a friendly farmer took pity on me, and we put my bike in his truck and took it down the road to his barn, where we invented a roller pin and made a master link for me.

It rained, as it always does when I am in a tent or on the road. Over the years and along the way, I have been hailed as a hero and savior for breaking droughts coast to coast. It has resulted in local folks buying me some drinks, and, on occasion, even a meal. I have been well-received as a rain maker most of my life.

On this trip forty years ago, it rained so hard that my ancient tent sort of slowed the rain down some rather than repelled it. Cowboys and Indians drowned on my sleeping bag, and everything I owned was soaked.

On this remembered ride, the road was as wet and cold as the camping. There were no Tote boots to keep your feet dry, just soaked, sodden feet. There was no rain suit, only a soaked leather jacket. Nothing like a windshield, just keeping your mouth shut and your eyes squinted as you leaned forward down onto the tank. No warm dry motel rooms, just the increasing water in the shallow depression you had managed to pitch a tent in.

There were no interstate highways, but there was a magnificent ride up the shore of Lake Michigan, long before the growth and development made it look like the shore of Disney World. There were no motels, but there was a truly fine ride through the forest before it became infested with tourist cabins and condos and Indian casinos. I didn't recall any amenities at all, but I did remember watching the dawn from the Straits of Mackinac.

There were some real nice Mexican boys who picked me up when I fell out of the cherry tree. I was in the cherry tree because I had run out of money and had to work the cherry harvest a couple days just to get home. I had fallen from the tree because I was weak and light-headed as a result of having spent my last quarter on a watermelon and then trying to survive on it for two days.

There were no credit cards or ATM cards or cell telephones to call home and whine for help on. But that cherry picking job paid enough in two days to get me the gas to get home on. And my fellow workers fed me some beans and rice and tortillas.

I continued my ancient reveries for several hours while the

rain beat down on the former used car lot roof, and I emptied my Thermos and Oreo package. There were memories of my misspent youth in bike shops and garages and junk yards and cherry harvest work camps. I thought about how heavy the old leathers and the older surplus pup tents would get when soaked, and how the bike would handle badly with all that extra weight. Those sleeping bags with the cowboys and Indians would weigh a metric ton when wet.

I thought about the time I rode three hundred miles on a 250 Yamaha, in the rain, most of it at night. And when I got there, she had already gone. That ought to be in the Long-gone Lowdown Scootertrash Blues.

There were memories of riding soaked cold and weary while the bitter wind bounced the wet snowflakes off my tinted and scratched face shield. No fairing, no heated handlegrips, no stopping to get out of the weather, no comfort. But I did recollect a BSA that had to be stopped and cooled down for a half hour or so every fifty miles whether it was raining or snowing or not.

I remained lost in my ancient memories long enough to lose track of the time and the weather both. Night was about to overtake me, and the rain hadn't let up much. This happens more frequently to me as serious senility approaches.

Just about then, as a testament and tribute to the irony in my life, two more kids rode by in the storm, into the increasing dark and gloom. Same deal as the two who had been behind me earlier. These boys each had a duffle bag tied on their mid-sized sport bikes. They waved as they rode by. One of them beckoned me to come with them. It looked like they were riding the roads of my youth, and momentarily, I was tempted to join them. This is another thing that happens as senility overtakes me. Oh man, youth.

I poured more coffee and swallowed a couple aspirins as I watched them ride away. I even thought about running after them to tell them. But, logic and arthritis overcame that temptation. Instead, I got out a map, figured out it was only about eight miles to an interstate where there would be a dry motel room with a hot shower and warm food and a light to read by. I had a good book, *A Hard Piece of Luck* by Tom Abrams. I put my rain gear back on, and was on my way.

As I packed and saddled up, I realized I had lost about a half day to the rainstorm. Then I figured out how much I had gained by settin' still, thinking about them olden days of yore. So maybe there is an upside to bad weather.

I have been involved in similar, sometimes non-motorcycle related, incidents with a couple of longtime old friends. Captain Zero and I have done some hard and glorious traveling together over the years. He helped me fix the air-conditioner and window locks at a lowdown motel in Huntsville, Alabama nearly thirty years ago during The Perfect Ride. And he just sat there and shook his head as I repaired the space heater and hot water heater in a low-rent motel in Arcata, California just a few years back. And he took turns with me guarding the bike in Orangeburg, South Carolina.

But recently, upon summarily rejecting my choice of bargain lodging at the Patel Discount Inn and Suites (Much Cheapness!), the Captain frowned at me and said, "Tiger we're all princesses now."

Then he led me to nicer, cleaner, fancier, roomier, and more expensive accommodations where we were not required to fix the door lock and bathtub drain, much less guard anything.

In a real similar situation awhile back, old Joe Taylor shook his head and laughed at me and said, "Damn Tiger, we aren't in grad school any more." On to the Hyatt-Hilton-Marriott-Howard Inn.

I recall a time I took a woman on a ride through a rainstorm for several days. First impressions are often lasting ones. This woman had not been on a bike before we took off into what became a storm of Old Testament proportions. She thought that's what a motorcycle ride was — an exercise in endless miles of damp misery and anxiety. And she never asked to be taken again.

I made that same mistake with this same girl when I first took her fishing with me. She'd never been fishing before, so I set up a trip with an old friend who always caught fish. He took us out into the finger channels below Miami, and we caught some fish. I mean it was steady action from the moment we dropped the anchor until we ran out of bait and tide several hours later.

We caught various snapper and assorted grouper and grunt

and flounder and drum. We caught some jacks and sharks and stingrays and other interesting yet inedible species. This was back thirty or more years when there either were no bag limits or they were universally ignored. I'm not going to mention total numbers, but the girl landed twenty-five or thirty fish herownself that day.

And she thought that was what fishing was. Next few times I took her, we caught little if anything. Yup, initial impressions and expectations. She thought I was retarded, or at least inept, and kept asking when my friend was going to take us "real" fishing again.

Now there are at least a couple morals to be gleaned from these parables. The second one, the fishing allegory, that one obviously leads to — Don't never lead with your trump card; save your best shot. After that, there is the maxim about showing off for the pretty girls. Might be an instruction or two about peaking early in there as well. Certainly a lesson on the nature of irony.
As for the Long Ride In The Rainstorm, I am less sure of the moral. She never again got up behind me except across town on a guaranteed sunny day. Well, part of the reason for that is that I had had a pretty bad wreck. And even though she wasn't with me, it scared her. Prior to that, she must have thought I was enchanted and impervious to getting hit and hurt. First impressions.

Got another story about irony here. Thirty-some years ago I had a bad wreck north of Durango, Colorado, up on Red Mountain, out there on the Million Dollar Highway. My Downfall In Durango. The details are in *Longrider*, and on my CD in a poem called "Lizabeth's Poem." I retain a personal memory of one of the doctors showing me an x-ray of my busted shoulder blade. There was a loose piece of broken bone in there that kind of looked like an arrow head. I recall asking the doctor about it, and he said there was no point in doing anything. When I pressed him on that, he said, "Oh, there may be a time years from now when it begins to bother you."

Well, that time is upon me here. Some mornings that left shoulder of mine hurts too bad to do much after I get up. Some mornings that left shoulder is the reason I get up. I am told I have a pinched nerve. No, I haven't done anything about it other than to increase my aspirin intake. And the reason for that is that I also recall that Colorado doctor's explanation when I asked what could be done, should it begin to bother me in the future. He said, "surgery."

And I've spent most of my life, with some degree of success, trying not to get cut or stabbed or stuck. No, I'll avoid surgery like I will avoid getting anything pierced.

A friend of mine, an absolute master of understatement, recently described Bike Week over in Daytona Beach as a hundred thousand drunk dentists with temporary tattoos on rent-a-Harleys, and another hundred thousand or so who trailered bikes in.

He didn't even address the issues of anti-nudity and noise ordinances or pudding and cole slaw wrestling. Nor did he get into the part about sport bikes in formation tipped up on their front wheels at stop lights. He didn't speak of fatality statistics. He went nowhere near the topic of the price of tickets or beer at the track.

Speaking of drunks and beer, I used to drink a bit. Been near thirty years since then. I wasn't much good at it. I made the decision that I would sooner ride than drink the same dark night I found myself trying to talk the cop into letting me push my bike home. I was about two hundred miles from home. Cop said he had clocked me at a little over a hundred.

I recall some advice I got along the way. I was young and foolish and daring and drunk. I was being picked up after a fall, and the man doing most of the lifting frowned at me and said, "Alcohol's got a flame that burns bright blue. Stuff will lift you up and take you down, too." That was about the third verse I learned of The Lonesome Lowdown Long-gone Outbound Scootertrash Blues.

chapter ten
THE TAKING OF CRAP, COPS,
and CONTEMPORARY TRENDS

Between the publication of *Longrider* and now, I have had to take some crap about several things. One of the main ones is that I spent little time and ink writing about the engineering, the aerodynamics, mechanical and technical aspects of motorcycles. I made no mention of competition, not even the Isle of Mann TT. Well, there is a real good reason for all that. I am neither a racer, an engineer, nor a mechanic. I'm a rider, a road rider.

And I am a school teacher, a poor person, unable to afford tours of Europe or anywhere else that you have to get to on a conveyance other than a motorcycle. I do enjoy watching motorcycle races more than automobile races. But I'd rather attend the all-night ratfuck on the banks of the Miami River than watch a car race.

As for the issue of the aesthetics of bikes, I ride old BMWs. Old BMWs have always been highly prized and praised for several things, but exquisite beauty has never been one of those things. I have grown to appreciate and admire the basic and classic old BMW design, but I still have to admit that it's an ugly bike, especially compared to an old Triumph or BSA. But back to that road rider thing a minute. I would much rather ride than wrench or watch or wash or invent an adventure.

And I always figured a man ought to try to write about what he knows about. So I have written mostly about the ridin' and about the road. Stories and epic poems about the whitelines and them good old times, tales of the distance through the handlebars and thousand mile days. Things like comparative horsepower and RPMs and relative Newton units and tire tread design just bore the hell out of me anyway.

So, regardless, I am neither interested in nor authorized to address technology, mechanics and design, or laps at Laconia. Sort of like along the way, I have had to explain to several women that my degree is in English, and I am unqualified to deal with madness.

Beyond that, I got a cycle to ride, not to work on or research or admire or adapt and modify or restore. Or wash. I have, over the years and along the way, also had to take a load of crap for not washing my bikes enough. Some folks have felt compelled to make the same complaint about my pickup trucks. Which brings me back around to I got the bike to ride, and I got the truck to haul hunting dogs and feed and hay. If I'd wanted something to wash, I'd have gotten dishes or nice clothes.

Looks, style, and fashion aren't very important to me. Anyone who has ever seen me understands that. And, living as I do on a dirt road, and parking my bikes as I do in an open carport, my scooters are always sandy and dusty. Sometimes I have to ride out through the mud of that dirt road. It's usually on these occasions that the bikes get filthy enough to embarrass even me into washing them.

Some people buy motorcycles to wash them, to polish and wax them, to make them look good. OK with me, as long as they don't get missionary about it. Awhile back, at a festivity of some kind, I listened to a man bitch about how every time he wiped his scooter off, it was scratching the chrome. He complained about the dust in the air. He spent far more time polishing his machine than he did riding it. You could tell by the shine on both the bike and the trailer, and the numbers on the odometer on the cycle.

And similarly, some guys buy cycles to work on them. They would much rather look at the insides of the machine than the scenery as they ride by. Hell, some people have a motorcycle so they can break down and have an adventure. And some of us, we'd just as soon keep the soapsuds off our bikes and the grease off our hands. We leave the soap opera roadside adventures and antics to Captain America and Billy, and old Todd and Buzz, and Bronson as we ride through it all.

A couple Summers back I was on my way to the BMW Nightriders Cornhusker Rally out in Nebraska. The site of the festival was in the south-central part of the state. I had some extra

The Lonesome Lowdown　　　　　　　　　95

time, so I came at it obliquely and roundabout. That route took me through Scotts Bluff.

I saw a big banner-like sign above the road as I swept through the curve. But I was going too fast to read it carefully, even though there may have been a blinking yellow light involved. When the curve straightened out, there were about a dozen cops, each with a radar gun and a violator at roadside. It looked real industrial-commercial; these boys were working an assembly line.

My personal traffic officer stepped out into the road in front of me and waved me to the side of the road. He was a young man, with dark hair and the obligatory cop haircut, moustache, and sunglasses. He was wearing shorts with his uniform, as it was hotter than the hinges of Hell in Scotts Bluff that August mid-day.

"That overhead sign said twenty-five, didn't it?" I was smiling and shaking my head in spite of my criminal nature and behavior. I handed him my license and took my helmet off.

"Yes sir, that's just what it said." The cop was smiling right along with me. He seemed to be a good-natured person with some humor about him, a rare quality amongst the current domestic enforcement corps. So I pressed on.

"OK, having gotten the toss-up question right, can I move on to — How Fast Was I Going?"

By now he was going along with it. Hell, he was laughing at me instead of with me by now, and I knew I had a chance. So I said, "I'm going to guess somewhere around sixty."

He glanced at his radar gun and smiled again. "That's very close, actually. I've got you at 62."

"OK, I'd like to continue in the category of — What Was The Speed Limit Before That Trick Overhead Twenty-Five MPH Sign, please."

The cop looked around to see if any of his brother officers were watching him having way too much fun. None were, so he kept laughing and told me to go ahead on.

I guessed, correctly, that the previous speed limit had been 65. Then I quickly went on to suggest that at 62, I was actually a paragon of highway virtue and law abiding righteous goodness.

For my next category, I chose — How Much Is A Forty Mile Over Limit Ticket In Scotts Bluff, Nebraska. I guessed well over a hundred dollars, and the cop confirmed that. He was still laughing.

"You going up to Sturgis?" He had already recorded my Florida license plate number.

"No sir, I am not. I am eventually going to a nearby BMW rally that is sort of the Anti-Sturgis. And along the way there, unless you incarcerate or bankrupt me here, I am supposed to meet up with a real pretty woman."

He looked at me like he figured I didn't even know a pretty woman, but he asked me where I was supposed to meet her.

"At a campground very near here. In fact, if you wouldn't mind, I could use some directions."

By now he had decided that he wasn't going to ticket me, but he didn't say that out loud. We chatted awhile about Sturgis and about highways and speed limits. He returned my license and asked where in Florida was I from. Then he asked about Bike Week, and I had to explain it was Sturgis with a beach and better weather. Finally he asked me how long I intended to stay in this area with this alleged pretty woman before going on to the alleged BMW rally. I told him two or three days.

He gave me some very good directions to the nearby campground. Then he put his ticket book and radar gun away and said, "Try to spend a hundred dollars into the local economy before you leave."

I was excused. And I did try hard to spend some money locally to make up for my lowdown ways and my having cheated justice and all.

Back to some more funny stories about book fairs and festivals and stores. The basic funny thing has to do with my rough and raggedy appearance I guess. At a lecture at a recent regional book festival, the moderator, a real pretty girl, introduced me by saying, "Appearances are deceiving. I would like you all to welcome the only man who has ever pulled a chair out for me at dinner."

When I stood, the audience didn't know whether to applaud or laugh or what. Undaunted, my hostess continued the introduction by complimenting my table etiquette and my manners generally, noting especially that she hadn't opened a door all day around me. She was particularly taken by that standing up when a woman entered the room thing that I was doing. Hell, I even got a piece wrote about me in a Panama City newspaper in which I was described as a True Southern Gentleman. My Grammaw would be so proud.

I probably don't look like I would know enough to have any manners at all. For sure I don't look like most other boys with doctorates in English, or anything else for that matter. And I have yet to see another author at one of the book fairs or festivals who looks like me. Back to that things have changed aspect of it all.

At one such giant huge book fair cocktail party awhile back, I was into my usual cocktail party behavior. I was standing off in the shadows in a corner at the far edge of the festivity. The shadows were made by several tiki torches burning around the periphery. The party was outdoors on a beach. Couple hundred people there in the evening. I was behaving myself, wearing my good blue jeans and my city boots in response to my agent's admonition to, "Dress up and try not to cuss." As it was a cool evening, I had my leather on.

Joel, my agent, he was out there in the crowd doing what he calls "networking" with other agents and managers and publishers and reporters and their ilk. He's good at such as that, and I am not. So he knows enough to abandon me to my own devices and go get some business done. Occasionally he would call me over to meet someone, most recently the president of the college that was throwing the literary to-do.

While I was standing there, copping a lean on a palm tree in the shadows, a really famous, really talented, Pulitzer prize-winning, best-selling author asked to be introduced to me. She said, "Who is the interesting-looking man who doesn't belong here?"

When I went to work at the place I presently teach, there were four of us riding in to work on motorcycles. One boy caught cancer and died. Another stacked up his scooter and had children and got a minivan. A third went over to the Dark Side and joined the forces of evil in administration. Apparently you can't be a corrupt corporate minion and ride a cycle. Currently, there is just me and a girl who works in Financial Aid riding to work. She rides that scooter, too.

Once again, I don't have definitive statistics to back this up, but it sure seems like a whole bunch more women are riding their own cycles anymore. Used to was you would see guys rolling cross country with their old lady up behind them. Then I began seeing more women riding their own scooters. But most of them were with their old man who was riding his own bike. Often he would be on a Gold Wing, and she would be on a Shadow. Anymore I have been seeing a whole lot of women out there, some of them in groups, some of them alone.

Both my previous books, like most of this one, were mostly about the way it used to be, about how I really am The Ghost of Scootertrash Past. Well, recently I have seen the future of motorcycling. And the future is filled with straight people, regular citizens with upright professional jobs, many of them wealthy folks. And a lot of them are women. Again, I don't have statistics, but I've heard that about ten percent of the registered scooters in this country belong to women. And I think that number is sort of doubling every year.

So, now we have middle-aged rich folks and women invading what was previously a poor young white male dominated subculture. Well, first of all, considering the escalating prices of new bikes, it really is no wonder that the affluent are who's riding them. That outlaw image is as dead as my chances of retiring early.

Furthermore, contemporary motorcycles do not require brute strength or much mechanical aptitude or heroic endurance to ride them. Many modern models now provide such things as adjustable brake and clutch levers and adjustable seats and shocks, both as selling points to accomodate women's smaller hands and often shorter legs.

Accommodation and convenience have overtaken motor-cycling just as they have nearly everything else. It began with electric starters. Somewhere in here I need to say that some women are just every bit as athletic and strong and coordinated and able to ride as some men; some of them much more so. And, I feel compelled to again state that none of this here is intended to disrespect or criticize anyone.

But it sure is a long way from the current convenience-oriented, technology-infested, computer-dependent cycles back to trying to get your BSA tuned and running. And it's another long way from pushing a button to start your new Epic Voyager back to being thrown over the handlebars of an Indian on the backsweep of the kickstarter. Long way from working hard not to fall off the Norton to listening to CDs to stay awake in the saddle as you glide down the highway on your air-conditioned Interstate Rover. Longer way from wrenching all day on your Bultaco to having a couple real expensive computer components replaced, by someone called a master technician, on your Vista Cruiser.

Seems like to me that most current bikes have so much computer technology that there just ain't much point to carrying tools no more. The cellular telephone has become the Tool of Choice. Long way from the crescent wrench and the screwdriver.

And it is an even longer way back to the way people looked at us back in '60 to the manner in which modern motorcyclists are perceived today. Turns out we ain't all scootertrash no more. And women have had a lot to do with that.

A couple summers ago I took that lesson on motorcycle rallies and women at rallies. I should preface this by saying that the only structured organizations I have ever belonged to were the Army and labor unions. The former by conscription, and the latter by necessity.

Organization, rules, allegiance, and compliance all disturb me. Beyond all that, I am not an especially social person. So, I had never been to a rally.

Unlike a lot of men, most women just love groups, being part of a group, taking turns being the center of attention in the group. Furthermore, they are far more and much better organized than men. Think little girl tea parties, pajama parties, birthdays, all major and some minor holidays, weddings, receptions, all Important Dates, dorm meetings, sorority gatherings, and workplace and office congregations.

Women are just far more social than men. Females, as a class, enjoy talking, sharing information, much more than most men do. And they enjoy talking to other women the most. They are way better at it than we are, so they should like it.

Ergo, the various feminist and all-girl rallies are bound to be successful and fun. Incidentally, I have found that the more women involved in the organization of any rally, the better the rally. But most women would rather be in a group of their own kind than with men. Again, you can't fault them for that. And again, let me disclaim any stereotypes and apologize to the women who would sooner hang out alone or with men.

Many women are highly fashion conscious, and the contemporary motorcycle aftermarket (motorclothing) has targeted that with pinpoint accuracy. Women love to shop; I suspect it has something to do with a primal instinct to gather or harvest. Guys tend to wear the same clothes from puberty to retirement. Most of the guys reading this probably have six or eight black t-shirts and four pair of jeans. Well, if there are any of those wealthy lawyers and business tycoons and doctors reading this, you all probably have suits and ties and such. Shoes with tassels. Maybe you guys are part of the target market with that motorclothing thing.

Girls will change costumes several times before deciding on which one to wear. And they will change into another one later that day, and then again for the evening's festivities. They do it for one another of course; most guys are too dense to notice.

And at the all-woman motorcycle rallies, there aren't any men there to bitch and whine and make fun of this behavior. Women can show off their pretty cycles and fashion finery to one another and get the proper feedback. They will comment on how well the flying wheel ear rings complement the faux diamonds around the license plate. And ain't the tattoo with the flying ponies pretty though?

Same deal with their bikes. Women are much more attuned to the aesthetic things like color and form and shape and appearance and impression. Guys are into loud pipes. Girls understand and appreciate one another and what they are doing way better than most men. Women will stop and admire one another's rides, comment on the detailing on the lovely saddle bags, compliment the air brush paint job of the roses on the tank. Guys are into checking out and measuring one another's tail pipes and odometers. Most girls don't play that stuff.

That brings me to another thing I learned, or at least rediscovered. Women get treated better than men. A man who has a woman with him gets treated better than a man alone. An old boy who has a pretty girl with him gets treated better than several men in a group. I have no idea what happens when numerous women are in a group without a man. But I suspect they are treated like visiting royalty everywhere they go. The workers in the American Hospitality Industry apparently figure that if you have a woman with you, you are probably less threatening, or dangerous, or have more social skills, or will tip better or something.

Then women will beguile the old guy running the campground or the clerk at the convenience store, and make friends with the girl at the motel desk, and establish a rapport with the waitress, and enchant the boys at the local scooter shop. And they get the best campsite and two beds in the motel room and fine food. And when it gets right down to the bendin' end, they will charm the native constabulary authorities and ride off without a ticket.

But that's not the point. The point is that I have been permitted to see the future, at least of motorcycling. And it is full of women. And they are having way too good a time. Someone ought to report them to the Fun Police.

chapter eleven
OLDFRIENDS, OLD TIMES, OLD SCARS,
and RECENT HUMILITY

I mentioned back there somewhere about how I used to drink some. Years ago, one of the first doctors who looked at my arthritic hands smiled knowingly, tut-tutted, shook his learned head astutely, and pronounced it the result of too many years and miles of motorcycle riding. And I had to explain that for most of those miles I had ridden BMWs. Then I had to tell him what that meant. Then I went on to reveal to him that I had gotten the arthritis from picking up wet bar change.

By the way, I have since found that good doctor I mentioned earlier. He explained it all to me. He said, "Tiger, you dumb bastard, it's arthritis. It doesn't get better."

Anyway, I also used to have a friend, a highway bloodbrother, back in Them Bygone Days of Yore. And we used to do some of our drinking together. Great big man. Utterly fearless, sometimes ferocious, especially when drinking. He rode a big Moto Guzzi.

And he'd show up on that bike, all packed and loaded, usually on a Friday after we had all been paid. He'd set there grinning in my driveway, idling his Guzzi, with a beer in his other hand, and holler, "Hey Tiger, you old gypsy, let's roll."

Invariably, I would ask him where to, and he'd grin at me and say, "We'll know when we get there."

Sometimes it was just the two of us. Other times he would enlist additional friends who were riders. We wound up in some damn strange places. As a result of some of these spontaneous trips, I have some old scars in strange places, too.

If I had a dollar for every bar we backed out of, I could give up on this Best Selling Author dream and get back to my Lottery Winner dream. And if I had another dollar for every place we coasted off the road, headlights out, trying to hide from pursuing police or others bent on ruining our evening, well I could probably work on that Man Of Leisure/Gentleman Scholar fantasy. And if I had one more dollar for every strange place we woke up in, I could just go ahead on and tell the folks I work for to kiss my ass.

I mean this guy could find and somehow insult the only girl at the dance who had a father, a husband, a father-in-law, and six brothers and brothers-in-law, also all at the dance. After we had fled the premises, he would lead us on to a bar, where he would manage to piss off the bartender's mother. Or he would find a card game in which we were the only unarmed participants or a pool hall in which we were the only English speakers.

As a redeeming feature of sorts, this guy could also manage to confuse people long enough for us to get gone. Like, as we bolted for the door, he would turn and announce, "Holy Jesus, owls!" He would do this with a dramatic gesture and a facial expression of the recently beatified. It almost always delayed pursuit.

One time, pool cue still in hand, he yelled in a high falsetto voice, "I intend to take trophies!" as he blew a kiss to the five or six guys following us out the door. We made a clean getaway, and this was back when you had to kickstart a bike. By then we had also mastered strategic getaway parking. Often as not, he could convince folks that besides big and mean, he was also insane and not to be messed with.

On two separate and unrelated occasions, in two different states, years apart, he found an off-duty cop to swing on. It was on the second occasion of police-punching that four of us woke up the next morning in a pavilion in a very rural churchyard on a dirt road north of Peoria, Illinois. As this was of a Sunday, the local congregation discovered and awakened us. Actually the church bells and choir awakened us. The flock became curious about what the four bikes were doing hidden in their pavilion. I recall that I had woke up wondering the same thing. And, as he was often prone to do, my pardner somehow managed to befriend everyone, and then he got us all invited to the after-church brunch.

Once, in a completely un-motorcycle-associated incident in the remote out islands of the Bahamas, he beguiled, seduced, and then abandoned Island Royalty. Her brother owned the jitney service. We feared we would never see America again.

This is the man who once called me long distance at around three in the morning to announce that he had hit the superfecta at the dog track earlier that evening for something like $20,000. Seems he had then made friends with a few dozen people around him at the track. Then he had rented a penthouse suite at a high-end hotel and threw a party for them. Apparently many of the other hotel guests and some of the staff had joined the party when their shift ended.

I recall our conversation ended with me asking, "No shit, man? You won twenty grand?" And I remember his long distance reply. He said, "Yeah. And, Tiger, I still got about six hundred bucks left."

We spent a lot of time fleeing, often with headlights on high beam in our mirrors. As often as not, I would be headed out the door and into the parking lot as I heard him holler, "I will smite all your borders with frogs!" in his Demented Old Testament Prophet voice.

We did a whole lot of getting out of Dodge, often with sirens and red lights on our tails. We kept making getaways into the night, escaping the scene, taking circuitous routes, eluding pursuers, splitting up, evading capture. One of the events he especially enjoyed attending was wedding receptions. No, of course we weren't invited.

As often as not, we were several hundred miles from home, and several continents and maybe a language or two away from the ethnic group celebrating the nuptials. He took particular joy in getting a bridesmaid to climb up behind him in a flowing dress. One time, we got about fifty miles down the road before he figured out he had ridden off with the mother of the bride.

One other time, at a Greek wedding reception, two of the bridesmaids came to blows over who was going to ride off with him. And then there was that particularly inauspicious occasion in Canada one time when he made a disparaging remark about hockey, eh. I think he pointed out that it was the last great athletic hope for medium-sized white boys. We went for separate exits during that incident.

There was that charming side to this man as well, and often he would enchant the assembly. And then we would remain and eat well and get even drunker before pressing on to the next adventure. We'd know when we got there. Often, they would be waiting there for us.

The two of us took a ride back in the middle seventies, when Richard M. (Tricky) Nixon had hidden the gasoline, and interstate highway speed limits were fifty-five. I recall we were headed down to Atlanta over a long holiday weekend. We must have been in a hurry. Somewhere in Ohio, a state trooper pulled us over. My old friend climbed off his Moto Guzzi, smiled at me, and said, "Be cool, Tiger. I'll handle this."

As he walked back toward the cruiser, I kept my eyes on my mirrors and my hands in plain sight. I may have whimpered softly in apprehension and anxiety. I feared my pardner would look heavenward and holler, "Holy shit! They put pepper in the ceiling," as he had at a bar the night before. I shut my cycle off and waited for the cop to call for back-up.

He and the trooper met about mid-way, and a discussion I couldn't hear ensued there at roadside. About ten seconds later, my friend was escorting the cop back to his cruiser, his arm around the trooper's shoulder. They stood at the door of the cop car a minute, still talking, amiably it seemed. Then my buddy closed the car door for the cop and began walking casually, almost sauntering, back to the bikes. And the state trooper drove off. I saw the officer shaking his head as he looked toward us on his way past. We waved.

My old highway brother was still smiling as he climbed back on his bike. I just had to know, so I asked, "Pard, what the fuck just happened?"

Still smiling as he started his scooter, my friend wiggled his eyebrows like Groucho Marx and said, "I told the guy we had gotten confused and thought 75 was the speed limit, not the number on the road." I was glad he hadn't threatened that frog smiting thing.

See. I told you that between his charming nature and his tendency to confuse folks he got away with some stuff. No, I have no idea whatever became of him. Last I heard, he was in Houston, or maybe it was Lafayette. I do know that he has been through at least three careers, two fortunes, a wife or two, and another Moto Guzzi after he stacked the first one up. I suspect that if he is still around, he is still confusing people. And I hope he is still riding into someone's driveway on payday and hollering, "Hey gypsy, let's roll."

They wrote a verse in The Outbound Scootertrash Blues about me and him. Some among us have been hard hurt, beat down, strung out, and used up way past compare. Most of us have just been bad wounded, in excess of what a man should bear. Others are weary and wasted and headed off into the distance, far beyond ever again bein' able to care.

Yesterday was a fine, fine day, the kind of day that will provide memories like those of my Guzzi-riding old pardner. I went to the BMW Owners Of Central Florida Rally just some to the north of here. What a great bunch of people, literate, considerate ladies and gentlemen, all. And it was a near perfect day for such an endeavor. The sun was shining, most of the northbound Winter tourists were in a mess over on the interstate, it was in the mid-seventies with a light and variable wind.

And I got to take that new Full-Time Good Woman, the Tallgirl, with me. The rally wasn't but about thirty miles off, but we stretched it out to about fifty each way. It was that kind of day. And she's that kind of woman. And I have gotten right fond of being with the prettiest girl at these assemblies.

Like most BMW clubs and rallies, this one was filled with old white people. In fact, these folks claim that the OFC really stands for Old Farts and Coots rather than Of Central Florida. I saw no one of any ethnic origin other than WASP. There were no badly behaving children screaming their way through the crowds. There were few crowds, and if there were any kids there, they behaved themselves real good. There were relatively few tattoos or pierced parts, and, thankfully, no one even suggested a frozen t-shirt contest or pudding wrestling. The atmosphere was real laid-back, the food was good and plentiful, the field events were orderly and pretty funny.

The crowd was friendly and erudite. I met an old boy from up in New England someplace. He was called Stray Dog, and he said he had admired my tape of poetry for years. We set and talked for most of an hour, comparing highway stories and such. I also ran across some old friends, some of whom I'd not seen in way too long. And, to top it all off, and to verify my findings that

BMW riders are more literate than most others, I sold a couple dozen or so books and some CDs.

Karl The Kraut, of Karl The Kraut's Afterhours Scootershop and Social Club on the Outskirts of Oneco on Dirty Street, he was in attendance. And while he did not win the field events, he should have. But he lost some points and was nearly disqualified for unsportsmanlike conduct. During the weenie bite contest, he choked, literally, and spit his bite of weenie into the air. He should have been hollered at for getting bits of weenie and mustard all over the pretty old antique BMW single he was riding.

Somehow watching Karl slow ride down the track during the slow ride event put me in mind of a couple years ago when I got to watch him ride under different circumstances. The dealership Karl The Kraut worked at had gotten in a used 1998 or '99 R1100 RT with about forty thousand miles on it. It was a former L.A. cop bike. Damn thing had two batteries and bullet-proof tires and a place to put your baton and riot gun and hide evidence and a host of other things that no one but an L.A. cop would want or need or even understand. Basic black and white cop cycle without the lights.

Anyway, Karl knew I was looking for a new bike, and he called and told me to ride on down and take a look at this machine. When I got there, I was quoted an insanely high price for the used cycle. These folks were interested in making money, not with putting BMWs or riders on the road.

Pissed off, but unsurprised, I was about to just head back home. Karl jumped in and told me I should at least ride the damn thing before I rejected it. I countered that for that price, unless it was going to tuck me in at night and protect my yard, it was too much money no matter what it rode like.

He persisted, and I finally climbed on. As I was in an unfamiliar area, and prone to getting lost in urban situations, I suggested Karl join me. I tossed him the keys to the Black Bike, the one he has been working on for years so I could put nearly a half million miles on it. It's a 1984 800 RT. I was on that L.A. cop bike, fifteen years and 400,000 hard miles newer and nearly half again as big.

I should preface this next part by explaining that I am no racer. I ain't even much good at going fast anymore. Karl is much younger than I, and he has done some serious racing. Furthermore, I was in an unfamiliar area, disoriented more than usual. And, as I was following Karl, I had to stay behind him. And, I did not want a ticket. And the sun was in my eyes.

Having gotten all those disclaimers in, I can continue that I couldn't keep up with him. Hell, some of the time, I couldn't even see him. I had no idea that old bike of mine could do some of the things I watched him do with it. He didn't rub a knee in the corners, but he got my crash bars on the concrete a time or two on a hard lean. And I've got to where most of the time anymore, I just don't much feel like getting bad wounded. Especially self-inflicted. When I caught up with him, I made him switch rides with me, and I rode on home on my old Black Bike and let him take the cop bike back to the dealership.

In both my previous books, I addressed the issue of highway humility, like trying to keep up with Karl The Kraut. I think modesty is a good thing. Most humbling experiences make us better people somehow. Usually we take a valuable lesson away along with the embarrassment. Sometimes the lesson is a review. My reviewed lesson here was that horsepower and computer do-dads and such do not make a motorcycle or a rider, either one.

I've had some discussions about what does make a rider. Turns out it has to do with a love of the road, not a line of credit. It's about the distance, not the chrome and computers. It's about getting off the superslabs and finding your own road, preferably one that twists and winds some. It doesn't have much to do with new-fangled technology or even old-fashioned engineering. It's not got a lot to do with fashion or style.

No, it has to do with gypsy nomad wanderlust. It's about waterfalls without names and views off into the distance. It's about pointing it toward a place on the horizon and listening to it rattle and watching it burn. It's about the coastlines of both oceans and both borderlines and the distance between all that.

Speaking of wanderlust, and I just was, sometimes it overcomes me when I am unable to do much about it. Like on a late Tuesday afternoon when I have to be to work early the next morning. And this is where some of the wisdom of my old mentor, Ed Calver, comes in handy.

Ed was no biker, but he understood us. And Ed was a teacher.

I recall a time when he and I had spent an afternoon beside a nearby river pretending to fish. Then we devoted the evening to setting in front of a small fire on his hearth pretending to gather more wood. Refreshments had been served on both occasions.

And I remember asking him, rhetorically I thought, what it was about big water, moving water, and fire that always seemed somehow soothing. Moving water and controlled fire invariably calm you down, always put your mind in a pretty good place. I've spent many of my days around or on big water, and I've passed a lot of my nights around a fire.

On this occasion, Ed was already an old man, and he had observed and studied the world around him for a long time. He was a good observer. Old Ed smiled, poured himself another drink, and began his explanation.

He used his Pay Attention, This Is A Lecture, And There Will Be A Test voice, "Well, Tiger, that's because both fire and water are always the same, yet they are always different. This somehow puts the human mind into a state of relaxation that permits us to wonder and ponder, to contemplate things that we would normally avoid or at least abstain from. Though both are elemental, the experience of being around them often results in some very creative and constructive thinking."

He smiled at me again in the firelight. His blue eyes twinkled and sparkled in the shadows. The lines on his old face, the ones he got from trying to straighten out the wrinkles in his life, were deep and creased.

He took a short drink, I believe it was gin, and continued, "I think it's because we can deal with the campfire and moving water on an almost automatic plain, at least a subconscious level. Maybe an unconscious one. You instinctively know how to pay attention to fire and water. We might know that on a primitive, genetic level. That sets the rest of your brain free to do better things."

Taking another drink, and pouring my glass full again, he gave me some time to work on that, to get my mind around it all. Then he concluded, "You know, Tiger, much like riding a motorcycle."

Since that incident, I have studied the subject on my own some. Several books I read referred to that mental level as the

Alpha State of awareness. From there it got pretty existential and effete, so I don't remember much more. I do recall that they explained that this Alpha State is supposed to engender creativity. But old Ed already knew that. And he taught it to me in front of a fire and on the banks of a river.

I've taken other lessons in other places. The view from Captain Zero's Pentshack overlooking San Francisco Bay is one such panorama and place. Always the same, yet always different. I have done some good writing and other creative things there at Zero Productions as the wind moved the water and the boats around in the bay.

Another such place I know of is south of St. Augustine there on the sand dunes by the shore, down there by them rocks. The ocean, beyond the short surf, is always moving, but hardly ever changes. I didn't do much creative work there, but I did regain my sanity. And I have always contended that most of us ride for the mental health, trying to keep sane and even.

So maybe real riders are the ones who achieve the Alpha State while they roll down the road. The road, the ride, is always the same, yet always different. And the ride goes on forever, and the highway never ends. The distance through the handlebars.

I do know that when I only have a few hours of road time to get myself healthy and sane, I often head for the coast or try to run along beside a river awhile.

The Lowdown Outbound Scootertrash Blues addresses this, if obliquely. Sometimes the highway conceals things, other times it reveals things, and most times you're just out there on your own. Sometimes the road leaves you with a sense of fulfillment, with the joy of peace and harmony. But either way, it always leaves you alone.

chapter twelve
MORE HUMILITY,
WHAT NEXT AMERICA?, and FLAMING SOCKS

Went and got pretty esoteric myownself there, didn't I? In order to counteract that tendency, I should confess to a more recent occurrence that involved some more of that highway humility. Or I might ought to write some about technology, the anti-Alpha State.

Couple years back, I found myself in the Berkshire Mountains of northwestern Massachusetts. Ed Calver Country. There was a regional New England motorcycle rally there. And the chief of police, Lorin Gowdy, is a rider and a good guy. I introduced myself to him and asked him did he remember old Ed Calver. Of course he did. Then he looked me over careful, pointed at me with his trigger finger, and said, "You're the one." He nodded with authority and smiled.

It always scares me to damn death when people say that to me. Often, I AM the one, and it's usually a bad number to be. And it scares me even worse when it's a cop, even a friendly one, who decides that I'm the one. I hastily denied that I was the one, but it was too late. The Chief began telling the story to a dozen or so nearby riders.

He began, "Let's see here now, Ed used to tell about how you came through here one year, ayuh. Let's see now, this must have been, oh hell, back thirty or more years, in the early seventies sometime. If I remember this right, you taught with him at that university Ed had retired from. Ayuh, and you were all pissed off about your job and everyone you worked for and a whole bunch of other things. And, let's see now, Ed said you showed up at his place in the afternoon bitching about it all as you got off your bike."

Here, the Chief paused to dramatically light a cigarette and gather his thoughts. He smiled at me the whole while. The audience waited in eager anticipation. Some of them called their friends over. They sensed this would be a good story. They had discerned that humiliation would be involved.

"Anyhow, I remember Ed said he'd heard enough of that shit by about early evening. Ayuh, he told how he got five or six pieces of construction paper or cardboard or something."

Here the Chief paused again, took a long drag off his cigarette. He looked around to make sure everyone in his captive assembly was listening. The whole group was attentive. Several others, also sensing imminent mortification, had wandered over.

The Chief continued, "And old Ed said he made you write a name of one of the bosses you were mad at on each piece of paper. Seems like I remember, let's see now, there were some deans and vice presidents and department chairmen involved. It was quite a list."

He was smiling one of those cop smiles. The kind you get when they've smelled your breath and threaten to go for the damn Breathalyzer.

Another slow drag on his cigarette while I sweated it out, and then he went on, "And then old Ed, he made you take those signs with the names on them out into the woods all around his house. Ayah, they were all over the damn woods there when he walked me around to show them to me."

Now the story had more authenticity. The Chief was a near participant now. It was more than historic hearsay, and I didn't have a hope in hell of denying that I was The One. The Chief took another drag on his cigarette. Someone in the group opened a beer and handed it to him.

Continuing to smile at me, he took a long drink and another drag before continuing, "And then, every time you began to bitching about your situation at your job, Ed made you go off into the woods and piss on one of the signs there."

He covered his own laughter with another drink of his beer, but the assembled gathering was slapping knees and turning away in general mirth. The Chief was a good storyteller. Some of his audience had tears in their eyes already.

And then the Chief delivered the epilogue, "Ed said he went

through nearly three cases of beer before you finally stopped your damn moanin' and pissin'."

Now on to the embarrassed by technology portion I promised. There I was westbound, I disremember when. But I had stopped to visit the nice people who published *Longrider* and *The Ghost of Scootertrash Past*, there in Livingston, Alabama. When you think of great literature, think west Alabama. I had spent most of a fine morning there, and I was on my way out the door when the editor hollered at me to come on back and sign a dozen or so of my books for him before I left.

So I did. I set my helmet and my Thermos and my laptop down there by the pile of books and commenced to signing copies. I had my helmet with me because I have always been afraid someone would steal it off my bike. I had my Thermos with me because they are generous folks who always have pretty good coffee there at Livingston Press. I had my laptop with me because I had been taking notes. My laptop is a legal pad and a #2 pencil. The pencil has an eraser in case I need to go into Delete Mode.

But my laptop is vital. It's a daily calendar with notations of what it is I am supposed to do and when and where it is I am supposed to be every day. It's also a journal of what I have done each day, places, names, roads, mileage and such when I am out on the road. It's a place to take notes, write pieces of potential poems, jot down lyrics to The Lonesome Lowdown Long-gone Outbound Scootertrash Blues as they come back to me. And, in the back of it, I carry a list of addresses and phone numbers I may need. There are also emergency, in case I am found dead or confused on the roadside, instructions, the phone numbers of insurance companies and such, and other critical stuff in the back of that legal pad. The complete laptop.

And I left the damn thing lying there in the offices of Livingston Press as I wandered off. And I didn't figure that out until I had gotten nearly to Texas and tried to find an address to send a postcard to. And then I panicked. I was disoriented and confused. I was forlorn and disheartened. I was pissed off and frustrated. While I drank a cup of coffee, I was surprised and grateful I hadn't forgotten my helmet and Thermos. And I didn't even have the Livingston Press phone number. No, that was in my laptop back in Alabama.

After that, I scrambled hard to come up with names and numbers of people I was supposed to stop and see along the way. I made up addresses on post cards. I spent some time studying foreign phone books and asking directions from cops and mailmen.

And when, a week or so later, I got out to California, to Captain Zero's Pentshack on Russian Hill, there was my laptop. The editor at Livingston Press had found it, and he had heard me say where I was headed. Then he found the Captain's address in the back of the laptop and mailed it on to me there.

The note with the returned laptop read, "Tiger, in your encroaching and increasing senility, you seem to have forgotten your laptop. I am surprised you didn't leave your helmet, too. I am returning your techno-legal pad. Now you owe me, big."

The Captain, always up for a challenge, immediately asked me if Livingston Press had a website. When he saw the stupid look on my stupid-lookin' face, he realized who he was talking to and that I don't know a webnest from an e-fax. So he looked at one of my books.

He got the interweb address and e-faxed back to them on my behalf, "Dr. Edmonds is in receipt of his laptop, for which he thanks you. However, it would appear that along the way, the laptop became infested with the Love Bug Virus. He blames you all, and he anticipates remuneration."

I asked him to explain to them that I had moved all my holdings offshore just in case they intended to counter-sue. But Captain Zero, he said that the only offshore holding I ever had was bait.

If you ask me, computer technology is itself a virus upon the land, especially upon the literacy of the land. We are, after all, in the Post-Literate Era. There are a lot of reasons contemporary kids can't count, read, write, think, or solve problems, and technology, beginning with television, is at the heart of it all. Anymore, students really do think Being Educated means knowing which button to push.

But, back to me and technology. Several years ago, a new member of the faculty where I teach, a young man, began taking me to task for refusing to use computers. He didn't know me well, yet he felt a need to take offense at my rejection of technology. One of the problems with the Post-Literate Era is that the computer geeks are real missionary.

Put me in mind of when people take insult at my lighting a damn cigarette. Ain't got nothing to do with them. I don't bitch because they are breeding inferior children or because they are obese. I ain't on a crusade to try to get them to stop using so damn much cologne. I have no hope of improving their manners. It is not my intention to try to make better drivers of them.

Anyway, my computer-unfriendly attitude was none of this new colleague's business. But, as with so many before him, he took offense at the way I live my life. And I was about to straighten him out on that point when an old secretary came to my aid and stepped between us. Margaret Lois JoAnn Linda.

Good secretaries have pretty much made me the man I am, at least professionally. Blessed secretaries have covered for me when I screwed up, and warned me about impending problems. Often they have provided me with solutions to the imminent situations. A couple of them have taken partial repayment from the bottle of Jim Beam I used to keep in my bottom left desk drawer. A few have permitted me to give them game and fish as a means of acknowledging their help. Others have allowed me to take them to lunch, buy them flowers and candy, chip in big on the office Christmas present.

And I should chip in big, because secretaries have made sure I remembered hire dates and birthdays and retirements and other Important Events. They've gotten me various greeting cards to sign and send on Important Occasions. Lately they've spent a whole lot of time trying to save me from technology. Secretaries have consistently rescued my sorry ass on more occasions than I will ever be able to thank them for.

And old Margaret Lois JoAnn Linda had known me the whole of the twenty or so years of my employment there. We were friends. She knew me well enough to step in and speak up for me. And what she said to the young techno-pro computer geek as she got between us was, "Professor, you don't understand. The only button Tiger knows how to push is on a knife."

The epilogue is even better. The students started a rumor that this new guy was actually my illegitimate son. As he isn't, and as he is a handsome devil, prone to wearing suits and ties and has a hundred-dollar haircut and a sporty car, he resented the gossip. As the official den mother or faculty advisor or something to the school newspaper, I made sure my staff covered this campus rumor story. They even printed pictures demonstrating how much we look alike.

Speaking of smoking and the anti-smoking movement, and I was back there someplace, I have a notion that isn't the end of taking things too far. I saw an article in a newspaper the other day. It said that obesity is killing near as many Americans as cigarettes. Actually, I suspect they count all lung cancer cases as demon cigarette inspired, so obesity might be tied with or even ahead of cigarettes on the body count. There were two anti-smoking pieces on earlier pages of the same section.

I'm curious to see how this one goes. Personally, I hope to see fat people segregated and treated like pariahs. I hope the tubby are made to stand around outdoors in poor weather and designated uncomfortable areas to eat. I foresee obese sections in restaurants. My vision involves huge price and tax increases on fattening food to punish the portly. I really hope the overweight are forced to go for long periods of deprivation without food.

And I genuinely long to see follow-up studies indicating that there is collateral damage due to second-hand fat. I hope people catch on that the halitosis from multiple meals is worse than that from cigarettes. Wouldn't it be ironic if someone figured out that fat people sweat a lot and are actually more odiferously offensive than fiendish cigarette smokers? Anyone who has been on an airplane seated next to one of these overweight folks understands the nature of second-hand fat. I would love to see ad campaigns and children's brainwashing commercials aimed at anti-eating.

But I doubt it. Actually it probably would be good to ban folks from walking around eating and drinking, much like we have been forbidden to smoke in public areas. But I suspect they'll just let this one be, as it was never about health to begin with. If it was about health or safety, there would be a ban on using a cell telephone in your car.

Besides that, I have a personal axe that needs grinding here. All my adult life, I have worn the same size clothing. For near fifty years now, I have been clad in size small Fruit of the Loom black, pocket t-shirts. I have worn Levi blue jeans in a 28X34 size for the same period of time. And, similarly, I have always worn a size 10 A Redwing Boot. Within the past couple years, all these sizes have been discontinued due to the fattening of America. So the thin have already been subjected to prejudice, bias, bigotry, discrimination, and deprivation. Skinny smokers are twice damned.

But obesity has already been classified by our federal government as a handicap, right up there with being crippled or insane. And, the corpulent, like the disabled and the demented, will, according to federal law, be accommodated. It is already required and mandated that the obese be provided with special parking places nearby their building at work so they won't have to exert themselves with a long walk. And they must also be provided with over-sized chairs and desks, and work stations, and elevators to haul their big butts upward instead of taking the stairs. There is little chance societal bigotry will reach into the realm and ranks of the fat and punish them for their unhealthy habit the way smokers have been castigated. No, we've already determined that the overweight are victims.

Understand, now, I am in no way advocating smoking. And I've got nothing against the obese. Some of my good friends are fat. Nor do I have anything against the incapacitated or the mad. Similarly, many of my good friends are insane. But it seems like to me that fat is in a category with smoking. It's something we did to ourselves. Physical handicaps and mental illness, on the other hand, are seldom choices. But the fat could decide to put the fork down just as smokers could decide to quit.

No, the reason I hope the obese are chastised and publicly scolded and ridiculed is because that might move us some toward getting rid of all these totalitarian fascist behavioral-conditioning laws. It's still America, after all.

I am confident that alcohol kills more people, ruins more homes, causes more public expense, fetal damage, and probably more fires than cigarettes. But they tried that one once, and the boozers rebelled. We're overdue for another rebellion.

Maybe, having made smokers miserable, they really will turn on the fat next. Then maybe they'll go after the juicers again. And then, there will be another revolt, and we can get rid of all these unnecessary, excessive laws.

I have the same problems with helmet laws and seat belt laws and a whole bunch of other such ordinances. I think there should be Seat Belt Good Ideas and Helmet Suggestions rather than bullying authoritative commandments, criminal discipline and punishments. Maybe they could spend the money they now use up on Seat Belt Cops to catch some real criminals. Hell, maybe they could go after some of the boys in suits who are robbing us all blind. Or maybe they could inform and educate the public. You know, teach some of the children to read and write. It's America, land of the free and home of the brave. It's not America, land of few choices and home of extremes and the easily persuaded and the overzealous illiterate missionary.

I am curious to know when the federal government, or any authority, took charge of what was good for me. Is that really the function of government? Let's review. I am a mature, moderately bright, well-educated, old person. I can decide such things for myownself just fine. Hell, given the opportunity, I could have made a learned decision in the 2000 presidential election. But, as I live in Florida, I was not permitted to do that either.

However, I am quite competent to determine what I want to eat and drink and smoke and read and think and say and buy and believe. I might need protection, but not from myself. Such bullying and domestic terrorism, often in the guise of personal or social protection, extends, like surveillance cameras, into far too much of current America. Literary censorship, especially in public schools, is more prevalent than it has been in decades. And many public schools really do require students to wear uniforms.

The public school curriculum often has more to do with embracing and advocating political correctness, safe sex, anti-smoking, responsible drinking, diversity, personal self-esteem, and becoming enslaved and misinformed by technology than it does learning to read and write and think. And I still haven't figured out that diversity part while everyone is in a uniform.

Tolerance can't be regulated and legislated. Appreciation can't be standardized and forced on a group. Just because someone is not a white, Anglo-Saxon, Protestant, heterosexual, middle-class individual does not automatically make him or her a good person.

America has been turned against smokers, and maybe the obese are next. Perhaps now that our steward government has adopted an in loco parentis approach to running our country and our lives, fat folks will be ostracized if they take a chicken leg or an ice cream cone out in public.

The real point, of course, is that none of us has a choice. You just can't do that nomore. The self-righteous crusade did not say Think About Smoking. It said condemn it and try hard to force that opinion on others. No one suggested we ponder the badness of drugs; we were told of the evils and provided with the consequent denouncement. Say no to drugs; drop a Prozac, drink a Bud. Same deal with insisting we talk in politically correct terminology; can telling us how to think be far behind? Yesterday, smokers. Today, the fat. Tomorrow...?

What if our caretaker government determines that tattooing and piercing are, like smoking and overeating, bad for our health? What if our custodian government puts the tattooed and pierced in a category with smokers and fatsos? And what about the bald and those who dye and bleach their hair? Those who wear glasses? How about those not in uniform?

When I got drafted, I never dreamed that my efforts on behalf of my country would be protecting the future of an America whose children are in uniform, studying the Righteous Wisdom of Political Correctness and the Re-Written History of Just About Everything, all of it on a computer.

Lately I have heard a lot of talk in which folks compare much of what is going on presently to books like *Brave New World* and *1984*. Some even allude to *A Clockwork Orange*. And while I am in accord with most of their thinking, I think we should fear the scenario of an old movie, *Soylent Green*. What would the obese do then?

But, back to scooter stories. A couple summers back, I returned to Michigan, where I did most of my growing up. And I ran across an old boy I knew forty years back when he was cutting meat at a place I delivered meat to. Several of us were gathered in one place on this occasion. Most of them were butchers and grocery store workers and drivers and such, many of them retired by now. We got to talking about old times, and my friend narrated a tale about me and him from forty-some years ago. It involved one of those old Bultacos of my childhood.

"Tiger came by the store one time on that damn bike. I don't remember why, but I got on behind him to go somewhere."

Before he could continue, the gathered audience provided a number of potential scenarios. As the guy telling the story was a chubby youth, and I have always been the same size, real skinny, that was the basis for some of the possibilities. The listeners postulated that I had turned the scooter over on top of us, that we had done a wheelie through the parking lot, that the rear tire went flat. But that wasn't it.

Others suggested that I may have been drinking a bit back then, and that the resulting drunken episode was probably the point of the story. Some recalled that both of us used to drink, and some of the speculations went that way, too. Nope, that wasn't it either.

A few remembered those old Bultacos and thought perhaps the bike had broken down. But no, although that used to happen a lot, it hadn't broken down on this occasion. Some of those listening to this old story had been drinking themselves, and they suggested we had been captured and taken off by a band of gypsies, or we had run off to join the circus, or were abducted and probed by aliens. Others proposed that perhaps we had done something stupid and been incarcerated for our misdeeds. The suggestions went on far longer than the story itself.

Finally, they all gave up and turned to my old friend to hear the true ending to the story. He looked around kind of sheepishly and apologetically before he cleared his throat and said, "Tiger had some kind of goofy snuffer pipes on the damn thing, and my socks caught on fire."

That should be a whole verse of The Blues.

chapter thirteen
HARLEY GUYS, FINAL SIGHTINGS,
and FOREIGN FANTASIES

I went to church last Sunday. Many thought it would herald Armageddon or at least cause local floods and pestilence. Those who know me well, they understand that I am a deeply spiritual man with little inclination toward organized religions of any sort.

Seems a Christian Motorcycle Association outfit was having a service at a church over by the Gulf Coast, all riders invited. And, the Tallgirl wanted to be taken to church. And one of the women she works with is married to a rider, and they were going, so we should too.

But this isn't about the religious service or the blessing of the bikes or even about comparative religion. Comparing religions is a whole lot like comparing cornflakes. This service was more a karaoke performance than an ecclesiastical endeavor, and there was just way too much indiscriminate hugging. The bike blessing thing, that might be a good idea, as the preacher spoke of keeping us safe from idiots driving cages. No, this isn't even about the nature of women who want to be taken to a church. This is about Harley Guys. You know who you are. So do the rest of us.

The Tallgirl's co-worker's old man rides a Harley, and his old friend rides another one. They were, both of them, individually and collectively, damn good road riders. And they bought us lunch, and we had a real fine Sunday in spite of that karaoke-church-hugging thing. And, I would enjoy to ride with them again any time, any where.

However, as the guy who had no idea where the hell the church or lunch or anything else was, I rode behind them. And it was late Monday before I entirely regained my hearing. Loud pipes save lives? Well, if you're riding drag behind them, you can sure tell when they are gearing down or fixin' to turn it on hard.

I recall the New Full-Time Woman shouted something to me like, "..xt time...ri...ith...em...rplugs."

And I replied, "Huh!? What?"

Now, beyond that, most Harley Guys are pretty predictable riders. First rule is, they're going to stop every forty miles or so. If they are in a state with no helmet law, they will not wear a helmet. If they are in a state with a helmet law, they will wear a half-hat.

Second thing about Harley guys is that they consider their scooter to be something to attach aftermarket lights and chrome to. The bike itself is like a blank canvas. Some Harley Guys kind of get monomaniacal about this, and their cycles are tricked out beyond all understanding. I had this confirmed awhile back when I talked to a factory certified Harley mechanic. He was working at a little independent shop, and I asked him why he had quit his job at the Harley dealership. He smiled wearily and said he had just got real tired of spending his whole life strapping chrome on new bikes.

After that, Harley Guys enjoy stopping for red lights. Some of them try to get caught. Then they jump the green light and run through the gears fast, hard, and noisy. And then they get it up to twelve or fifteen over to cruise, often out in the passing lane, which is where they should be.

Most Harley Guys will wave only at other Harley riders. They will invariably slow down unnecessarily going into a curve, maybe shift down one. Then they are going to turn it on hard, again unnecessarily, coming out. They often do the same thing on inclines. And always, without fail, they will either speed up, go for the Johnson Brake and drop it a couple gears, or just pull the clutch and rev it up hard under bridges. Loud pipes save WHAT?

Now, other than that noise thing, I had a fine time riding drag behind these boys. Within a few miles I had ascertained that they both had some miles on them and knew what they were doing. Better still, they had done a lot of their miles together, and they rode well with one another. All I had to do from my place in the rear was to keep track of one of them. And, as they were good at what they were doing, there was no problem at all except for that hearing loss problem.

This is in no way intended to castigate or cast aspersions. If I was going to cast anything, it would be dice or bait. And if I had a Harley, I would do all the same things the Harley Guys do. I had a Harley for awhile back in them Bygone Days of Yore. And I did all those things and a few more. I suspect if I were to climb on one today, I would do all those things. Something about that noise. Even setting still, there is the need to turn it on a time or two, just to listen to it. Sort of like a chainsaw.

Over the years and along the way, I have rode with a whole lot of Harleys, and around them, and past them going the other way. I've spent time behind them and in front of them and beside them, and a little time on them. I once spent most of a day broke down at a lowdown motel listening to hundreds of them pass by. And, thanks to the kind of analytical approach to understanding that Ed Calver espoused, I think I've figured it out. Not sure I get it, but I have come close to comprehension.

Harleys sound like gunfire. There is a belligerent pop and snarl in that exhaust noise. They have an aggressive, angry sound about them. The damn things make a noise like a gunfight. They sound like automatic small arms fire. Sometimes, under bridges for example, they can sound like something heavier, a medium serious firefight. Sometimes, you get into a bunch of them, and you can hear bayonets and sabers clashing. Sounds like a damn cavalry charge sometimes. You can hear the war horses. The fucking things sound like a battle. And war is a real adventurous and romantic concept, especially in the National Guard, movies, and on the TV.

Now, just so you all will know that I am getting smarter in my old age, please note that I did not say a single thing here about women who ride Harleys. Yeah, I've become one of them Sensitive Guys of The New Millennium.

And, in all fairness to that patented Harley exhaust noise, I rode some a few months back with a pair of Ninja sport bikes behind me. I kept wanting to turn around and swat them.

Funny how the way a scooter sounds has such an effect on us, ain't it? Used to was a real old German boy came around to buy used textbooks where I work. He was a pretty cool old guy, spoke an interesting broken English, and always told some good stories about old BMWs and his childhood in Nazi Germany. He limped badly, used a cane. And, although I never asked, I think he got stacked up on a cycle.

One day I encountered him in the parking lot on campus. He was standing beside my scooter, just looking it over, smiling. We talked a minute, and then I started my bike to leave. I was on a 1978 R80 roadbike at the time. As it fired up, I glanced over to the old German guy. He had a look of rapt nostalgic pleasure on his face. As a tear formed in his eye, I looked at him questioningly.

"It zounds like ven I vas a young man." He looked like a conductor pleased with his orchestra as he nodded in time to the engine firing. I suggested he could climb on it if he wanted. I held my helmet out to him.

He smiled at me and said, "Danke, no." Then he limped off to find more used textbooks to buy.

I know just what he means. Years ago I found a shop full of old Bultacos out in Colorado Springs. The smell of those old two-stroke Spanish scooters hit me hard as I walked in the door. It drove me back in time to when I was a kid. For a minute, I was fifteen and didn't know no better. Hell, back then I thought I was indestructible, that I would surely live and ride forever. And a hundred miles an hour in the dark of the night down an unfamiliar road with a half-assed headlight didn't seem stupid. Then I heard one of them old Bultacos start, and that just made it all worse. It sounded like when I was a young man.

Speaking of nostalgia, me and Zero were talking the other day about it all. He's still here. Linda The Hawk moved into his Pentshack when he left San Francisco. He got a letter from her just awhile back. Said she had put up lace curtains and doilies, and he ought not bother to never come back home. So I guess I got him for awhile. And that's OK, even if he is retired and won't work.

Me and him, we got to remembering some of them Bygone Days of Yore when three or four of us would leave out of Michigan westbound headed to Captain Zero's home on the far left coast. Then, when we got there, we'd swarm and scatter off into the mountains and the valleys and all up and down the west coast highways. By then, we were no longer fifteen and indestructible. No, we had another ten or fifteen years or so, and we had some high mileage on us by then. By then we knew some of the verses of the Lonesome Outbound Blues, and we had begun to develop some appreciation for it all.

I recalled a ride from the real early seventies sometime when three of us took the southern route to Captain Zero's place. We crossed the Brazos and the Pecos in the high heat of Summer, and we rode beside the Rio Grande under a massive full moon. The next morning, the setting moon lay balanced on the western horizon out beyond our handlebars. The rising sun rested on the eastern edge of the world behind us in our mirrors. We listened to the Spanish Angels singing the Scootertrash Blues in the canyons there as we passed through.

We continued on into the Del Norte Mountains, on to Marathon and Alpine. We rode across the Maravillas, and we stopped awhile in Lajitas and in Terlingua as we rode west to Presidio. And there we turned north to Las Cruces. I couldn't remember where it was we finally stopped that night. But I was able to recall the nature of the conversation around that campfire.

The full moon came back up in the east, behind us. It came up red as if to remind us. That night by the fire we reviewed some of the lyrics from The Outbound Long-gone Lowdown Scootertrash Blues. We spoke of the dead and the dying, about riding through The Crossfire, about the blood on the whitelines, and of the others who have somehow or another given in or given out or given it up before their time. We talked of the price we have to pay for being allowed to follow one another on down The Lost Highway. Told you we had acquired some appreciation by then.

By then, we had cultivated more than appreciation. We had come up with a system in which the boy running lead had the fuzz buster. And we pissed off cops all the way west.

When we got to San Francisco, I needed a rear tire. So I took my bike to a dealership in downtown San Francisco. There I was treated badly and overcharged. I remember they would not let me go with my bike back into the service area. This was the first time I had encountered that approach to service. I was invited to set in the waiting room and watch corporate color TV infomercials about their business and their products, while I sipped on a really bad complimentary frothy weak coffee drink. This was also the first time I was introduced to the concept of the infomercial. I took a lesson on corporate greed. But I was forbidden to go watch them wrench on my scooter.

When they pushed my ride back out, I inspected their work and determined they had put the tire on backward. I pointed to the German directional arrow and explained I intended to ride the machine going forward. Not only were they not embarrassed, but they tried to charge me for the hour and a half it took them to take it apart and put it back together right while I had another latte and further TV brainwashing.

That was when I began to develop some appreciation for the old and the true ways, for the old dealerships and shops and the old boys who ran them. Those places and them boys are getting fewer and farther between anymore. Prior to that unpleasant experience in San Francisco, I had always gone with my bike back into the garage. There I was often called upon to help, to run for tools and parts and coffee or beer, to answer the phone and take messages, to listen to the mechanic as he worked on my machine, to learn something. Onliest thing I learned out there in San Francisco was that my dollar wasn't worth near what it was back home.

Lately, I have run into far too many dealerships who forbad me to enter the service area. There was one place, they let me go back into the garage with my scooter. But I was required to stand behind a line they had painted on the floor there. And I was prohibited from talking to the mechanic while he worked on my ride. I am not making that one up. Toes behind The Magic Line during The Grand Silence. Instead of color TV infomercials, I got a guy followed me around trying hard to sell me a new machine. The mechanics there were not permitted to turn on a radio or talk to one another, either. Damn place didn't even smell like a scooter shop. Once again, it would appear the whole country is following California's lead right on into cultural ruin and fascist corporate oblivion.

In part, I blame our custodial government and commercial motorcycle corporate suits for this. Lawyers, most of them. God forbid a customer slip in some oil or bust a knuckle trying to help the mechanic; lawsuits could result. There is more concern that a handicapped toilet facility and wheelchair ramp be in place than there is about fixing a bike and getting us back out on the road. At this rate, the whole damn country is going to become one giant huge Mart-Mart Store in a plazamall. My hope is that someone spills an especially hot cup of weak, frothy latte on her lap and sues. That might put a stop to some of it.

I got a hunch there are some dealerships where they would take offense at you stopping there for any reason other than to spend a lot of money, preferably on a new bike that they weren't going to maintain for you very well. And they would prefer all transactions be done with a credit card. Impersonal corporate greed, the demise of the little Mom and Pop businesses, is going to ruin what's left of this country.

Once anything, a government, a police force, a hospital, a college, a motorcycle dealership, gets big enough to consider itself an American Institution and a Corporate Entity, it no longer does its job. No, the job of an American Institutional Entity is to perpetuate and increase itself, always from the top. That's how we got so many suits. And when the budget crunch comes, as it always does, they lay off the workers, the beat cops, the nurses, the teachers. Never occurs to them to clean things out from the top and try to do with fewer administrators.

This is how we got the governments and police departments and hospitals and public schools and scooter shops not doing their jobs. They don't care if their citizens are free, their neighborhoods safe, their patients healthy, their children educated, or their motorcycles running well. They are far too busy with growth and development, with making more vice presidents, deputy chiefs, sub-CEOs, assistant deans, and district sales managers with corporate perpetuation and bottom lines.

Used to was old Coach Robinson or Oren Gassel or Charlie Syms, they would either remember or write down on a piece of paper that you were a few dollars short. They would trust you to bring them the money next time you were to their motorcycle shop. Then Oren would pour you a cup of coffee and show you the new models. Old Coach would want to talk about the past weekend's races. Charlie would holler over to the house to see if Mildred had enough supper for you to stay and join them. And there was a radio playing at all them places. They smelled of grease and oil and gasoline and exhaust fumes and coffee and cigarette smoke. They smelled of tools and rubber tires and riders.

There are still a few locations like that. I wrote about a real fine and inexpensive morning at BMW of Detroit in *The Ghost of Scootertrash Past*. I told a story about a wonderful place called Cycle Works in Del Rio, Texas in *Longrider*. And, thanks to Karl The Kraut, I still have a place like that to go to regular. And besides being better mechanics and more caring people, and besides saving you money and teaching you something, these little shops provide a much better time there and way better stories afterward.

On my last trip down to Dirty Street, we all discovered that Sam's, of Sam's V-8 Engine Refurbishment, daughter is the pretty girl who works at the bookstore I was at the previous weekend. Karl The Kraut had come by the bookstore to help me shill books and had shown some romantic interest in the girl. Discovering that she was a friend's daughter put a whole different focus on things for Sam and Karl both. Confusion ensued. We all agreed that the pretty daughter would figure it out for them both.

Then Jimmy G., of Jimmy G.'s Detail and BMW Restoration and Storage, he showed up on a screaming 250 Yamaha. We all got to hear about how it is a much better idea to truck your 250 up to your in-laws' place in Tennessee, unload it, and then run Deal's Gap and the Dragon's Tail with it rather than the big road bike you rode up there on. He said he was blowing Gold Wings and Valkyries and test-tube Harleys and real Harleys off into the woods at every curve. And then he told of the aftermath of one of the bad wrecks he had come upon.

Rebel, of Rebel's Paint, Trim, and Other Stuff, came by awhile and brought beer. That somehow attracted another half dozen denizens of Dirty Street. Dirty Street, as you might expect, is a pretty noisy place. One guy is always running his power sander in his shop where he makes surf and boogie boards, Bob's Boards. There is another boy who is always working on boats with power tools. The guy who repairs large appliances has got a whole bunch of noisy hydraulics going on. Several kinds of engines are always running in several garages. Two or three air compressors. And everyone is playing a radio or tape or CD player. But them boys can hear a beer get opened from a couple hundred yards off in spite of the ambient noise.

Dirty Street smells like old times. There are the mingled odors of motor oil and grease and high-test gasoline and hot engines and exhaust smoke. It smells of old bikes and hydraulic fluid and take-out food and beer and coffee and cigarettes. You can smell rain and dust and hot asphalt and the canal behind it all.

Old Doug rode in with more beer. Doug teaches school, too, so he and I bitched to one another about contemporary students. Other guys drifted over, drank a beer or maybe a soda pop. Karl saw I had my Thermos and asked for a cup of my Cuban coffee. Some set in the shade and told a story, laughed with us awhile, then wandered back to work. Topics ranged from women to motorcycles to politics to literature to fishing to old times.

The stray brown dog that has been around for years, sensing a potential opportunity, came by. A collection was quickly taken up. As the perpetual designated sober gopher, I was dispatched for more beer, dog food, and a couple quarts of motor oil. There were two dogs when I returned. They were given potato chips to supplement the dog food.

Karl The Kraut announced that he needed a particular tool that he didn't have. One was produced within minutes. He went back to work on my scooter, while a boy called Slow Poke (his nickname, oddly, is not Pokey, but Slow) bitched about how his ex-wife was still taking all his money. Jimmy G., who has a truefine good woman at home, he just smiled and began talking to me about how I needed to come take a look at an old wrecked bike he had just gotten in. He figured I might could use some parts.

Sydney and Cal rode on in to hear the last of a tale about outrunning a cop one time in the Ozark Mountains of Missouri. Then talk turned to the new auto-ferry boat service from Tampa to Merida down in the Yucatan of Mexico. Sydney teaches Spanish, and it's Cal's mother tongue. So if we go, we want to go with them.

I told about how the last time I was in Mexico, I was driving a Ford Bronco through to Central America. My pardner, Tommy, he had learned how to say, "More beer, please." And I had mastered the phrase, "Where is the bathroom?"

I explained that a couple days into it, in the middle of the Mexican nowhere, the Bronco blew a wheel bearing. We were so far in the wilderness that the Tool of Choice was a machete. Hell, it was the only tool. But we were rescued and well treated by the locals; Tommy bought a couple rounds of beer for everyone.

We had encountered nothing even remotely like anything other than warm hospitality and friendly, helpful local people on that trip. But I recall saying to Tommy back then that I was glad to be in a vehicle rather than on a scooter. The damn roads looked to be made of adobe in some places, especially during and after a rain. As it was August in the Yucatan, there was much rain. We were in a few spots that I didn't think could be ridden on a road bike. I was sure they shouldn't be. And everywhere we went, the local folks admired that pretty green four-wheel drive Gringo Bronco to the point of covetousness and near theft. They did the same with many of our other possessions. I suspect I would have feared walking away from a packed and loaded motorcycle to get another cerveza or look for the baño.

We discussed the nature of foreign travel awhile there on Dirty Street. That time me and Tommy took the Bronco through Mexico, we had to get our Very Important Papers in order at the Mexican Consulate in Tampa. It was located in the back of an auto parts store, and I had to sit on a case of oil as Tommy occupied the metal folding chair. But the staff, Maria, was very helpful.

Everyone there on Dirty Street agreed that the roads had to have been improved over the ensuing ten or twelve year period since my last run down there. We were in accord that buying a round of beer for the locals is a good idea no matter where you are or what the language is. And they also concurred that if we were traveling in a pretty sizable group, we would surely be near as safe as in a vehicle. And with professional translators, we weren't likely to piss nobody off accidental.

Then I told the story about the time in the Army, when, trying to quiet the troops, I told about a hundred Puerto Ricans, in bad Spanish, to shut up their cows. Everyone laughed, and then we all tried to remember the prices we had heard or read or seen about the new ferry service. No one could recall any specific figures, but we all agreed it had sounded reasonable when we first heard it.

After discussing this potential foreign travel fantasy, we began to talk about other rides. Sydney and Cal had, awhile back, put their machines on the Amtrak AutoTrain northbound to New York or someplace such as that. They knew right off that I was going to take knee-jerk offense and have a bad reaction at them having taken the rubber off the road. It's not quite trailering, but it ain't riding neither.

And they explained that if you don't run inland to the Blue Ridge Parkway and through there, that there just isn't a whole lot to see between of here and New York on I-95. You can try to ride the coast, but it's a mess and takes forever. The Georgia and Carolina and Virginia lowlands and midlands are interesting places, but not real scenic. Cal and Sydney pointed out that Washington, D.C. is a clusterfuck. The train was easier, faster, more pleasant, and far less hassle. Both these folks are high-milers, so I didn't say a word.

A couple months later, my friend, Chopper, did the same thing to get up to The Rolling Thunder Ride up in D.C. He was pressed for time and pointed out that the train continues to roll right on through the night all the way. Chopper is a hard man, and no one could ever accuse him of being a highway weenie.

The moral seems to be that we are, anymore, all of us princesses now that we ain't grad students no more. And before Karl The Kraut finished with my scooter, we all reviewed a long verse of the Long-gone Outbound Scootertrash Blues, the one about how, The highway is like a woman, and both of them are like horses, and we couldn't have rode them any different if we'd tried.

chapter fourteen
MY STAFF, RADIO SHOWS,
THE MART-MART MASSACRE, and PREDICTIONS

In *The Ghost of Scootertrash Past*, I made reference to an eighty-three year old Midwestern mother of eleven who just loved my books. I think my point was that demographic niche market thing was a myth. Got a letter from that girl here awhile back. She told me she thought that might be a reference to her, but, as she was only eighty-one, she doubted it. I spend way too much time writing disclaimers and apologies. But I have some help.

My staff here at The Redoubt all have dual functions, some have several. Captain Zero, for example, he's my graphic artwork/retirement/spiritual advisory staff. Joel Lee is my literary agency/legal staff. Jan is my personal shopper/computer and telephone technology organization. Chopper is in charge of security/publicity. Terry, he's my farrier/real estate agent. My dad continues as my top salesman/work-ethic model. Bosco The Bandit is in charge of all electrical problems and keeping me even. Bill Dudley remains my audio engineer/production staff. Karl The Kraut is my motorcycle mechanic/shill. My Uncle Keith works as my financial advisory staff/guy who found a good woman and didn't fuck it up model. Jimmy G. is in charge of obscure parts, great deals, and general counseling. Marty The Big Guy Francis is my radio mentor/bargain finder. The New Full-Time Good Woman, her name's Juanita. And she has become my logistics organization/charming woman with me at them whoopie-do functions I am required to go to. They all take turns making sure I don't fuck up. They also take turns picking on me. If I ever make any money at this, I am going to hire me some praise singers.

Now you all have already read some about Captain Zero.

He and I have been friends for over thirty years, way longer than anyone else has ever tried to be friends with me. We've done some time and miles together. He knows how to play with computer technology, so he got put in charge of the artwork on the jewelbox of the second CD of epic motorcycle poetry. And, as a former member of the clergy, he is, of course, in charge of matters pious and ecclesiastical. As my longtime old friend, he often begins his advice with, "Tiger, you dumb bastard." The problem is, of course, trying to get him off his retired ass long enough to do any of this.

Joel Lee Sherman, Esq. is, among other things, a true Southern Gentleman. The fact that he is a lawyer doesn't detract from that a bit. He is also a former student of mine and another longtime goodfriend. For years, while he was living up in D.C., I would route my Summer travels so I could roll through the nation's capital and spend some time with him, even before we went to work together on matters literary. You know someone is a good friend when you will go to Washington D.C. to visit him. Joel has guided me through the maze and morass that is contemporary publishing and promotion and sales. Without him I would still be writing poetic stanzas on matchbooks and bathroom walls.

Jan is the Benefits Lady (woops I mean the second double under-associate vice president for getting hurt and sick, tooth doctors, paychecks, workman's comp., and retirement) where I work. I was gone out on the road when she took that job. Our corporate group insurance was changing, and she somehow managed to find me at Zero's house, three thousand miles and a whole continent away, while I was on sabbatical that year. This was no mean feat, and it was my first hint of her amazing abilities. When she got me on the phone, she introduced herself and said, "Do not fall off that motorcycle until I get your new health insurance card to you."

Since then she has fed me repeatedly, and we have become great friends. She is also most adept at finding the sort of obscure things I need (ancient computer printer cartridges, rawhide chewies for my dogs, little-known books), often at a discount.

Bosco The Bandit is another former student of mine, from about thirty-five years ago. In those years, he and I have ridden together more than anyone else I know of. We have been to both borders and both shores and most of the in-between together. We've picked one another up after a fall.

Chopper is a damn cop it turns out. I first met him when he telephoned The Motorcycle Riders Radio Network call-in show, hosted by Marty The Big Guy Francis. The show is based in Orlando, airs early Sunday mornings, and Marty often has me on the air as his co-host. Old Chopper calls in from his extra part-time work as traffic coordination and parking control officer for a giant huge church. He really likes my books; in fact he describes himself as my groupie. Having him say flattering things about my work on the radio has sold more books for me than taking out ads in magazines. The problem is that Chopper once announced loudly on the radio that he had finally figured it out. Said he had gotten as stoned to read my stuff as I was when I wrote it. Told the entire of the Greater Orlando Metropolitan Area that it made infinitely more sense that way.

I've known Terry Horsefeet for years. He takes such good care of my little mare's hooves that she runs right to him when he comes by whether he is going to trim her feet or not. When some acreage immediately adjacent The Redoubt here came up for sale awhile back, Terry pointed out that I would surely kill whoever moved in there. Then he went from farrier into his real estate agent mode and set it up so I could buy the land.

There were eleven people there at the formal signing of documents ceremony. In the middle of it all, Terry leaned over and whispered to me, "Tiger, you are the only person in the room not making money right now."

I near bolted for the door. He is further renowned as a chef for Terry's Flippin' (NOT Dade City) Chicken and for feeding me Thanksgiving dinner. He has also single-handedly raised two of the truly nicest and prettiest girls in Pasco County, maybe in the entire of the Free World.

I've known my dad longer than I have known anyone else. I wasn't there to see how he got through the Great Depression and other early hard times. But for years I watched him get up every morning in the dark and go to the first of his day jobs. I saw that job go to hell for him forty years later when the company folded, and the suits absconded with his pension money while he was right on the brink of retirement. Then I witnessed the

Reagan Administration screwing him out of a sizable portion of his promised Social Security money. And then I watched while he got another job, even though he was too damn old for such as that. I saw his first wife leave him and his second one die on him. And I was there when he had to bury his parents and a whole lot of other folks he loved. And through it all, he got up every morning and went to work. Through it all, he has been my best friend. Around all that, he has sold more of my books for me than Barnes and Borderline and Amazoncomdot put together.

William B. Dudley is a damn genius. I have mentioned this before. Bill did all the production and engineering and mixing work on both my early cassette and the newer CD of epic motorcycle poetry. He also played some of the music on both of them. Hell, he took some of the pictures for the new CD, too. Anyone who has ever heard this stuff, even if he didn't like it, would agree about that creative genius part. Bill is also a good friend with whom I have enjoyed some fine times. He has been a great source of support and help on a whole lot of things that have nothing to do with poetry or recording work.

Karl The Kraut is maybe the best scooter mechanic I have ever been permitted to watch work. But he should be. His dad ran a legendary BMW dealership for a half-century or so while Karl was growing up. Besides that genetic thing, and all kinds of schools, and the life-long experience, Karl has a hell of an instinct about diagnosis and trouble-shooting and predicting problems. I have learned a whole lot from Karl The Kraut over the years. And, he often comes to book stores and rallies and tells anyone within listening distance that they ought to buy my books.

My Uncle Keith is another damn genius. This is manifest in the fiscal advice he has provided me over the years. Had it not been for Keith, I would be trying to live on the several square inches of land in the Klondike I got from eating all that shredded wheat in my childhood. As further evidence of his genius, he has managed not to mess things up and has been with my Aunt Dorene for the past thirty-five years.

Marty The Big Guy might be another genius. I have seen him ride a dozen different bikes over the years, and he has yet to buy one. And he is convinced that God created gentiles so there would be someone to pay retail. Marty possesses the kind of demented strategy and twisted humor that makes him a huge success on the radio. He has an amazing ability to throw nine things in the air and have them come down just in time and in chronological and alphabetical order. And he always knows just where to send me for the best deal on leathers or a helmet or a rainsuit.

Juanita puts up with me. Beyond that, she is really good at finding the way to the obscure bookstore or local book festival I am scheduled to appear at. And she always makes sure I have a pen and books and CDs and bookmarks and all the other right stuff with me. And then she charms the locals and confuses the hell out of them as they wonder why the tall pretty girl is with the old burnout.

Speaking of Juanita, she moved her little dog, Lucy, and Julio, her jackass, into The Redoubt here lately. My remaining dog, Louise, and the little dog were already great friends and thoroughly enjoy one another's full-time company. But my old mare wasn't real sure about that donkey at first. They've got it sorted out now and are getting along just fine except at feeding time.

Some of my new noisy neighbors, the ones who imported a giant three-story tall blow-up waterslide and forty or fifty screaming kids in for a birthday party, they actually had something to say about the jackass braying in the night sounding like someone getting killed. I told them to wait until I moved the peacocks in. Actually their comment confused me, as I was sure they thrived on noise and would like Julio. Apparently it's just noise of their own making that they love to hear.

I tried to feed Julio from my hand once. He bit me. And I hit him with a right hand that should have taken him to his knees. He blinked. So did I as I turned away trying hard not to cry. Think I might have broken something in my hand. There were a couple things moving around in there that didn't used to. The really scary part isn't that I am that dumb. No, it ain't even the part about how I didn't hurt the damn donkey, or even that I hurt myself. No, the scary part is that it was purely instinctual. If someone's nasty pre-socialized kid had bitten me, I would surely be in jail now.

The other scary part is that the New Full-Time Woman has six more dogs, and seven or eight cats, and enough birds to make a National Geographic Special, and four horses, and forty or so head of cows. Utterly fucking terrifying.

While I am on the topic of scary things, this is a story about a good ride and a spooky experience at the Mart-Mart Store, not in that order. I don't recall ever having a good experience at a Mart-Mart Store, but this time the corporate clowns outdid themselves. Seems the Mart-Mart Stores had declared war on ignorance and were sponsoring some kind of nationwide stamp out illiteracy campaign. Apparently they also sell books there at the Mart-Mart Store. The Mart-Mart Empire has become the epitome of The American Institution. Anyway, they were seeking authors to come to the Mart-Mart Stores to address groups on this fine effort and noble topic, to assist in the elimination of illiteracy.

Even though I would normally rather have a stopped up toilet than go to a Mart-Mart Store, I couldn't refuse this one. I have spent most of my life in such an effort. I feel passionately about the radical and steady decline in literacy in this country. I have lots to say on this topic. So I told Joel Lee that if he would come with me, I would go. He agreed, and 'Nita said she'd go, too, if for no other reason than to see me in a Mart-Mart Store.

We got up early in the cold morning and rode cold the fifty or sixty vicious miles down the nasty interstate to get to the urban Mart-Mart Store in the bowels of Tampa by ten o'clock. It was of a Saturday, and the traffic was abominable. We met Joel in the Mart-Mart Store parking lot. It was one of those Super Giant Huge Mart-Mart Stores, and it had a giant huge parking lot, and it was filled to capacity with frenzied Mart-Mart shoppers. There was no shade to park the bike in, and there was nowhere remotely near the store to park either. It was not the sort of place you wanted to leave your cycle unattended for a couple hours.

When we got into the store, through the monumental crowd, and past the corporate greeters and all, we eventually found someone in a management position of some sort. We had got there early. Good thing, as that finding a manager part, that took some time. A boy in a nametag, necktie, and colorful company vest eventually showed up and listened to our story.

Then he had to find someone in a higher management position, and that concept and task seemed to just flat baffle and befuddle him into slow motion. 'Nita and Joel Lee and I stood out of the way, uncomfortably. The swarming bargain hunters pushed and shoved around us. That higher management finding thing, that took some more time. By now it was a quarter after ten, and I was getting angry.

Eventually someone, whose nametag identified her as an Assistant Manager, sort of slowly wandered over to us. Joel told her who we were, and why we were there, and what was going on. That seemed to displease her somehow. This confused me, as I thought I was the one who should be unhappy and angry. She got on her cell phone or walkie-talkie or something and angrily shouted at someone. Then she nodded at us and strode off, annoyed and enraged, yet very slowly. Time passed. Shoppers pressed and shoved around us. My scooter sat forsaken in an urban parking lot. Finally, yet another management type showed up. By now it was 10:30, and I was up to pissed off. This guy's nametag on his colorful corporate vest identified his as The Manager. Well, it turns out that not only did they not know who we were or why we were there, they did not know that it was Mart-Mart Stamps Out Illiteracy Week. Hell, they didn't know what day it was or where they were or why. I doubt if they could have described their jobs. They damn sure couldn't do them.

Juanita and Joel each took an arm and led me back out into the parking lot and listened to me rant awhile about the immorality of corporate greed and computer communications. I did a half hour on the evils of big plazamalls, franchise chain businesses, and the demise of the little independent stores. I pointed out that books should be sold at book stores. Joel Lee and Juanita were patient.

I would like to take this opportunity to beseech all riders, in fact anyone who reads this book, to boycott the damn Mart-Mart Stores, especially the Giant Huge ones.

But when we left the Mart-Mart Store, me and the Tallgirl went for a ride. It was 'Nita's idea. As I've explained, she has known me a real long time. Long enough to know how to calm me down and get my mind off the Morning Mart-Mart Massacre.

Traffic was light, as everyone else on earth was at the Super Giant Huge Mart-Mart Plazamall Store being illiterate, especially the management. We rode easy and unmolested through the Springtime of Central Florida that day. It had been a bad Winter down here. We'd had too many hard freezes and twice that many bad frosts. Beyond that, it had also been an unusually wet Winter. I was about to run out of firewood. But me and 'Nita, we got to ride out into it on the afternoon that the weather recovered and turned to Spring. We rode off into the country away from the city and the noise and traffic and all. We rode on the two-lanes. We rode into areas that had no Super Giant Huge Mart-Mart Stores.

The cold morning had become a nice day. It was near seventy degrees and mostly sunny, with a cool north wind blowing some sparse clouds around in the sky. We rode along the Gulf shore awhile, past the salt marshes and sawgrass prairies. The tide was out, and we could smell the salt and mud and fish.

The Gulfside was turning green that afternoon. Then there was a gentle, turning, incoming tide, and the sawgrass fluttered and undulated in the easy breeze and easier current. Mullet jumped in the mouths of rivers. Beyond them, dolphin waited for the tide to increase. Gulls and terns wheeled past, screaming and calling. Above them, black frigate birds sailed effortlessly, never moving their wings. The shoreline palm trees were recovering from Winter and beginning to leaf out and turn a brighter shade of green.

We stopped awhile in Aripeka. The town is named for an old Indian who fled with his people into the swamps rather than take The Trail of Tears. The U.S. Army spent lots of money, several years, and a whole bunch of boys dying of snakebite and fever looking for him. And they never ever even saw him.

There were new calves and colts in nearly every pasture we rode by that Springtime afternoon. Birds filled the air between the butterflies. Every tree, every vine, every weed, every shrub, and every wildwood flower that could, came to bloom that day. The roadsides were festooned with wild violets and phlox. The dogwoods and the chinaberry trees were in bloom, and the swamp lilies had come back and were blossoming stark white in and around the lakes we rode by. The lobelia and water hyacinths were in purple blooms all around. Wading birds were nesting along the shores. Sawgrass was bright green and had blossoms on thin stalks. Ospreys hunted over the alligator-infested waters for fish for their own new nests. Scissor-tailed kites wheeled overhead.

We rode along beside lakes and rivers.

The air was wet with Spring. Everything looked fresh and new. It smelled that way, too. Tiny new leaves were coming out on some of the trees and bushes. The cypress trees were turning back to a hazy shade of green. The citrus trees were trying hard to make some blossoms. Vines, climbing high in the live oak trees, were leafing out and blooming. The fields were poking up new grasses in various shades of verdant green. Some of the raintrees and redbud trees were beginning to bloom. We rode through the forests and by the fields.

And by the time we got home, my anger had dissipated in favor of being glad I rode a scooter and live in Florida and have a good woman.

Next day I was back on the interstate to Orlando. Marty The Big Guy runs a biker talk-radio show on Sunday mornings out of Orlando, and he often invites me to come be the periodic guest co-host. Marty is the self-proclaimed Hero of Harleys, Bozo of BMWs, Terror of Triumphs, Harlot of Hondas, and Yahoo of Yamahas. He once made an announcement on the air that the next day was National Ride Your Bike To Work Day. Then The Big Guy looked over at me and began laughing so hard he nearly had to go to commercial. He continued, "Or, as Tiger calls it — Monday."

Marty bears watching, himself, but he knows some folks who make him look pretty normal. And he gets them all to call in to his show. He usually does that when I am co-hosting the show with him.

There is one regular caller who is actually six or seven. I've not ever been permitted to meet him personally. But I am told his real name is Jimmy, and he has a beautiful wife and a straight job. He has several radio personas. I suspect the man is also on some serious medication and several government lists, so I am not going to mention his last name or location.

My favorite is when he calls in as Ranger Rex Rage of the Rainbow Riders ASSociation. Rex is flaming gay and as out of the closet as can be. He claims the Rainbow Riders all have pastel painted scooters with patent leather saddlebags.

He contends that most of them are so hard-core that their cycles have no seats, just the post. Rex lisps into the telephone, and it is broadcast throughout the Greater Orlando area on the air waves and all over the world via the interweb.

"Tigger, sweetie, you should give it a try. All you macho boys are so scared, afraid you might like it."

I reply, "I don't think so, Rex."

"Tigger, you big closet queen, you! You're just frightened that you will realize the wonders of it all and come over to our side."

"Rex, sit on it."

"Oh you marvelous man! I AM sitting on it, sweetie."

I look to Marty for help, but Marty is seldom any real help. He adjusts his headset with a demonic twinkle in his eye and says, "Tiger, try to sell some of your books. Hold that one closer to the microphone for the folks out there in Radioland."

Another of Jimmy's characters is the Reverend Billy Bob "Bubba" Beaudine, a self-proclaimed, self-ordained, twice born again some more evangelist who is on an extensive Greyhound Bus Tour ($49.95 package) of the country spreading the Gospel of Jaysus. He calls in to condemn Rex for his filthy heretical gay ways. The Rev also chastises me for encouraging Rex.

He usually begins screaming. We all turn our volume buttons down as he starts out, "Tiger, ya know whut them gay homosexual queer faggots do, don't ya? It ain't RIGHT! They prevertin' the youth of Amurika with they aberrant, unnatural, preverted, deviated behavior. Tiger, boy, ya need ta git right with Jaysus, and see if ya kin git that Rex boy ta see the light, too."

Frowning at Marty, I reply into the microphone, "Rev, I've done explained to you that I'm a practicing animist/ancestor worshipper. And I really think it's too late for Rex."

Marty contributes a weary, "Oh, man," and lays his head gently on the microphone.

With a deranged scream, Billy Bob "Bubba" continues, "Tiger, son, that idolatrous, heretical, stuff you talkin' about, that there's near as bad as faggotry."

He pauses and takes a noisy wet breath, "Tiger, it ain't never too late. Just lean yer haid up against the microphone there and he'p me in a prayer for yer own damned soul as well as that of that poor queer Rex boy. See can ya git that pagan Big Guy to join us. Lean over there and smack him upside his haid a time er two and git him right up there ta the microphone."

Marty perks up, "Don't get me involved in this, Rev. You know I'm Jewish."

The Reverend Billy Bob "Bubba" near loses it, shouting, "Them are the folks what kilt Jaysus! Marty, them people are near as bad as that Rex boy."

The advantage here is that Marty can hang up. He does.

Jimmy calls right back as Fukayu Yamhonzuki, an angry Japanese businessman who yells at everyone for making fun of Asian bikes.

He begins his frantic tirade, "Tigah, you know da same people make dat BMW what build Volkswagens and Auschwitz. Same people make brud sausages and sauerkraut! And dey eat it, too. Dey bad people, Tigah! BMW mean Bavarian Murder Weapon! Dem people, dey try to kill Marty's people. Tigah, you need to do what da Rev tell you and rook at da right and buy a lice burner. BMW! Bavarian Meat Wagon!"

Most of Jimmy's characters have an agenda.

Speaking of characters, one time on a ride back north to Michigan years back, my pretty cousin Lee Ann made me go to a gypsy fortune telling psychic woman. Actually, she made me take her, and then she and the clairvoyant mystic prophet lady ganged up on me and insisted I also have my fortune told. Before I make too much fun of things I don't understand, I should point out that this fortune teller is also an ordained Christian minister.

I have no real memories of that supernatural psychic reading other than to recall that the girl said some real vague, generic, imprecise things about me. I remained unimpressed and on the edge of telling her so. Then she smiled, unperturbed, and said, "I see you surrounded by books."

I blew up. I told her that I taught English. Of course I was surrounded by books.

She continued to smile peacefully and said, "No, no, YOUR books."

And I hadn't even wrote that first book, *Longrider*, when she told me this. I scoffed. But since then, I've rode by to visit her several times. Her bearing is dignified.

One time she asked me what color my motorcycle was. And I told her black. She predicted that I was going to get a red bike. When she told me that, I told her right back that I was NOT going to get a red machine. Told her that was in a category with a haircut, a necktie, and a full-time woman. She smiled, closed her eyes a minute, and said, "Oh yeah. It's your bike. I can see you working on it." Her manner is serene.

She foretold that I was going to buy that piece of land just to north of The Redoubt here. She also predicted that I would have more books and a second CD of poetry published. Hell, she even suggested that I might wind up making some money with my writing.

But she has made a couple mistakes as well, so that wealth thing, that could be a trick, false-positive prediction. One time she talked about how she saw me in a strange place.

She began, "There are people not like you all around you. Tiger, they are all watching you. Some are wearing uniforms and have guns." Sometimes she makes those kind of real general statements that could refer to most portions of my life.

But she continued, "And you are trying to find something, to select something. But you keep rejecting your choices and trying others. It's very bright. Bright, bright sunlight is coming through the windows. It's dry. It's quiet. And you can't seem to find the one you want." She paused here to see my reaction.

Turned out she was describing, with some scary details, an incident from a few months prior to this. I was coming back east to home and had stopped by one of the trading posts the Navajos run out in New Mexico. It was a hot, dry, bright day out there in the desert, and I had gone into the place mostly to get out of the heat and into the air-conditioning awhile.

It was a slow day there on the Rez, and I was the only foreign gringo tourist paleface white boy customer in the place. And the trading post seemed to be the preferred air-conditioned gathering place for idle Indians, including the on-duty Tribal Police.

A display of native pottery had caught my attention, and I was examining little handmade vases for a gift for some friends back home. They were small enough to fit into a saddlebag easily. And all the damn things had non-flat bottoms and would not stand up straight and solid. I spent some time going through the tippy selection before finding one that would set solid upright.

So I said to the fortune telling witchy woman that she was telling me about something that had done happened already.

She smiled, unruffled by the error, and apologized, "Sorry. That happens sometimes."

Last time I saw her, she told me I was going to wind up with a Full-Time Woman. Remembering that red bike thing, I didn't say a word to the contrary. She missed a couple details, got the name and eye color really close. She prophesied Juanita in my life just about as sure and tranquil as that red bike prediction.

Between the calling of former occurrences and some of the inexact but close predictions, I suspect that prophecy about me making some money probably meant I was going to die a little less broke.

chapter fifteen
MORE WOMEN, THE LAST WOMAN, PACKING, and PENINSULAS

I used to know a woman who rode a Harley. This was a real long time ago, back before many women rode motorcycles, much less Harleys. Back when you had to kickstart your machine. She was a pretty girl with way too many tattoos and pierced parts. And this was back before hardly anybody had too many tattoos and pierced parts. Girl used to quote Rilke. But she was also disposed to saving rent money and wound up living in places that looked like where everyone would eventually come to overdose on heroin. And her dental hygiene left something to be desired. She was also a devoted breeder. Named her girlchildren Leavenworth and Attica. The boys were called Raiford, Chico, and Jackson. Had something to do with the locations of their various fathers.

Used to know another girl, also a real long time ago, who rode a Triumph, one of those big Tridents. Although she had no pierced parts or tattoos, she, too, was a dedicated procreator. Named her kids after her moods I guess. There was Maliss, and Regrette, and Ire, and the twins, Liberty and Harmony. She had a dog called Spot.

Met a girl one time named Cyrilene. I asked why. She explained that her parents, Cyril and Roberta, first had a girl, whom they named Jane. Then they had another daughter and called her Mary. When they had a third girlchild, daddy panicked and named her Cyrilene. Then they finally had a son. Named him Bob.

I used to work with a boy named Moses Christian, and then there were the Brothers Smith: Cool Breeze, Mad Dog, and Little John. When I taught at that Great Northern University, I kept having classes full of Polack kids who had nothing but consonants in their last names. Now, down here among the Italians and Irish, my roll book looks like some kind of weird vowel festival.

Up north, I had kids named Stan and Atilla and Jolene and Loutullus and Yorbalinda and Horst and Jesusa. Down here, the ones not named Jennifer and Jason are called Tara, Amber, Heather, Brittany, Jeffery, Josh, Jeremy, or Justin. I don't really know whether the differences are ethnic, geographic, economic, or chronological. And I have no idea what that all means or where I was going with it.

But just to prove that I can still recover when I've confused myself, I met a woman at a motorcycle festivity awhile back. I was there to sell books and tapes and CDs. It was hard to sell tapes and CDs, as they had them a band there. These musicians were way too loud and completely unafraid to fuck up anything they had ever heard.

I engaged the folks in the nearby t-shirt booth in a contest of sorts. "This one here, this is either 'Stairway to Heaven' or 'The Yellow Submarine,' right?" And they would shout back, "No, we're pretty sure it's 'Proud Mary,' or maybe 'Respect.' " Hard to play a CD with poetry when the band is messing up the words to "Louie Louie."

Anyway this woman walked purposefully up to my little table full of books and CDs and a silent CD player. Her name was Froggy. I suspect it was a nickname, even though she had a happy looking green frog sewn on her hat. She introduced herself and said that she had just read about me on the interweb that afternoon. Fearing for my personal freedom, liberty, privacy, independence, and confidentiality, I inquired as to what the hell was I doing on the worldwide interweb. I looked heavenward to see if there was a surveillance satellite twinkling among the stars. Then I looked around the crowd to see if any of the bikers were wearing wingtips.

Froggy laughed and told me she ran an interweb webnest for women bikers. I disremember the call letters or cyber-address or hyper-site or whatever it was. Anyway, she said a girl had e-faxed in to her webnest asking for some good books to read. Apparently she had stacked up her ride and was going to be down awhile. And someone else, another woman we presume, she e-faxed back in and recommended my books. I was delighted to learn about this turn of events. I was even happier when Froggy bought both books and a CD. I remain frightened at being on the interweb.

Like cellular telephones, credit cards, computers generally, cable satellite TV, AM&T cards, traffic camera scrutiny, discount cards, random crowd surveillance video, debit cards, and maybe the new impregnated-with-a-chip American paper money, that interweb thing ain't nothin' but thinly disguised surveillance.

In review, now my books have been acclaimed as "great airplane books," "perfect bathroom books," and now "commensurate recovery and rehab books." And some places are using them in their Literature of The American Road classes. Hell, I might have arrived. Just ain't sure where it is I am.

Got back here from a weekend ride with The New Full-Time Woman just recent. It went really well. We left out of here in the pre-dawn darkness to get over to Orlando to Marty The Big Guy's radio program. Marty was in top form. And pretty Biker Babe Michelle had rode her Harley in to co-host with us. Chopper called in to say he was soon headed up to Washington, D.C. to The Rolling Thunder Ride. Told me he was taking copies of my books to pass around.

Rex called in to see if I had come over to his side yet. "Tigger, Sweetie, it's going to be Gay Day at Disney World soon, and I don't have a date."

Fukayo was in his usual mood, angry. "Tigah! Them BMW people same people make schnapps for god's sake!"

The Rev reported in, "Tiger, son, ya need ta just drop ta yore heathen knees and repent!"

Then Marty got a call from a real person. Susan Buck called all the way from New York to report on a news story. She told about how someone, a vehicle driver, had killed a rider someplace. And the penalty had been a six-hundred-dollar fine and an hour and a half community service, or something like that. She was pretty upset.

I told her it was better than back in them bygone days of yore when there was a bounty on us. And Marty announced my next half- dozen book store gigs and tried to sell some books for me.

Juanita and I got back on I-4 eastbound toward Daytona Beach from Orlando about mid-morning. I figured to turn north there and run up the coastline on A1A north to some south of St. Augustine. Her family was gathering there for a graduation or Mother's Day festivity or something such as that. Riding the coast is almost always a fine ride.

However, heading up A1A this Sunday, that turned out to be a dumb idea. The traffic stacked up and got weird and potentially lethal on us long before we could smell any saltwater. These fools were ignoring that rule about personal space at high speeds and were bumper to bumper jockeying for position at ten over the speed limit. I blame NASCAR on TV.

But I had a little while to ponder this traffic, and I think I figured it out. It was Mother's Day. People in the central part of the state take their mothers to Disney World for Mother's Day. Folks on the west coast take their moms to Busch Gardens or Tarpon Springs. And on the east coast, Mother's Day is celebrated on Daytona Beach. I have no idea what they do in Miami or Tallahassee.

As soon as I could, I headed north via an inland road I used to know from twenty-some years ago when I first moved to Florida, Highway 11. Parts of it had been built up and developed enough to make me sad. But it's still empty and beautiful for miles and miles. We rode mostly alone and unmolested. I recalled a ride through here on Christmas Day in 1980. The dappled shadows on the concrete as the bright sunlight came through the tall trees hadn't changed much. And the Tallgirl learned which one is the near and which one is the off saddlebag.

We made the turn east toward the coast on Highway 100. Since I lived in this area, they have replaced the old bridge over the Intracoastal Waterway. The new one is real tall, puts you way up in the air so you get a magnificent perspective and first look at the Atlantic Ocean from a fine vantage point. The sun was behind us in the clear afternoon sky. The ocean before us was a hundred shades of blue. 'Nita took a deep breath of salt air and began recalling her childhood on the beach south of there.

It was about then that the traffic locked up and got to potentially terminal. And this is where I found out how good she is behind me. I had to swap lanes twice, once gearing down, and the next time getting on it hard, just to avoid being sandwiched between a semi-truck and an idiot in a giant huge SUV.

Juanita saw it all coming about the same time I did. And she just settled in and relaxed and let me ride it out. I know some girls who would have tightened up and tried to help. Some people would have attempted to climb up on top of my helmet for a better perspective. I know some who would have made it all much harder as they tried to play defense against everything I did. Hell, I know some women would have tried to bail off the bike.

Next chance she had, 'Nita asked me.

And I told her. "The idiot in the SUV didn't see me."

She thought about that some before saying, "But the bike is bright red, and the headlight is on."

"Sometimes there's a bounty on bikers."

"But it's a bright red bike. And the headlight is on."

She had even noticed that I had hit the high beam trying to avoid the confrontation.

I told her, "He didn't see the semi-truck either. I suspect he was on his cell phone."

A few miles down the road, she spoke up again. "OK, Tiger. Now I get it."

I believe she does, too. Told you all I had me a Good Woman here.

A1A is one of the finest rides in all of America. As it is located along a Scenic Southern Shoreline, it should be. There are several miles of the road between Flagler Beach and St. Augustine where you ride with nothing but sea oats and sand dunes and a beach between the road and the ocean. But anymore, much of A1A is being ruined with overdevelopment. Instead of looking at the short breakers, you get to see the backside of condominium complexes the size of major military installations or large maximum security prisons. They all have just about the same aesthetic charm.

Along the way, I got to ride Juanita past Camp Granada, down there by them rocks near Painter's Hill, where I lived my first Winter here. It still looks like the kind of low-rent deal it was back then in '80. Three bucks a night when the old guy running the place got sober enough to collect it. Non-potable water. Ten miles to a store. Lukewarm showers if you got to it before dark. I learned to situate my campsite far from his office. Usually he had collected enough money for a couple six-packs long before he got to me.

That Winter I also learned that a bluefish will bite you, that rattlesnakes are quite at home on a beach, and that a motorcycle will damn near dissolve if parked by the ocean for a long time. I saw rainbows in the moonlight and a UFO in the night sky. I got to watch sunrise and moonrise, and dolphins playing offshore. This time there were massive, monstrous time-share condominiums on each side of the old campground.

When we got to 'Nita's family gathering, and I was offered a place in an enclosed garage facing away from the saltwater, I jumped at it. After a couple real fine days on the beach south of St. Augustine with Juanita's people, with the scooter closed up in a garage, she and I turned it around and headed back home here to The Redoubt. This time she got to do a hundred and fifty miles straight through a bad wind. I kept to the back roads the whole way.

It was the kind of wind that doesn't really damage anything but motorcycle rides and semi-truck driver schedules and the flight of birds. The TV weather reading meat puppets astutely reported strong winds on the news that night. It was generally a hard wind ahead of a front from the north, but there were those trick gusts that come out of nowhere and move your cycle around some. It never got downright dangerous, but it was the kind of wind that kept you alert all the time. It was the kind of wind that wears you right down to weary and fatigued with painful crap in both eyes. You are damn glad to be off the road finally.

I have discussed the nature of the wind in both previous books, sometimes at length. In *The Ghost of Scootertrash Past*, I quoted my daddy when he once opined, "Sometimes I bet the wind is as bad as rain out there."

Uh huh.

And the Tallgirl now also understands some about the wind. It was a cloudy day, sometimes on the edge of sprinkling, all during that bad wind. So she also figured out that windburn is as bad as sunburn.

First time she climbed up behind of me, I said to her, "Do not try to help; let me ride it. And if we go down, get the hell away from the bike."

Since then, she's asked some real good questions about it all. She understands about how the cycle will hurt you worse than the concrete. This trip, she commented on the nature of big, over-dressed road bikes that have a rear seat that looks like an escape-proof Barca-lounger. It was then I confessed that when I bought my new Red Ride, it had a backrest attached to the stock seat. Told her I had removed and hidden it. She just smiled, as she knew the Red Ride had preceded her into my life by a year or so.

The only lesson we may have to review is that one about how little you can carry on a motorcycle. For the forty or so years I have been at it out there on the highway, I have been an advocate of the light, low, and horizontal school of motorcycle packing. I try to stay way under whatever maximum weight specifications and limits the manufacturer suggests, whether I'm alone or with a companion passenger.

But I'm going to have to make some personal adjustments when we take off for the long ride this Summer. As this is, I hope, the first of many such long rides, I want to make sure this new Full-Time Woman has a good time, that fun is had. And one of the best ways I know of to piss off a woman is to tell her she is restricted in terms of shoes and/or underwear that can be taken. Right up there with telling one that she has limited time to prepare for something. Not quite in the deadly category of answering the fatal questions, "Do you like my new haircut?" and "Do you think I look fat?"

And it turns out, once you have done took them to church, next thing is, they want is to be taken dancing. It's all beginning to come back to me now. Including putting the lid on the toilet down, that separating the laundry thing, and the balanced diet obsession.

For most of my life, especially the last real long time, I been out there rollin' around on my own, stone solitary. The isolation and hush are refreshing, in a real Zen kind of way. It is an important element in maintaining sanity, especially after two semesters of listening to freshmen and suits. There is little interaction, few compromises, fewer consolations. There are no schedules, few decisions. I had it right down to the basics, right out of the Long-gone Scootertrash Blues. Find food, find shelter, find gas. Figure out when to stay back out of the way and when to come out and pass.

Other than the occasional roadside rest area conversation with another rider, I seldom talked to people other than to say thank you when they handed me my change. I recall a run to the far left shore of California and back a few years back. I believe I was on sabbatical. And I didn't hardly talk to nobody from one coast to the other. And back. In between, I talked to Captain Zero and my old pardners Kenny The Hammer and Linda The Hawk and Dr. Johnson and Sandra Mae and Chuck The Nurse and Ralph The Sailor and Davey The Driver and his kid, Sidekick, and them other boys out there.

Besides that unaccompanied, isolated thing, the other advantage is that I had the whole damn scooter to pack with my own stuff. And, it turns out I got way more stuff than I used to.

Typically, anymore I leave out gone wearing a pair of jeans and a t-shirt, leather vest, socks and boots. And I pack five more pair of socks, two more pair of jeans, four more t-shirts, a long-sleeved shirt with buttons and a collar and all, just in case I wind up someplace unusual. I always take my denim jacket and my leather jacket, no matter which direction I am going. I picked up a real nice poncho down in Mexico years ago. It has proven to be the perfect multi-use travel garment, so I always tie it on behind me.

And, if I am headed north, I usually include a heavy warm shirt, maybe two, or a sweatshirt. If I am going north before or after Summer, I pack my leather pants and heavy gloves. Anymore, in the high heat of Summer, I've got to where I also take a light, long-sleeved shirt to get between me and the sun before cancer sets in again.

I have a set of Damart long underwear that, tops and bottoms both, take up about as much space as a couple pair of socks. And, as I would sooner be hungry than cold, I always take my Damart long underwear. Sometimes I will include a down-filled or thermal vest of some kind. Anymore, I toss in a pair of cutoff jeans, just in case swimming is required or judicious. And I take a pair of sweat-pants that double as pajamas. No, I don't wear no underwear. Not unless I'm goin' to the doctor. That saves a little room. I usually toss a towel and washcloth in there, too.

I put all this in two or three layers of plastic bags. Then it all goes in an old round heavy canvas bag that I picked up for five bucks back in 1970. It's the perfect solo motorcycle bag to tie on behind you and lean back on. I've never seen another like it.

Normally, I don't even try to haul a second pair of boots. If I am going someplace where I will be required to walk a lot, like San Francisco or with someone who wants to take me on a hike in the city/forest/mountains/desert/along the river/shore/path, I pack a pair of walkin' boots.

Similarly, if camping is required, like at most rallies and other such festivities, I have a lightweight tent and sleeping bag. They are bulky and take up some room. But they weigh little, and they are nice and soft and malleable and easy to tie down and on. Now besides all that, running solo like I been doing, I can also pack my entire kitchen. I have a one-burner propane stove and a coffee pot and a tiny, one-egg frying pan packed into a single bag that I bunji down on the tailrack. Also I have the aluminum canteen cup with the issue canteen I carry for water. I make my breakfast café con leche in that canteen cup.

In the off saddlebag, there is a quart of motor oil, a bag with silicone, two kinds of glue, JB Weld, spray cans of Chain Wax and WD40, a plastic honey bear with a few ounces of 90 weight, a long skinny funnel, some clear nail polish, duct tape, electrical tape, a spray can of engine de-greaser, some Armor All, a few zip ties, some heavy cord. There are always a couple rags in there, maybe an extra cable or two, some extra bunji cords, and probably a tin of mink oil for the boots and leathers. My rainsuit and face shield and rubber overboots are in this saddlebag, too.

One fairing compartment has a little tool kit and the owner's manual and repair books, a tiny flashlight. The rest of the tools are under the seat. The extra fuses and bulbs and spark plugs are in the little cargo area under the rear fender. The other fairing compartment has a tire gauge, gloves, a clean rag, and usually one of those throw-away cameras, maybe a bottle of sunscreen.

In the near saddlebag is a little bag with a toothbrush and toothpaste, deodorant and shampoo, some Band-aids, a needle and thread, and, anymore, my pain pills and Rolaids and such. This saddlebag is also where I keep my Oreo cookies and Thermos and a road atlas and my laptop legal pad and other things I might want to get to in an easy hurry. Copies of my books and tapes and CDs for highway gifts and promotion, whatever other book I am reading, some extra cigarettes and such.

And around all that, I always had plenty of room for any extra junk I picked up along the way. Usually that was limited to small rocks, bird feathers, and an occasional sea shell. Sometimes, in a low-tax state, cheap cigarettes. And even if I got two or three cartons, I was never pressed for space or weight.

And then There Was Woman. And I am having a hell of a time remembering how I used to do this with a passenger. I mean I understand she needs all the things I do, including a leather jacket and a rain suit. Hell, in my real old age here, I even understand that, as A Girl, she has a natural and inalienable right to more stuff and more room and space than I do. I've even got to where I understand that it is not a simple double standard; it's a damn complex multiple standard, applied whimsically. And I don't think it's a bit funny when she pats me on my head and says how cute I am for thinking I have a say in it all.

I've about got too damn old and lame to be sleeping on the ground, especially if I want to get up and walk around the next day. So there goes the tent and the sleeping bag.

But I sure would hate to give up my kitchen. I don't ask for much in this life, but good coffee is real high on that short list. And I would prefer my own home-made espresso coffee to the useless warm brown water they get a buck and a half for in most modern restaurants. But this New Woman, she don't drink no coffee.

And I would regret having to leave my long underwear and warm flannel shirts and sweatshirt to home, especially on a ride north like the one we are about to undertake. But the Tallgirl, she don't much mind being cold. Same deal with the sweat-pants. Probably same deal with the cutoffs, extra boots, leather pants, and a sock.

I've got to where, unless it's brutal, sweating all over everything hot, or I somehow wind up getting myself real dirty, I can go for about a week between laundry events out there on the road. I often wind up standing around the machine in my sweat- pants and boots with no socks while my clothes dry. Between hand laundering my delicates in a motel sink, commercial laundromats, friendly truckstop facilities, the occasional motel with a washing machine, and some good friends, it's been real easy.

But the New Woman tends to change her clothes frequently,

including underwear and shoes. And she is a real bargain hunter shopper, always on the alert for a deal, on damn near anything. Yeah, it's all coming back to me now. It's like the Lowdown Blues reminds us, The times have changed, and I have not. I'm still an old believer, but I can't hardly remember in what. Yeah, I am a recurring rumor in some places, but mostly I am forgot.

Other things, however, remain kind of creepily similar. Some years ago, I found myself engaged in conversation with the nice folks who run the Official AMA Museum and Everything Else up at Pickering, Ohio. My mission was to try to get my books in their gift shop, so I was being polite and agreeable and behaving myself and all. As I have pointed out, relative to selling my books and tapes and CDs at least, I am a good whore; I am congenial and polite with the customers.

I have no idea how the conversation took such a turn, but at one point, I said something about motorcycle riding in Florida. And the guy I was talking to said, "Oh, it's so flaaat!"

As he was a native Midwesterner, he said it just like that. I recognized it from my youth when I often listened to the same flat, nasal negative tone of voice and sentiment when I heard the pessimistic oft-repeated fatalistic Midwestern Naysaying Phrase, "Oh, you can't do thaaat!"

It was in the same tradition of the reactions I got when I told people I was going to get a motorcycle, or that I was going to go to a college, or that I was going to write a book, or that I was going to try to make something of myself, or that I was going to escape from that region. Something about the weather or the water in that part of the country that just naturally lends itself to such pessimism and negativity.

And, instead of sucking it up and agreeing with the dumb bastard, I took mild offense and commenced my rebuttal. I began by explaining that, for openers, all of Florida ain't all that flaaat. I continued that one of the reasons I moved to Florida was so I could ride every day of the year, including Christmas, New Year's, and my birthday. I pointed out that the seven-week "riding season" in the North had grown tiresome. I said something about cabin fever and spending November through May sitting around indoors looking at maps. I mentioned the joy, as a Florida resident, of not having to find Winter storage for my machine. I believe I commented on the fact that I had put around seventeen thousand miles on my scooter so far that year, most of it in Florida.

I fear I may have gotten a little overzealous and said something sarcastic about the nature of Ohio's scenery and how it was a rider's paradise with its twisting, winding mountain roads, high snow-covered peaks, and the miles of road along the scenic Ohio shorelines. I know I mentioned the breathtaking rivers and magnificent waterfalls. I am confident I commented on the majestic virgin forests and on the impressive overabundance of scenic highways. I even said something about Ohio rivaling Iowa for fine motorcycle riding.

And I suspect I remarked sarcastically on the horizontal, level nature of most of the roads in the Buckeye State. I may have mentioned the Dayton Alps or the Scenic Sandusky Seashore. Perhaps I also said something about Cleveland being The Mistake By The Lake and the River On Fire Festival in the Summer there. I may have even made passing reference to the vicious nature of the police in Defiance and the Magnificent Toledo Sunrises. In my zeal, I might even have said something about Columbus being the cultural epicenter of the entire Free World.

As I recall this, I became foolish and went on to try to defend Florida. It's hard to defend Florida. It's difficult to extol the wonders of anyplace with well over twice as many residents and nine times the tourists it had twenty years ago. I mean, Florida is pretty much the posterboy/spokesmodel for the horrors and perils of overpopulation, over-growth, and over-development. The state is proof of what happens when greed, growth, and development are the trinity. It's impossible to laud a state that has the construction crane for its state bird, asphalt as the state gem, a mouse on its state seal, and a population with an average age equal to that of most of the cypress trees. And I haven't even mentioned that voting thing.

But, it is not entirely flat. There are no more winding mountain roads than there are in Ohio. But if you look hard, you can discover some twists and turns and moderate inclines. You can't find them along the beach or in the Everglades. But a ride beside any Florida beach is better than the run from Cincinnati to Akron. And a run through the Everglades is certainly superior to the road from Mansfield to Massilon. And, it's even more superior on Christmas Day.

Actually, Florida, in spite of the crowds and traffic, has some incredibly beautiful roads. Many of them are, indeed, along the coastlines. A1A along the Atlantic is a real fine run almost anywhere on the east coast. The Gulf Coast highways, mostly U.S. 19 and 41, mostly don't really run along the Gulf Coast. You have to take some side roads down to the shoreline to see the Gulf water until you get up in the Panhandle. And those side roads are a damn good idea all through the Big Bend area. Some real fine side roads in here.

There are some good roads inland, too. U.S. 98 runs beside the shoreline most of the way across the Panhandle. Much of it is truly spectacular. The problem with coastal highways is, of course, traffic. But sometimes, even in the Summer, you can still manage a good ride beside the water through here, especially on the far east end of 98. And some of the inland alternatives in the Panhandle are full of short hills and little traffic, very scenic.

That Highway 11 I just mentioned is a fantastic ride. Same deal with that Highway 100 I wrote about. Many of the coast-to-coast two-lane roads are well worth the traffic and trouble of the small towns along the way. Notable among these are State Highways 44, 42, and 24. That last one terminates on Cedar Key. Real fine place to terminate, Cedar Key. A whole lot of the central Florida inland two-lane roads are pretty good rides.

Actually there are some wonderful rides in the southern portions of the state as well. The Tamiami Trail is, indeed, flat and straight, but it sure goes through some interesting country. Damn spooky road at night, too. And the Panhandle, up there in Baja Alabama, really is full of genuinely great roads once you get away from the beach and the interstate.

And, with the possible exception of Michigan, I know of no other place where you can watch the sun come up on one coast and then watch it go down on another. But in Michigan, as in Ohio and Wisconsin and Minnesota and Indiana and Illinois and Pennsylvania, you will often be told, "You can't do thaaat!" And, as both shorelines of Michigan are customarily frozen in the icy grip of a northern Winter, they're probably right.

chapter sixteen
OLD AGE, GREAT MEMORIES,
and GREAT LITERATURE

In the previous chapter, I commented that I ought not be sleeping out on the ground no more, especially if I want to get up and walk around the next day. I have gained new insight into old age and increasing infirmity just lately. Consider this advice to the elderly.

On Memorial Day I got early up and climbed on Juanita's tractor and finished mowing the five-acre pasture next to The Redoubt here. I refer to it as The North Forty. About the time I finished, 'Nita came home from a half-shift on the holiday and announced that I should take her for a scooter ride. So we climbed on the old Black Bike and spent three or four hours and a hundred and fifty miles on local roads. It was a pleasant, if warm, day and a real fine ride. Then when we got back home, the Tallgirl decided I should saddle my mare and help her chase some of her cows. We did that until near dark.

Let's review. That was three or so hours on a tractor, three or four more hours on a motorcycle, and then three or four hours on a horse. If you ever have a day like that, the thing to NOT do the next day is climb in a canoe and head downriver toward the Gulf of Mexico. Captain Zero pulled the canoe on shore and sort of tipped it sideways and dumped me out. I felt like the guy on the tricycle on *Laugh-In*. Yeah, there was a time. But it was long ago and far away. Good damn thing I have my memories.

There was a time I rode 1180 miles one day with a busted shoulder and my arm in a sling. They had to tape my left hand to the grip first thing that morning. I once took it from below Miami to above Detroit in about nineteen hours, most of it in the dark. I have kept it upright all day long in the Tehachapi wind with my windshield in my lap, and in a Montana wind with my crashbar scraping the centerline, and all day long down out along the Platte when there were whitecaps in the ditches, and everything else was layin' flat.

There was a time I rode the Skyline Drive and the Blue Ridge Parkway from the top to the bottom in a single day. Done it the other way, too. I have rode around the Olympic Peninsula in a day, and around Nova Scotia in a day. But that was all in a previous century.

Anymore, I celebrate a five-or six-hundred mile day as if I have accomplished something. Hell, I've got to where I find myself in my pickup truck in a rainstorm or real bad traffic, thinkin' how glad I am I ain't on a bike.

But I have memories of riding the ridge of the Rockies and both borders. I recall riding The Avenue of The Giants, and The Trail of Tears, and The TransCanada Highway, and The Great River Road, and the Old Hillbilly Highway, and Route Sixty-Six, and The Old Lincoln Highway, and The Pacific Coast Highway. I remember riding beside the Hudson's Palisades and along the Trinity and the Columbia and the Red.

Lately, as a genuine book author, I have been doing a whole bunch of telephone-radio interviews. Turns out some of my memories are worth sharing on the air-waves. Most of the time, the radio station is in a little town someplace in the Heartland or a remote village someplace on a crossroad in the hinterlands. Sometimes, it's a station in a city. I've been on the radio in Topeka and Miami, Lake Osage and Las Vegas, Scotia, N.Y. and Hofstra University, Kitchener, Ontario and Billings, Montana. Like most of my activities anymore, selling my books is at the heart of it all. I almost always get to begin the interview by saying to the local radio host, "Hey man, I been through your town."

I have gotten to talk on the radio to some places that have touched off memories of times gone by. I spoke with some nice folks in Alton, Illinois awhile back. Got to read them the story of how I sat out a monumental rainstorm in their town one time years ago. It's in *Longrider*. And I had a real good time on the air with the radio folks in Broken Bow, Oklahoma awhile back. And I have been on the air in Dubuque with Chris and Rachel a couple times.

Anyway, it set me to thinking about the little towns and the two-lane highways between them. One time, long ago, in real rural Iowa, I stopped to visit an old friend. She had a couple little kids who wanted to be taken fishing. So I rode back into town to get some tackle so I could take them out to fish the local waters. Downtown was about three blocks long. There wasn't a building over two stories anywhere. Many of these Midwestern towns have the same basic business pattern: courthouse, hardware store, feed store, gas station, barber shop, grocery store, library, Dairy Queen, farm implement dealership, Christian book store, and usually a restaurant called the Dew Drop Inn or Mom's.

I stopped at the local hardware store to get some fishing tackle. I am always aware that, damn near no matter where I am, I don't look or sound like I am from right around there. Without the double hammer hanger overalls, Massey-Ferguson cap, and brogan shoes, I am immediately identified as an outsider in these little Heartland towns. With my full beard, a pony tail hanging to my butt, a helmet, leather and boots, they know right off that I don't belong there. Then I open my mouth to talk, and they are reassured that I am not from right around there.

So, there I was in downtown wherever it was in rural Iowa, and I went into the local hardware store to get some fishing tackle. As I stood in front of the small display of hooks, sinkers, and bobbers, an elderly woman cautiously approached and asked if she could help me. I explained that I had been put on taking little kids fishing detail, and we needed some gear.

She smiled, I presume at the idea of me with small children, and took me by my arm and began walking me back toward the door. As I have been thrown out of nicer hardware stores in nicer towns, I figured just to go along with it. But as we walked toward the door, she explained that I could get a cheaper deal on what I wanted across the street at Vern's Barbershop.

I stood on the sidewalk with her and raised an eyebrow in skepticism. I figured this was a Midwestern comment on my general appearance, perhaps even a mean trick to get me into a potential haircut situation. But she assured me it wasn't. Turned out, old Vern had a box of assorted fishing tackle in a box under the counter that he sold real cheap.

That's pretty typical of how you get treated out there in

middle America. I've had whole towns like this gather in a meeting to help me in whatever it is I am working on, whether it's fishing tackle, or parts for a bike they've never heard of, or finding an obscure place that should be nearby. This time in Iowa, old Vern, after taking minimal money for the fishing tackle, he told me a couple places to fish. He never even offered to cut my hair, but he did assure me that I would not need a local license. His nephew, also named Vern, was the only local cop.

Over the years and along the way, I have been turned on to some great fishing places, beautiful campsites, scenic local wonders, little-known mechanics, hidden caches of parts, wonderful meals, fine roads to ride, festive local celebrations, and ways out. Much of this is pure country people friendliness. Some of it is the fact that folks in such places are just used to helping one another. Part of it is surely a desire to get me on my way the hell out of there. But I think most of it has to do with boredom and a desire to talk to someone who ain't from right around there.

Once they figure out that you're not dangerous, and that you have some social skills, they will often invite you to hang around some and maybe spend the night there. Sometimes they suggest you would be welcome if you came back through there in time for the Sugar Beet Festival next month or the Annual Tumbleweed Jubilee and Prairie Dog Race in a couple weeks.

One time, deep in the Heartland, I barely escaped being made to stay a week there so I could be an impartial judge in the Miss Millet & Milo Contest that was the main part of the county fair. I had to wait until I saw the local cop head out of town with his lights and siren on so I could depart the other direction. Didn't stop until I had crossed a state line. They were quite serious about the Miss Millet & Milo Queen thing.

Sometimes the first person you get to talk to is the local cop. And most of the time, they are pretty good guys, often more human and humane than their state highway and county sheriff counterparts. Once they figure out that you ain't there to convert and pervert their children, or run off with their women, they pretty much leave you be.

I've got to where I often seek out the local cop. Whether I need it or not, I will ask them for local directions or advice on where to eat or something, let them know I got some money and intend to spend some there. This way I can identify myself as articulate and polite and harmless. I can thus establish a rapport before they go into automatic Running The Scootertrash Out Of Town Local Cop Mode. Some of the younger, more zealous uniformed authorities still approach things with that attitude, but most of the time the local cops are pretty good to you.

People often categorize parts of America. Hell, people tend to codify and stereotype just damn near everything. I guess it helps life make some sense. Anyway, I have spent most of my life reading and hearing that New Englanders are terse, taciturn, and unfriendly, that Southerners, hospitality aside, are slow talkin' and suspicious, that Midwesterners are gullible and conservative. Texans are braggarts. Though W. Bush may have broke them of that. Florida is one big beach full of damp Cuban refugees and old folks. Californians are, of course, all young and suntanned and homosexual and liberal to the point of anarchy. Although I think Ronnie Rayguns may have dispelled that generalization. People in Wisconsin pray to cheese, and every white person in the Deep South is a devout racist.

Minnesotans will feed you dessert with miniature marshmallows in it and over-cook your meat while they say "Aw Jeez," a lot. Iowans live on corn and pork. People from New York are rude, talk fast, and bitch about everything. Folks from Michigan have no manners and want to tell you how they do things Up North. There are more horses than people in Wyoming, and Arkansas is full of hillbillies who talk like Li'l Abner and Snuffy Smith. And beware of Georgia, especially if you hear banjo music.

Well, there is truth in all stereotypes. That's how they get to be stereotypes. The exceptions prove it. I have found helpful, talkative, friendly, funny folks in New England, and fast-talking, open, trusting, non-racist Southern people. I've eaten fine salads in Iowa and had some relatively rare beef in Minnesota. And once upon a time I had a brief relationship with a pale heterosexual girl from California until I found out she had voted for Reagan.

My own classification instincts, developed from forty-some years of riding around out there in America, is to divide the country into cities, urban sprawl, and country. Back when I first began rolling around America, there was a lot more country. Back then, even the cities had some charm and local flavor. They were still cities, but they were unique, interesting places, even if they were no place to be on a scooter.

But anymore it's hard to tell if you are in Cleveland or Tulsa or Nashville. Chicago can look frighteningly like Atlanta. Ain't a lot of difference between Omaha and Jackson and Albany and Indianapolis. It's even medium easy to get confused about Seattle or San Francisco. All them damn Starbucks. About the only other similarity among American cities is that most of them are dying. And the sprawls all look so much alike as to cause confusion, disorientation, and sometimes panic. Development, construction, traffic, and overpopulation dominate. The chainfood places and other franchise outfits in the American Hospitality Industry are so much alike as to be interchangeable. Once you've seen a McDenny's/Howard Hilton Marriott/Pizza O' Plenty/Sleepy Inn 7 and 8/Family Golden Sizzler Platter/Super Giant Huge Mart-Mart Store, well, you've about seen the American Sprawl.

It's out in the country, out on the two-lane roads far from the cities and impending sprawls that I have found my own America. Couple years ago I was wandering around out in the Sand Hills of western Nebraska, an exercise I would recommend. Pretty country and really nice people. Not much good to say about the weather, but it was a fine ride. Very little in the way of big cities or urban sprawl out there. Whole lot of country.

Actually, there is another category. Turns out all of America is divided into four parts. The fourth classification is Amusement Parks. I use this term generally, disparagingly, and inclusively, much like I use the word Winnebago. These places are where we find The Amusement Park Impaired. While these folks can be pretty funny on public transport, they are a dreaded menace on the highway. Much of Corporate Commercial Business America is devoted to entertainment, recreation, and amusement anymore. You don't believe that, ride around Orlando for about five minutes. And Los Angeles, and Six Flags Over Damn Near Everyplace, and San Francisco, and Daytona Beach, and Recreated History In Costumes Is Us, and Gatlinburg, and any coastline or beach, most lakes, all National Parks, Las Vegas, Branson, and countless local periodic celebrations. All these things attract people, and people make crowds and traffic.

And these gatherings are hard to avoid. I have, unwittingly, stumbled into such things. And once you've done that, it is often hard to escape. I've gotten caught up in several motorcycle festivals that I was unaware of over the years. Anymore, no matter where it is, the whole place is gridlocked with trucks dragging motorcycle trailers.

But I have also wandered, completely oblivious, into hot air balloon festivals, annual color tour holidays, classic old car cruise-in week, the steam engine enthusiast festivity, vintage motorcycle/auto/bicycle/boat/tractor days, all kinds of local pioneer day jubilees, assorted local food festivals, various pow-wows and rendezvous, and sundry conventions.

Years back, a former student and friend of mine wound up teaching at a little college in eastern Wyoming. She said her classroom was full of cowboy hats with boys named Clete and Hoot and Hoss underneath them. The rodeo team. She told her dean that she had determined these young men were uncomfortable with a woman in a position of authority. He explained to her that most of those boys were from the Sand Hill country of Nebraska and had probably never seen a woman before. Turns out if your folks live around there and name you Guido, your name is Guide-O.

On this recent ride out there, I wound up in a little town out on the scenic two-lanes in the northwest of the state. It was a slow time of day, and I had an opportunity to talk to the few other customers and the restaurant staff. Among other things, I took a lesson in local geology. Turns out the area used to be a sea floor. Some interesting geological formations out there. Nice folks, too.

There is a part of William Least Heat Moon's book, *Blue Highways*, that offers a theory about restaurants. He claims there is a simple ratio; the more local calendars from the insurance agent, hardware, bank, feedstore, and such on the wall, the better the restaurant. The local calendar count, according to this theory, pertains to and reflects both the food and the service.

I noticed seven such calendars on the walls of the Nebraska Sand Hill restaurant and explained the Heat Moon theory to the waitress there, Molly Margaret Mary Maeve. Then when I went on about how I never seen any calendars on the walls of a McDonald's, she told me she had never seen a McDonald's. One of the other customers opined that he thought there might be one over in Casper.

On my way to the Nebraska Sand Hill country, I rolled across Iowa. And in spite of the fact that there are fewer designated scenic highways in Iowa than are in Rhode Island, I found some beautiful places. The Amana Communities were pretty places, and the roads through them were a treat. And along the way, I found some places to ride beside and across the Mississippi and Missouri Rivers that did not involve interstate highways. And there really is some pretty scenic country up in the northeast corner of Iowa, across The River, west of Prairie du Chien. Wonderful rides and fine river crossings out there on the two-lanes.

I offered this categorization and preference in a conversation recently. I was selling books at a local motorcycle rally and was talking to three older couples, folks my age, all of them on Gold Wings, two of them hauling trailers behind their scooters. These folks had some miles on them. They had come a long way to attend the festival.

When I suggested that the two-lanes were the best roads, one of these riders countered with the standard, Oh The Inconvenience Of It All argument: Sometimes it's hard to find gas or other services on the blue highways. Cellular telephone reception is uneven. Same deal with your laptops and GPS machines. And then you get lost and wind up in weird places. There are too few motels, and if you do manage to find one, there is seldom color cable-satellite TV, internet access, a nearby restaurant or a laundromat or a store or a gas station with an ATM. Worse yet, some of the more remote places refuse to take credit cards. You never know where or when or what you are going to eat. There are so few convenient shopping opportunities out on the two-lanes.

My rejoinder, rebuttal, and response was the same as it has been for years. I said, "Uh huh."

If I thought they'd have stayed and listened, I'd have quoted from The Long-gone Blues. When we rode that first road the first time out, that was when the highway took a real firm grasp. The future was flatout inevitable, and the die was firmly cast. Once the highway had a good hard hold, we were forever bound to be lonesome outbound scootertrash.

I mentioned in a previous book about how I thought I was getting treated generally better in my old age than I did as a youth. In retrospect, I think I have figured out some of that. Much of it, obviously, has to do with the changing of the times and the advances of technology between of then and now. Folks, even those in the little towns out in the middle, are far less isolated and suspicious.

But I think most of it has to do with, now that I am an old man, I am no longer a threat; they know that I am not going to mess with their women.

Also, there are some tales in those books about incidents when somehow I did wind up with a local girl. I have some fine memories of a couple such occasions. But that was years ago, and it ain't happened in a real long time. Yeah, busted dreams and broken hearts, and one headlight in the dark of the night. And I forget how the rest of that verse goes.

As a result of that first book of mine, *Longrider*, I began an informal, but pretty extensive, study of Literature of The American Road. An old friend of mine, a boy I used to ride with, he was teaching such a class at a SUNY campus. He and I put together a book list. He was kind enough to include my book.

I had read Kerouac's *On the Road* years ago. Same deal with Steinbeck's *Travels with Charley* and William Least Heat Moon's *Blue Highways*, and Dr. Hunter S. Thompson's *Fear and Loathing in Las Vegas*. Likewise, I had read Wolfe's *Electric Kool-Aid Acid Test* back when it first came out. Memorable on the list was Robert Pirsig's *Zen and the Art of Motorcycle Maintenance*.

And this was just the literature from the past century or so. We didn't even approach the topic of Road Songs. Someone is surely going to do that. That list will surely begin with the Lonesome Scootertrash Blues. Having thought that one through, I suspect the whole phenomenon of having a need for going, of migrations and road trips and all, is distinctly American.

Anyway, I wound up stealing most of the course from SUNY and taught such a class myownself a few years back. I found that, while all these books held up real well over time, my experience in reading them years later was much different than it had been in my own youth. And the re-reading was a fine personal literary experience all the way around.

The other discovery was that the contemporary young people in my class, which they called Road Lit., They Got It. I feared some of the works would be dated and obscure, that they might not hold up over time. But the students in my class thoroughly enjoyed and understood Kerouac and Wolfe. They got hard into Steinbeck and Least Heat Moon. Hell, they even figured out the lineage from Kerouac to Alan Ginsberg to Wolfe to Hunter Thompson to McMurtry, and who and what came in between.

The Road Lit. class became a valuable lesson in history and sociology and geography and economics and literature. You can tell how well your class is going by the serious questions the students ask, the spontaneous discussions that erupt. This was a truly great course. They learned about America.

When given the choice between taking a final exam or taking a road trip and writing about it, the entire group went for Option B. I got some damn good papers from that assignment, and the students got some wonderful experiences.

They were so involved and enthusiastic that they insisted we spend an extra week on *The Electric Kool-Aid Acid Test*. That was the first time in thirty years I have seen students take charge of their own education like that. I was near moved to tears.

Beyond these books, I came up with some other titles. Peter Beagle, as I have mentioned, wrote a book about a cross-country trip on a Cushman scooter back in the 1960s. It's called *I See By My Outfit*, and it is one hell of a book about one hell of a ride. And I got hold of a copy of Woody Guthrie's *Bound for Glory*, and I was also turned on to a contemporary book by Robert D. Kaplan called *An Empire Wilderness*. The former is an autobiographical look at the past, and the latter is a scary as hell prediction into the future of America. Based on my own personal recent travel observations, it may be a scary as hell account of the present.

Larry McMurtry, one of the best modern writers in America, also contributed to the book list. His is called *Roads*, and it is about U.S. interstate highways. Oscar Zeta Acosta wrote a book called *The Autobiography of a Brown Buffalo*. It's a fine road trip book in the Gonzo tradition of Hunter Thompson.

And lately I have run across a pair of books by Englishmen who recently drove around America. One is called *Almost Heaven* by Martin Fletcher. It was a lot of fun. The other is by a guy named Bill Bryson, who is really from Iowa, but who nonetheless takes a really mean, snobbish British viewpoint of The Colonies. It's called *The Lost Continent*.

One of my favorite authors, Andrew Vachss, has one called *The Getaway Man*. It's about driving rather than about the road. Kind of like Thompson's *Hells Angels* is neither about the road or the ride.

And someone recently gave me a copy of a book by a black guy who climbed in a canoe up in Minnesota and paddled south to Grand Isle. Hell of a book, even if it isn't technically about The Road. *Huckleberry Finn*, one of the very best stories American Literature has to offer, is really about a road trip. Again, the road was the Mississippi River.

Many of these works aren't entirely about road trips. The authors use the road and the journey as a basis for their story. Sub-titles are a tip off. Pirsig's book is sub-titled "an inquiry into values." My students agreed that it was mostly about madness. Steinbeck's classic has the sub-title "in search of America." The students understood that he found it, too. So did they.

Least Heat Moon's tale is sub-titled "a journey into America," and the students got out a road atlas to follow him along. Kaplan's piece is called "travels into America's future." The students are closer to the future than I am, so they understood this one better than I did.

Fletcher calls his "travels through the backwoods of America," and Bryson's is sub-titled "travels through small town America."

Even my own *Longrider* has the sub-title "a tale of just passin' through." My students understood that this is what we are all doing. And my second book, *The Ghost of Scootertrash Past*, is subtitled "memories and rants of a longrider." Yeah, we all got our own little agendas.

The most important things I learned from this study of Road Lit. is that it is universal, and it is eternal. The very earliest, and probably some of the very best literature is Road Lit. *The Iliad* and *The Odyssey* are good examples. So, too, are *Beowulf* and *The Canterbury Tales*. Damn near all civilizations and cultures have produced some kind of epic literature about a hero of some sort and the journey he undertakes. Check your *Old Testament* out for earlier examples. I may try to include at least portions of "Exodus" next time I teach the course.

I came to understand that it ain't just me. The need for goin' is intrinsically human. And the need for coming back and telling the others where we have been, what we have seen, is just as natural. I am confident it pre-dates writing. I suspect it somehow even pre-dates speech. Might could be instinctive.

chapter seventeen
PLACE NAMES, LITERACY, and BAD WEATHER

Another way of dividing the U.S. is into sections by names. This is pretty easy, as most places are named for the early pioneer folks or initial inhabitants or a local historic hero one way or another. Seems like about half the states follow this practice and are named for the native Indians of the area. A lot of sites in the country, especially the East, have a "New" in front of the name of the place. I think this usually indicates where the early white pioneers came from. Most of the time you can pretty much tell where you are by the place names around you.

Used to was, you could tell where you were by the way the folks around you talked. I spent a few pages in each of the previous books discussing this sad phenomenon of dialect leveling. Forty or fifty years back, you damn near had to take a translator out into the hinterlands with you. But TV and such have taken a bad toll on the varieties of American English. And current high school graduates are using two-thirds fewer words in their vocabularies than we did forty-five or fifty years ago.

There are still some pretty obvious regional dialects and differences remaining out there. As you run from one end of the East Coast to the other, the waitresses begin, down in Miami, with "Con I help joo, mon?" Then, some to the north, they'll inquire "Kin I he'p y'all?" Farther north, it becomes "Cayan I hayulp youse?" In New York City, they just sort of frown at you like they wish you'd go away. Sometimes they demand, "Yeah?" or sometimes, "What, dammit!?" And eventually, farther to the north, you'll hear "What can we get fer ya, eh?"

But there was a time when, if you wandered into some remote place in south Alabama or north Minnesota, you were listening to something approaching a foreign language. Thirty-some years ago, I was called upon to translate for some Michigan friends I was riding with and the locals up around Asheville. That long ago, I was often baffled by the speech of folks in New England. And, anymore, not only does it all look alike, especially near the cities and sprawls and interstate highways, but it sounds pretty much the same, too.

One of the first rules of dialect is that mobility, even vicarious, levels it. And we are the most mobile society in the history of people, at least vicariously. Ask any kid if he has been to Africa, and he will tell you about a popular webnest, or a full-length feature animated cartoon movie, or something on the Adventure Channel. Yeah, they think that counts. We took their imagination away from them with TV and computers, and now we are destroying their sense of reality.

But back to that thing about riding around the country encountering specific place names. New England and New York are full of mostly British and a few Dutch designations. And you also get a whole lot of indigenous Indian names, too.

The Middle Atlantic States are kind of culturally and geographically amorphous, but they have a whole lot of imperial, royal-sounding names. They also have some real interesting Indian names, too.

Once you get into the Southeast, The Confederacy, there are a whole lot of towns and cities named for war heroes. I think there is some kind of zoning legislation that requires several variations on Calhoun, Jackson, Gaines, Lee, and Jefferson in each former Confederate state. And then there are lots of places with Indian names. They have some hard to say Indian places in much of the Southeast. Way different Indians than the ones in New England or the Middle Atlantic States.

The Southwest and most of California are full of Spanish-named places. It's hard to get far away from El Someplace or Santa Someplace Else out there in the former Spanish Empire. Sometimes the translations are pretty interesting. Sometimes it turns out to be corrupted and badly translated. Key West was Cayo Hueso, the Island of Bones, but that isn't what the Crackers heard or said, either one.

Up and down the whole length of the Mississippi and

around the Great Lakes you get all kinds of French-sounding places, many of them beginning with a Saint. There is a town in Michigan named Grand Blanc, after the fat French fur trader who ran a post there in the 1700s. Parts of the upper Midwest are full of Scandinavians and corresponding, appropriate place names. There is a really neat picnic area just outside Standquist, Minnesota. Other parts of this region are equally Germanic and Nordic in their origins and names. And all of these areas pay homage to the original natives they killed and starved for the land, so there are local Indian names.

And then there are the anomalies and the just plain strange names. Like where the hell did Yankeetown, Florida come from? Panacea, Florida and Hell, Michigan kind of make sense. But Manhattan, Kansas will make you wonder about it for awhile. Sort of like West Thumb, Wyoming (no, there is no East Thumb), and Upper Southwest Mabou, Nova Scotia, and Opp, Alabama. Some places take you a minute to figure out. Show Low and Sixes made me think about them. Turns out to be references to games of chance. Lum and Guber and Flushing were surely christened after unfortunately named founders. And if you work at it some, you can come up with an explanation for Bad Axe and Blue Ball.

But Atlantic, Iowa don't make much more sense than Zap, North Dakota or Buffalo, New York. And then there is Mexico, Missouri? Oxford, Mississippi? Moscow, Idaho? Toledo, Ohio? Paris, Texas? Cuba, New York? Athens, Georgia? Arab, Alabama? At least the folks in Cairo, Illinois and New Madrid, Missouri mispronounce the names of their towns so you'll know you're not in Egypt or Spain. Then there are the names of local Indians, most of them long dead.

Sometimes, in these places, I try give my books to people who resent it. They do not read, they do not want to be given any kind of print assignment, and they damn sure don't want to attend to anything not presented in special effects animated cartoon fashion in a color digital format that can be manipulated by a mouse on a great big TV screen. Sometimes, when I hand someone a copy of one of my books, he asks, "Does it have pictures?"

Sometimes I tell them, "Yeah, one on the front and one on the back."

It's sad, this Post-Literate aspect of modern America. I mean it is hard to teach anything. But teaching writing, or literature, or selling books, or promoting a documentary Literature of The American Road project, that's a task of Herculean proportions. Sometimes I feel as if I am teaching The Legend of Literacy. But beyond that, it's sad.

Reading requires and develops imagination, and contemporary young people have been cheated out of acquiring any kind of real inventiveness. They are, individually and as a group, just flat out unable to play like.... This is the fault of telephones, television, computers, computer games, e-faxing on the damn interweb, and other anti-literacy technology. Radio required imagination.

Beyond the fact that these non-readers are never going to experience the absolute joy of a good book, it's sad because they are never going to figure much out. If you can't imagine, you won't be much good at determining alternatives or making informed choices. You might know which button to push, but that only works with computers, some of the time. Young people's decision-making skills, in their own words, suck. Had a kid explain to me awhile back that school prepares one for life, which also sucks.

Making pictures in our heads is much more satisfying and productive than watching pictures the government and the Global Corporate World Economy insidiously and constantly broadcast into homes and schools and restaurants and bars and cars and minds. No, these MTV/Video Game kids aren't much good at making up pictures in their heads. As a result of this, they also lack resourcefulness. When the power goes out on their video games and everything else, I suspect they will all starve and freeze from an inability to read the directions on a book of matches.

A few years back I found myself in conversation with a woman who was fourth or fifth in command of the U.S. Department of Education. Nice lady. I asked about current statistics on The Illiteracy of America. She had been drinking some, and she sort of conspiratorially told me that the official line was that about ten percent of America was illiterate. The unofficial reality was that forty percent of the people who should be able to read and write really can't.

My own personal observations confirm this. About a quarter

of the freshmen entering America's colleges each fall are unable to consistently compose a simple sentence. Most have never seen one.

When I inquire of them what the hell were they doing in high school, they explain it to me. Contemporary high school, in their own words, is a containment effort with occasional lock-downs and fashion shows. Many students are unaware that there was an American Revolution. Most don't know who we rebelled against or when or why. I guess we don't want them to have some sort of bad example. The idea of a revolt, of any kind of disagreement with authority or the current administration's policies, is perceived to be politically incorrect, if not criminally questionable.

Beyond my personal sorrow for such a state of affairs, I am also saddened because it's America. And we are consistently coming up about 73rd in the world in terms of public education and smart, literate kids. Right behind San Honduragua and Yoohooistan. Real easy to lead stupid people. For example, not only is no one doing anything about this situation, but no one really seems to give a damn.

And it seems a pretty easy fix to me. Obviously bigger isn't translating to better, so let's exercise the Wisdom of old CalTran Dan and try for smaller. Smaller districts, smaller schools, smaller classes. And, yeah, smaller football teams and such, too. Teach the children how to read and write instead of how to push a damn button. After that, all we need is fewer suits and better teachers.

There seems to be a general consensus that those of us who graduated from high school in the early-middle 1960s were the last entire literate generation America has produced. And we are all real old people now. And that's sad for a whole bunch of reasons.

But, I will soon retire and be done with the hindrance that is work. Then I can concentrate on other sadnesses. One of them will be the Summer weather in Florida. We have dropped into the Typical Summer Pattern here recent. What that means is It Rains. Usually it does that in the early evening, so that you have to plan your riding around it. Sometimes it rains well into the dark of night, so you have to get back home early to feed your dogs and horse. And sometimes, it rains all day long, for days on end sometimes, so you're just pretty much screwed.

Besides taking the riding away from you, the weather turns all your leathers and belts and boots green with mold. Everything made of paper swells up and sticks to whatever is next to it. Envelopes seal themselves. Matches won't light. Guitars go out of tune. Sinus infections bloom like mildew.

Last time I was down to Karl The Kraut's, he suggested some transmission and rear bearings and seals for my new Red Ride would be prudent preventative maintenance. And I had to truck the damn thing down there to Dirty Street because of the torrential rainstorms. I mean it has got so damn Typical Summer this year that the best move is to get up early and try to get some riding done before noon or so.

The other thing the rain is affecting is this book. When it thunders and lightnings, I have been told to turn this here computer off. Otherwise it will explode or something. That's problematic in that if I ain't riding, chances are I am writing, usually about riding. And the rain is screwing up both them endeavors.

Years ago, there was a terrible storm came upon us at work, and some of the students asked me should they turn off or unplug their computers. I told them I didn't know. Told them I had never been real comfortable on a scooter in lightning storms. Said if they were on horseback in such weather, they ought not wave a shotgun around in the air.

But, it turns out the answer to that turning off the computers question was Hell Yes. Seems it is also prudent to turn my own computer machine off in such weather. I don't recall this problem with the Smith-Corona portable I used from high school through my doctoral dissertation.

One other time, the new suits where I work decided we were going to have a hurricane. We weren't, but these New York Yankees had just taken over, and they didn't know much, beginning with where they were. So they panicked. First thing they did was, of course, to tell everyone to unplug the computers. You can't run a business without them. Then they dismissed classes and began putting sandbags around everything they could find that would hold still. I wished I had the local sandbag concession and moved my scooter to high ground in the sunshine just in case they were right.

Someone in a position of authority came by and issued

big plastic garbage bags to everyone. This time I wished I had the local garbage bag franchise. I stood there, stupidly, with my garbage bags. I just couldn't imagine what I was supposed to do with garbage bags. Finally, I put one on each foot and held them up with rubber bands. I figured if the suits were right, maybe I could wade around in the flood and keep my feet dry. Turned out the administration wanted us to cover up the unplugged computers with the garbage bags.

They were confident that disaster was imminent, and they put up shutters and plywood, and sequestered students and collected drinking water and all. Batteries were counted and catalogued and rationed, equipment was moved to high ground, other emergency procedures were begun. I moved my scooter again, this time to over near a building with an overhang and some shade from the bright sunshine. Was hard to do with them garbage bags on my feet and all.

A work crew was formed, and they began cleaning out all the ditches and gutters. Orders were made to ensure everything of value (computers) be put up high off the floor. A few pieces of equipment were tied down. The school nurse, a local girl who knew better, was put on Red Alert. She rolled her eyes and sent someone out for a pizza.

When they began putting sandbags around the outside doors on the third floor of the buildings, I figured I'd seen enough, and I rode on out between the sandbags. I feared they would find my sandwiches and ammunition up there in the bell tower where they were sure to sandbag next.

As I recall this one, it was such a nice day that I rode off toward the middle of the state someplace where I pondered the words to The Lonesome Scootertrash Blues.

chapter eighteen
WRECKS, ANGELS OF MERCY, and SCRABBLE

I mentioned the School Nurse back there. Hell of a girl, the School Nurse. I have known several many of these women over the years, and they are always True Angels of Mercy. The current one where I work, she took care of me the last time I went down on a cycle. Come to think of it, she took care of me the time before that, too. The last time I went down was stone stupid. So was the time before.

The most recent one was early in the morning. I was on my way to work on the old Black Bike. I had been following the crazy old bitch at fifteen under the speed limit for several miles, so I knew better. But when she turned on her left turn signal, slowed down even more, and then dropped over into the passing lane, I figured that meant she was going make a left turn. That was the stupid part. I started around her on the right, and she speeded back up and came back over onto me nearly sideways. From experience, I understood that the next ten seconds were going to be an eternity.

I leaned hard right and got on everything that would slow me down and somehow avoided contact with the vehicle. But I put the scooter down hard. Fortunately, just me and the insane elderly woman were the only ones out there the early morning highway. Also fortunately, I had it slowed down to thirty or so when it went sideways on me, and I dropped it.

It went down to the left, and I made contact with the pavement mostly with my left hand and arm and hip and my head, which was fortunately in a helmet. I recall the helmet made a weird noise as it bounced off the cold, hard concrete, twice. I slid some and bounced once before I could kick loose of the scooter. And then somehow I managed to get my legs under me and stand up and slide on my feet for maybe another ten or fifteen feet. It was a great vantage point. I got so see the scooter pancake twice, shedding busted parts with each flip-flop. Then it skidded to a bad stop and turned over once more.

The lyrics came to me before me and the cycle had come to a stop, Sometimes the highway will exact a sacrifice, demand an offering for the freedom and the solitude. Sometimes the road requires only smoke and blood. And sometimes it insists you give more than that to show your gratitude.

The crazy old bitch continued slowly on her way, left turn signal a-twinkle the whole while. I doubt she was ever aware of my presence, much less of the mess she had made of a real fine machine. I am pretty sure she is unaware that automobiles have a rearview mirror.

I limped and hobbled to where my scooter lay and got it back upright pretty quickly. The windshield and a big piece of the fairing were gone. I had staggered through the remnants and debris of both on my way to the down bike. There was nothing to salvage.

What was left of the fairing was twisted at a bad angle. The handlebars were pinched together pretty hard, both the footpeg covers and the handlegrip on the left side were shredded, both mirrors torn off, the left front crashbar was bad bent, and the right rear one was busted. A side panel had come loose and was sort of dangling at a bad angle. I pulled it all the way off and stuck it in my saddlebag.

I hummed the rest of the verse, Sometimes it wants sadness, sometimes it needs sorrow. Sometimes the highway takes away your yesterdays, and sometimes it robs you of your tomorrows.

Then I started the bike back up and rode it slowly home. It ran good, especially considering that bouncing around part. And it handled just fine, especially considering that bent handlebar thing. All the damage, of which there was lots, was cosmetic. I got it home and leaned it against a wall to get off it. I stood there shakily a moment, sadly inventorying the damages to the cycle. Then I stumbled in to see how bad I was hurt.

Well, I had ruined a pair of jeans and a denim jacket and made a mess of a pretty good helmet. That left boot was scuffed up all the way to the top. And somehow I had busted my pocket watch. When I pulled my lighter out of another pocket, it was mashed beyond repair and maybe recognition.

After that, I was bad roadrash all up and down my lower left side. I had to peel my shredded blue jeans away from my bloody left leg. The bruising had already begun. That hand was a bloody mess. There wasn't anything like a fingerprint left on any of my digits, but nothing was broken. So I washed off as best I could, took a handful of aspirins. Then I grabbed my stuff out of my saddlebag, and jumped, well, crawled, in my truck and headed back to work. Got there in time for class, too.

. As I stumbled into the classroom, by now dragging my left leg behind me, I realized I was bleeding some from two places on my face where either the windshield or mirror pieces had come at me. I tried to casually wipe the blood away as I wrote an assignment on the board. One of the kids finally inquired as to what the hell had happened to me. And I told him. When I spoke, I realized I had a loose tooth or two.

As I handed blood-smeared papers back to my still-stunned students, they murmured softly about how this old hillbilly-hippie-biker-cowboy son of a bitch was stone crazy. This was early in the semester, and they didn't know that yet.

After class, I went to see the School Nurse. She took one look at me and just shook her head. She had taken care of me the wreck before this one, ten or so long years ago, and she knew what had happened without asking. In fact, she knew that the first question is always, "How's the bike?"

Told her I had rode it home, and she told me to take my shirt and pants off. Last wreck before this one, when she had told me to take my britches off, I had demurred. She explained that she had been a nurse a real long time, been married twice, and raised three boys, and I should take my damn pants off. So I didn't even bother to try for modesty this time. I got the typical peroxide wash, followed by some kind of iodine stuff, followed by some kind of salve, then gauze and tape and such. There was some examination to determine that I had not, in fact, broken anything. Just badly bruised.

. She offered no help at all for my broken watch or mashed lighter, but she did light a cigarette for me when we stepped outside after she was done with me. She inquired about being up to date on my tetanus shots, and I was. She asked did I need some pain pills, and I told her I had plenty.

Then she told me she would expect me to report to her every morning until she told me to stop coming. As I could reach most of the wounds, I was given gauze and tape and salve to take with me for nightly dressing changes. As she and I have done it all before, I wasn't even given care and feeding of the open roadrash wounds instructions. As my left hand and arm were a mess, she didn't even suggest a cane for my beat-up left leg. Then she sent me hobbling on my way to confuse more young people.

About a week later, I was upgraded to reporting to her every other day. About then, I went wading, well, limping, to fish the by now chilly waters of Tampa Bay. The saltwater had a healing effect on the roadrash. That cold water drew the bruise out real good. My whole left side looked like an over-ripe eggplant when I staggered to shore. Caught some fish, too. I was walking pretty good again within a month.

Took longer for the bike. Over the miles and along the way, I have been down a few times. I don't want to enumerate, but counting the early downfalls as a kid, I must be up in double digits somewhere. Some have been spectacular and horrifying, a couple have been near fatal, one or two were self-inflicted, some have been just plain ugly, many of them have been basically uninteresting, and a couple have been downright funny, at least years later. I walked away from some, and I had to be carried away from a couple. But they all have had two things in common.

First thing is, one way or another, they were all of them avoidable. Comes down to paying attention. Second thing is that I have always felt terrible bad and guilty about what I had done to my motorcycle.

This somehow goes back to that thing about old scooters having a spirit. Those old Bultacos, they had Iberian souls. There was a particular British essence to those old Triumphs and BSAs and Nortons. Moto Guzzis and Ducatis were distinctly Italian. Even the early Japanese bikes had an Oriental soul. Same deal with old Harleys and Indians. Hell, even those old Cushman and Vespa scooters had souls. I mean some of them old machines, they knew the way home. And you feel bad about wounding something with a soul, especially a Teutonic one.

I recall one time back in the middle distant past when I was riding with a woman on her own bike. We got hung up in a bad construction-inspired traffic mess out on the Delmarva Peninsula someplace. Bumper-to-bumper stop and then go a little ways slow, feet-on-the-pavement slow for miles and hours. Just to make it all memorable, it was near a hundred degrees out there. As bikers know, it is hotter down on the pavement than the weather reports indicate. As everyone knows, this is not a real good thing for air-cooled engines.

This was a real happy, optimistic woman I was riding with. Girl smiled a whole lot. Earlier that ride, we had gotten lost in Columbus, Ohio one night. I was about half pissed off, but she was laughing through it all. I remember she looked up at a near full moon, smiled, and said, "What a beautiful night to be lost in Columbus, Ohio." That kind of girl.

She had been enjoying the slow ride through the construction mess, taking advantage of the opportunity to see some scenery at a sluggish pace, talking to me when we came to a lengthy stop, getting a drink, engaging our fellow highway captives in brief conversations through their windows. Some time and a very few miles into it, she saw I was frowning, and she asked me what was wrong.

And I told her, "We're hurtin' the horses."

So I always feel terrible over putting a bike down, dropping one hard on the concrete, turning it loose while horizontal, watching one come apart as it bounces down the road. This last wreck was no exception. I called my pardner, Ron, that night. He's been down a time or two himself, and after he asked how the bike was, he inquired as to what I needed. I told him I would need some help getting my busted up ride down to Dirty Street.

A small crowd of the usual spectators gathered as we (by that I mean everyone but me) unloaded my cycle down there. They could all see how the bike was, so they silently helped unload it. Then they asked about my well-being.

Jimmy G. had a wreck with a similar fairing, so we got the two busted up fairing panels right away. They were green. That same wrecked bike's fairing brace was in much better shape than mine was now, so we took it, too. Another wreck of Jimmy's had handlebars and footpeg covers. Karl had to order the mirrors and handlegrips and a new windshield for me.

Ron got a long, stout pry bar and four big guys to hold the bike solid while he straightened the front crashbar. The rear one had to be removed and welded. And that all got accomplished by the time I was able to move around and ride good again.

The lesson of all that is the same as it has always been. If you are going to drop your bike, try to do it close to home where you have help and friends. Try to do it near enough to ride it home and find a local Angel Of Mercy.

And the moral is, of course, from The Lowdown Scootertrash Blues. For every gift the highway bestows on you, it requires you give back something in return. And most of the gifts the highway imparts are lessons, and then it tests you on what you've learned.

On to lighter topics and more uplifting tales. One time, a long time ago, four of us were headed up The Blue Ridge Parkway. We stopped for something awhile, and as it was a warm day, some of us took off our leathers. When we saddled back up, all of us got back into our jackets. All of us but Bosco The Bandit. No, old Bosco left his leather lying on top of his pile of gear that was bunjied on the back of his seat. The jacket caught in the wind and blew off about a half mile down the line, before most of us had got into high gear. Bosco was unaware of its departure.

As I was next behind him, I stuck my leg out and caught it up off the pavement with my foot as I rode by. I held it out beside my bike a moment, and Scottie pulled up and reached out and took it off my boot. Zaf blew by him and took the jacket and sped up to the front, where he handed it to Bosco. The Mexican Bandit looked briefly confused, then he took the jacket from Zaf and put it back on.

The whole thing didn't take a mile or a minute. It looked like we had practiced it, like we were preparing for some kind of drill team event. And when we were done, I was riding drag like I should have been.

One of the other advantages to traveling in a group like that is spare parts, especially if you are on similar machines. You can spread things out, give one guy the extra cables, and another guy the spare lightbulbs, and the third guy gets the inner tubes, patches, and air pump, the last guy packs spark plugs and such.

That way, we had some extra room so one of us could bring a real dictionary for the Scrabble games.

That became important when we were setting out the highway storms or around a campfire playing cut-throat, buck-a-point Scrabble. One time Bosco spelled "squoutada." He insisted it was a word, as in "Squoutada kitchen and get some cookies." Another time he spelled "nazi." We all tried to explain the word was a proper noun and had to be capitalized; and, it was therefore illegal in the game. He countered that he didn't mean one of them Hitler German kind of Nazis; he referred instead to just regular nazis, like at work.

One time on the Outer Banks of North Carolina the same four of us came across a pier with an old tugboat moored to it. The sign on the dock and the boat both said, "Ol' Ugly." I was made to park beneath the sign for pictures. Same thing happened over in Spain, Europe. Me and my pardner Tommy had taken the night train down to Gibraltar. When we got out on the far end of The Rock, out where you can see Africa across the windy straits there, Tom found a sign that said, "Land's End — Much Cheapness." I was made to pose under that one, too.

Speaking of pictures, Juanita has put together a little scrapbook of pictures and newspaper articles and book reviews and such for me. It's quite a collection and really nicely displayed now. We take it to bookstores and motorcycle rallies and put in on the table with the books and tapes for folks to look at.

She gathered a bunch of old photographs from the walls of my office, collected newspaper stories, got hold of bookstore and motorcycle rally announcements and newsletters. Then, being an artistic girl, she arranged them in a real logical and pleasing manner. I can see that the old pictures touch off fond memories in some of the folks looking at them.

chapter nineteen
MORE RIDING IN THE RAIN
and MORE ANGRY WOMEN

I just had a memory here myself, and not an especially fond one either. I mentioned back there someplace that it had been raining here. Well, it still is. And I got caught in it earlier today. It was coming down hard already as I bailed off the highway into a convenient abandoned little strip mall with an advantageous overhang. Like I said, it was raining hard, and it had come up sudden. I didn't have my rainshield on yet, just my wet sunglasses and a wet windshield to look through. Vision impaired, I slowed down as I rode in through the chuck holes and puddles.

There was a chain around the damn parking lot. It was strung about headlight level, real taut. One of those outdoor dog chain kind of chains. And I damn near didn't see it in time. As it was, I wound up kind of sideways in the mud parallel to the chain.

Put me in mind of a similar time. This was maybe back five or so years ago, maybe more. I was in the mountains of West Virginia, also in the rain. This one wasn't a Florida thunder and lightning downpour that has you scurrying for cover in a wet hurry. No, this was one of those all damn day long, steady rains that has you longing to see a color other than gray. The sort of weather that has you frustrated and angry because you know how pretty the area would be if you could only see it. I was on some kind of divided, limited access road. The weather was bad enough that there was very little traffic. There was very little of anything out there. Just rain.

I had been in my rainsuit and faceshield and rubber boots since first thing that morning, and I was just tired of it all. I was looking for a place to get off the road and out of the rain awhile. Figured to make a pot of coffee, smoke a dry cigarette, wipe off my glasses and face shield and windshield. Get out of the rubber rainsuit. Listen to the rain fall on something besides me. I had been looking for just such a place for quite awhile.

And there it was, an abandoned gas station with a huge tin awning. It was maybe a quarter mile off to the right on a cross-road, up on a steep hill, as things in this area tend to be. So I headed that way. As I came to the stop sign, I saw that there was another bike about to roll into my intended shelter from the storm. He had it first. I hesitated, trying to decide if I should force my company on another rider, or if I should just roll on and find my own dry place. That was when the other rider went down. I was maybe a hundred yards off.

As it is hard to see much when you are looking uphill into a rainstorm, I wasn't close enough to observe details. But my first impression was that the guy had been shot off his ride. I figured that the sound of the storm had deadened the noise of the gunshot. Then, as I got closer, I could see it was a passenger that had come off the bike.

While I rode closer, looking around me for sniper positions, the other bike immediately went down with the rider still on it. It did about two and a half pinwheels on its side before coming to an ungraceful, horizontal halt against one of the abandoned gas pumps. The guy had held onto it and been underneath it during the whole thing. Now I was looking for snipers and wondering if the down scooter sliding across the cold concrete near the gas pumps would throw a spark and blow the whole world up in my face.

By the time I got up to it all, the rider was trying to get up, still holding onto his bike. I figured he was OK. By now I was close enough to notice that his glasses were kind of diagonal on his face under his face shield. I turned my attention to the passenger. She was already up and headed toward the bike. She looked at me with a stupefied expression on her pretty face as I rolled by her.

The next thing I attended to was riding on into the shelter to park my own ride. That was when I saw the guy-wire that had flat-out clotheslined these folks clean off what turned out to be a really pretty Kawasaki Concours. It was a thin-gauge rusty airline cable hanging sort of slack just exactly at eye level, especially if you were setting up straight looking for a place to put your machine out of the rain. It was a full-dressed, dark green bike with local plates.

By now I was going about two miles an hour, so I just sort of tipped my cycle some sideways and reached and lifted the wire out of my way. By the time I had parked mine, the other folks had their bike back up. They were holding it upright between them. The man, with his glasses remaining cockeyed on his face, still had hold of the handlegrips. I parked my ride on the dry concrete up near the abandoned building. Then I climbed down and took my helmet off and put it on my bike.

When I looked their way, I could see he was bleeding all over his left handlegrip. His hand was white and shaking from clutching it tightly. I could see the stunned, dazed expressions on their pale faces as I walked toward them. They didn't say a word, to me or to one another. They just looked at each other across the tank of their machine, which was pointed away from the cover of the awning. I could tell that the woman's confusion was being replaced with anger.

As I got closer, they both turned to look at me. They were old folks, nearly my age. It was obvious from their confused expressions that they simply did not know what to do next. They looked to me, clearly seeking advice and help. Having been in their situation, I recognized the look. They wanted someone to tell them that none of the horrible weird bad shit that had just befallen them had really happened. That was beyond optimism. The rider had a dark slash across his visor where the cable had hit him about eye level.

He was standing on the left of the machine, so I suggested he might want to put the sidestand down. He seemed to think about that a minute, then he nodded his head. Took him a couple tries, but he managed to get the kickstand down. Then they turned back to me with the same quizzical look. So I told him to turn loose of it and walk around some and over to where I was parked, see if he was hurt.

That turning loose of the bike thing, that took him a couple tries, too. He shook some blood back into his hands, and some blood on the concrete. This time he reached up under his face shield with his other hand and straightened his glasses and smiled sheepishly when he looked at me. Then he looked at his bloody left hand. By now some of the color was coming back into their faces. I could see the woman building up to serious angry.

She strode around the machine and walked beside him as they made their way over to my scooter. He was limping some, but she was moving just fine. She was talking OK, too. Mostly she was telling him he was an idiot. There was a suggestion that he had less business buying a motorcycle than he did an airplane. She went on some about the expense of the cycle, in specific dollars. And she was pointing out what they could have had instead when they got out of listening distance.

They both removed their helmets and put them near my cycle. I pushed their machine over to a place near mine. As I pushed it, I noticed a bad scrape up at the top of the windshield where the cable had hit it first. It looked kind of burned.

When the rider started to take a seat on the dry curb there by my bike, I told him not to. Suggested it would be better if he kept on moving around some. Told him to walk over there and inspect the wire that had taken him down. I quickly looked at their helmets to make sure nobody was going to have a concussion. Nope, the passenger had landed on her butt, evidently in a puddle. You could tell by the big wet spot on her pants. And the rider had gone down to the left. The shoulder and elbow of his jacket was a mess, and I could see the left knee was gone from his jeans.

I began to look their machine over. The mirror on the left side was cracked bad, but still in place. That handlegrip was in bad shape. The fairing and the saddlebag on that side were scuffed up pretty hard. So was the front fender. One muffler was scraped up some. And the top of that windshield was opaque, looked damn near scorched, in the top couple inches or so. There was nothing to do about the machine.

Instead, I turned my attention back to the rider and the passenger just in time to see him tear the wire loose. He had three wraps around his arm, the left one with the scarred jacket. He put his weight into it and ripped the whole thing, about fifty feet of it, loose. Then he coiled it up and threw it off beside the building into the rain. I determined he wasn't real bad hurt.

Apparently neither was his woman. The sounds of the rain on the awning deadened most of what she had to say in spite of her volume. The parts I caught weren't pretty.

By the time they got back to me, I had gotten into my saddlebag and was able to offer them both some aspirin and water. The guy's hand had stopped bleeding, and he had apparently washed it off in some rainwater. They both accepted water and aspirin pills but passed on the coffee as I poured myself a cup. It was early morning coffee, and it did kind of look like lukewarm, used motor oil.

I lit a cigarette, and the rider looked at it like I have seen heroin addicts look at the orange juice with the methadone in it. "Here's to the monkey!"

He asked, "Could I please have one of those?"

"Raymond!" She was on top of that one quicker than management on a way to screw the wage slaves.

"Be still, Donna May." He accepted a light for the cigarette and inhaled deeply.

He was a big man, probably six foot two or three. When he took his leather off to check out his arm, I could see he was in pretty good physical shape. He was clean-shaven, but his hair was as gray as mine. His shoulder was going to bruise, and there was some minor roadrash on his elbow. He'd lost the fingerprints off a couple fingers, too.

"Oh, I'll be still alright!" His woman was scowling at him hard. She huffed and sniffed and scuffed her toe on the concrete a time or two. Her frown went from general angry to specific and personally offended.

By now he had smoked half the cigarette, and I could see that neither of them was hurt bad or going into shock. He smiled at me again, this time kind of sheepishly. Then he looked back at Donna May, who was still frowning. Then he threw the half a cigarette out into the rainwater as it washed downhill.

"Thank you, Raymond."

"You're welcome, Donna May."

I took this opportunity to gesture toward his bike and say, "Wasn't none of this your fault at all, pardner."

The man sort of shook his head, as if to clear his thoughts. Then he walked over to the left side of his bike to inspect the damage.

I got between him and the machine and said to him in a low voice, "Your bike ain't hurt much. I believe you can ride it away from here. Why don't you and your woman walk around the side of that building. Drop your britches and check one another out for injuries." I motioned to his blood- soaked knee. "Your old lady lit pretty hard, man."

He looked me over closely, I think for the first time. Then he looked at my machine, the twenty-five-year-old one with a half million miles on it. When he saw my age and miles, he smiled at me and nodded.

"You've done this before, haven't you?" he asked rhetorically.

"Repeatedly." This was neither rhetorical nor intended to be cynical or funny.

Nonetheless, he laughed a little as he took his woman by the hand and headed around to the dry side of the building with an awning. I didn't want to start his machine without him there, but I was pretty sure it would start and run. Further external observation indicated that his pretty custom seat was shredded on one side. I saw by his odometer that it was a real new machine.

"I don't care how far it is, Raymond! I am not getting back on that blasted motorcycle!" Donna May was yelling from around on the side of the building.

I turned his key on and made sure all the lights were working. I got under his machine to determine nothing was leaking, that no battery acid had spilled. Then I pulled both his clutch and brake and turned the throttle to ensure all the cables were still sliding. I looked up to see the fallen riders returning from their personal injury examinations.

"Raymond, I am not getting back on that silly thing!"

Judging by Donna May's stride and the way she tore her hand loose from Raymond's groping grasp, she wasn't hurt bad at all. Her eyes flashed, and her teeth were clenched. She shrugged off his attempt to put his arm around her.

"Donna May, it ain't but about seven or eight miles."

He turned to look at me and then at his machine. There was a question in his eyes. I nodded to him to let him know I was sure he could ride it away.

"It ain't no seven miles! How dumb you think I am, Raymond?" She took a stray swipe at him.

Raymond looked appropriately chastened, but he pressed

on.

"Darlin', the rain's lettin' up some, and it really ain't much more than fifteen miles."

Donna May was a pretty woman. She was near as old as me and poor Raymond, and her hair was dyed a fiery red. I presumed it approximated her former natural color. She had gray eyes, and they were flashing fire. She was a small girl and quite mobile and agile in spite of the recent accident.

She moved like a viper, got both hands on him and announced, "Don't you 'Darlin' me! You promised me you'd quit smokin'! It's better than twenty miles, Raymond! It ain't goin' to stop rainin' for another three or four days! And what we ought to do is sit me back up on that foolish motorcycle and then you push it there!"

The one-sided discussion continued as I walked off the other way to smoke another cigarette. A stray verse of The Long-gone Outbound Scootertrash Blues came to me there in the rain, And I could hear her good-bye comin' like bad weather up the road. Like when you first see the lightning, and you can see through things. And then the thunder does explode.

"Raymond, I'm soakin' wet, my butt hurts, and I ain't gettin' back on that motorcycle. I just do not care anymore!" Donna May was turning up the volume, and I could hear her in spite of the storm.

The rest of the verse ran through my head to drown out Donna May's tirade, I could hear her farewell break the silence like the screamin' of the sirens reminding us of the price we have to pay. Like the sound of brakes and the smell of burned rubber, and then denim, leather, and blood all over The Lost Highway.

Donna May lit into poor Raymond again, so I walked further off and pondered the many joys of solitude. I reflected on the pure absolute exhilaration of loneliness. I could still hear some of what Donna May had to say, but most of Raymond's replies were drowned out as the rain pounded harder on the tin roof of the awning of the abandoned gas station. Water ran downhill all around.

By the time I finished my cigarette and returned to my companions in the storm, they had resolved their dilemma. Donna May was on her cell telephone calling someone named Norbert, who, based on her volume, was deaf. He also apparently had a pickup truck.

And Raymond was, it would seem, trying to decide whether to put his bike on the truck or just put Donna May in it and ride his dropped and bent scooter alone back out into the rain. I was pretty sure I knew which way that one was going, but I remained stoically silent.

Raymond looked at his brand new cycle, then over to where the wire had cleaned him off it. He walked over that way to where he had thrown the torn down wire. He muttered about how, "Sidney Bob ought to know better than to do such a thing."

Donna May took a moment to stop hollering into her cell phone at Norbert long enough to point at where the wire had been and yell at Raymond, "I don't care if he is your second double step-cousin, I'm goin' to sue the little bastard."

Raymond just rolled his eyes and turned to me and said, "Mister, I sure do appreciate your help. We'll be gone out of here in just a little bit."

He was about to continue, but about then a brand new shiny black double cab Ford diesel pickup truck roared up the road toward us. Mud flew.

As I stepped out of the way, I heard Donna May scream, "Never mind, Norbert! Abel and Johnsie are here. No, you won't see me, Norbert! Norbert? Norbert, give the phone to Maybelle!"

Her volume decreased as I turned my attention to the truck. Abel and Johnsie climbed out and lumbered toward us. As they exited, the truck popped back up a foot in the air. Abel and Johnsie were big boys, probably six or seven hundred pounds between them. Both wore overalls and t-shirts and brogan shoes. They also had obviously gotten their haircuts at the same place.

"You hurt any, Raymond?" The bigger of the two asked this as they walked past me and Raymond and toward Donna May. It was obvious it was mostly a courtesy question.

The other one waited until Donna May got done yelling at Maybelle and put her cell phone away. Then he told her, "Granny called and said she saw you all go by in the rain on that new motorcycle of Raymond's. Mama told her she had been on the porch all morning and hadn't seen you all come past there. Then she made me and Johnsie come look for you."

Both boys stood massively in front of Donna May waiting for instructions. She stepped right up to that one. "Put that cussed machine in your truck. Then take me home."

She paused to frown at Raymond before she continued, "I don't care what you all do after that."

She turned and smiled at me. I don't know why. She really was a pretty woman. Then she went and got in the truck.

Abel and Johnsie pushed the bike over behind their truck. Raymond was there to drop the tailgate. Then the boys lifted that big road machine into the truck the way regular people would do it with a bicycle. Abel climbed up in the back and lashed the bike down with a length of stout rope. Johnsie climbed behind the wheel. I could hear Donna May issuing more directions.

Johnsie got back out of the truck and went over to where I was still parked to collect Raymond's and Donna May's helmets. He seemed to notice me for the first time. He frowned first at my helmet, then at me, and finally at my bike. It wasn't an angry frown, but rather one of confusion. Johnsie walked away and put the helmets in the back seat with Donna May.

And Raymond walked quickly over to me. "I just wanted to thank you again, mister. You were a big help here."

There was a silent pleading in his eyes as he glanced back toward the truck and then to me. He extended his hand to shake mine, and when he felt the book of matches and cigarette palmed there, he nearly crushed it in his happiness. I noticed he climbed in the bed of the pickup with his cycle rather than in the cab with the others.

As the big truck splashed off into the downpour, I walked back to my bike. I got my stove and coffee pot out, and made me some fresh coffee. The rain increased as it perked. I glanced over to where the cable had been strung through the air at eye level. It was pretty obvious that if Raymond hadn't gotten to it first, I would have been taken off my ride by it. No way in hell anyone was going to notice that thing in a rainstorm. Raymond was right, Sidney Bob should have known better. I poured myself a cup of new coffee, put the rest in my Thermos, and set the pot out in the rain to cool down.

While my fresh coffee cooled, I took my rainsuit and rubber overboots off. Shook the water off and hung them up to drip dry.

Then I broke the little propane stove down and put it away as soon as it had cooled. I finally got around to wiping my windshield and bike off. I also wiped off my faceshield and my glasses. By then the coffee pot was cooled down, so I flung the grounds out into the storm. They were gone downhill almost before they hit the ground. I rinsed the pot off with rainwater and put it away. Then I found an apple and a couple Oreo cookies in my saddlebag. Grabbed the book I had been reading, *The Drinking of Spirits*, by Tom Abrams, and had just settled in.

That was when Norbert arrived.

He drank my coffee with me, bummed cigarettes, and in a loud voice he harmonized with me as we sang a few verses from The Lonesome Scootertrash Blues.

chapter twenty
MORE DISTURBING THINGS
and TRUCKSTOPS

I came across a number of disturbing things on a ride to Orlando and back the other afternoon. To begin with, the back way over there doesn't exist anymore. The road is still there, of course. But it is no longer a sweet two-lane run through the swamp and pastures and citrus groves and a couple little towns. No, now it's all become American Sprawl. Mart-Mart Stores and plazamalls are packed in together between stretches of similarly ugly huge houses in cramped subdivisions and traffic and stoplights. The few areas that have remained unmolested the longest are now being landscraped for development. There was dust in the air everywhere. There were many bottlenecks and slow-downs that didn't used to be there.

And that's a damn shame, because it used to be a real fine ride. The portions through the swamp have generally avoided the development, but there was still lots of traffic. And I saw some dredging and filling that is going to solve that little problem of it being difficult and inconvenient to develop swampland. The parts that used to be peaceful cow pastures and pretty fields full of wildflowers dancing in the wind and aromatic orange groves are now all duplicated similar look-alike subdivisions and plazamalls, huge massive ones. Signs for GTI Ruby Chuckle Barrel Chili Wednesday Outbehind Appleberry's chainfood competed for space in the air and assured me it was an affluent area.

Second disturbing thing was that the alternative, the dreaded interstate, is a bigger mess than it used to be. Admittedly, this was in the late afternoon, but the early rush hour mess was down to a standstill before I could get to third gear. There were big lighted overhead signs that foretold of imminent construction, slow-downs, and "congestion" ahead.

And, it turns out the other alternatives are all new toll roads. Yup, the government figured it out, and now they are going to make us pay for it. I hate toll roads. Just isn't American.

The third thing I came across is even less American. There were surveillance cameras mounted at most of the big intersections and all along the interstate. Hell, they might could have had the damn things in the swamp, too. No telling what un-American stuff the woodland creatures might be up to. But my frustration was on videofilm. We ought to form a union and refuse to go on camera without a contract, a script, and a make-up girl.

While I am on this whole topic of the decline and demise of most things that made sense and were good, I got another one. A very few years ago, somewhere in the North, I needed to change my oil. I pulled into a little corporate franchise chain convenience store and put my scooter in the shade. All I needed was oil. And, anymore, with all the high-rev Jap cars out there, you can find 20w50 oil almost anywhere. But it takes forever to get in and out of the Giant Huge Mart-Mart Stores. Things are often overpriced at the corporate franchise chain auto parts stores. But this way, I wouldn't have to abandon my ride and most of what I owned in a plazamall parking lot while I got lost amongst several acres of stuff that has nothing to do with my life.

As I walked to the store, I was gratified to see a display of 20w50 right outside the door. There was a kid, a grown boy, sitting at a tall stool behind the counter. He was sucking on a Big Gulp around his lip, nose, and tongue rings and leafing through a dirty magazine. I was the only customer. He didn't even look up. The eyelid rings may have made this a difficult activity.

I walked over to the shelves containing motor oil, only to find there was no 20w50 there. So I interrupted the young reader and asked him to please take enough money for three quarts of oil, and I would grab them as I left. Annoyed at being bothered by business, he sort of wearily told me to go get three quarts from the outside display and bring them in to him. With the tongue stud, he sounded a lot like Sylvester The Cat. He casually waved me toward the door.

That was where I began to administer a lesson. I started by explaining that he worked there. And I did not. And it would seem to me that it was an employee's function rather than that of a cash-paying customer to fetch and tote. He angrily set his magazine down and told me, in an annoyed and sibilant tone of voice, that he was prohibited from leaving his post at the cash register.

And I had to explain to him that was the only way he was going to be able to get the oil. I suggested that while he was out there retrieving the three for me, he might bring in several extra quarts so this sort of thing didn't happen again.

He wasn't much of a learner. He frowned a lot, which was difficult with all that face jewelry. That bringing in oil in preparation for another potential sale, that just flat baffled him. He did have enough sense to get up off the stool and take a step away from me. I believe he knew that it would be prudent to move away from a man who was thinking about getting hold of some of his ear rings and banging his head sharply on the counter a time or two. I might even have suspected that such a thing had already happened to him. Was hard to discern scars among the acne on his face.

I asked him how much the damn oil was, so I could just give him some money, get my oil as I left, and be about my business. It was a buck and a half a quart. I dropped a five on the counter and told him to keep the change for a tip, for his commendable service and refreshing attitude. He said he had to have the containers to scan on his computer. And I explained that now we were back to him having to go outside and get the oil.

He protested and whined and carried on awhile. Finally, I just pushed the five across the counter at him and told him I was taking the oil on my way out. That was when he threatened to call the local authorities. That was also when he had enough sense to grab his cell phone and run to the bathroom where he locked himself in to call the cops. Turned out he could desert his post after all.

I waited quite awhile. Looked at most of the naked women in the kid's magazine, read the front section of the local paper. There was a story about a bad multiple automobile crash that had killed seven people.

Finally, I just left the five on the counter. Then I went out and sat on the curb beside the display of oil and smoked a cigarette.

Eventually, I picked up three quarts as I walked by the display rack on my way back to my bike. I took my time getting them put away in my saddlebag.

I dawdled while I put on my jacket and helmet. I considered just changing my oil there in the parking lot. I must have hung around there twenty minutes or so before I made my departure. My suspicion is that his cell phone didn't work. Most seem not to, at least not very well.

And that was the time I got off easy. This other one happened some time before the convenience store episode. I was with a young girl, about half my age. And what follows is just one of the reasons old men ought not try to hang out with young girls.

She made me take her to one of those counterfeit seafood chainfood places, Captain Admiral Frozen Foreign Unidentified By-Product of Mock McFish-Like Substance Nuggets Helper Ahoy.

I didn't want such near-food to begin with, and I damn sure didn't want to eat it there with the noise, the over-bright lights, and screaming children, some of whom were employees. But I did. She was a really pretty young girl. When we had finished our mock maritime repast, I got up to leave so I could smoke a cigarette in the quiet and comfort of the parking lot with my bike. That was when the young girl told me I had to clean up my table and throw the refuse away in the nearby garbage container. The container was shaped like a dolphin. The garbage was to be put in its mouth. I was apparently the only one there to see the irony.

It was just like the unfortunate incident with the kid and the motor oil. I explained to this young girl I was with that she had me confused with people who worked there. I was a customer. My job was to pay for my food, not to bus my table or total my bill or go get myself more coffee. I was not on KP. I concluded by saying that when some of the fake-seafood employees came to my classroom and erased my blackboard or graded some papers, I would be happy to help them with their job. Words were exchanged. As I recall, that was about all that got exchanged that evening.

Speaking of the perils of the present, I need to get back to that issue of government and corporate surveillance briefly. A few days ago, I was on the radio, via telephone, in Oklahoma City.

Actually it was late at night, and I was on for an hour. The topic was supposed to be motorcycles. But the host, a biker himself, wanted to talk about repression and control and information and surveillance. He was of a like mind with me on this whole topic. We agreed that it was America, and we didn't need a Patriot Act, microchips in our children or uniforms on them, or profiling, or surveillance cameras or piss-testing in the workplace, or helmet laws.

Just the previous weekend, I had been on the radio in Riverhead, New York. Some of the folks up there, members of the Harley Owners' Group mostly, were decrying a local police practice of stopping and frisking all motorcyclists. One guy reported that they had a scooters-only checkpoint set up with cops just waving all the cycles over into a roadside rest area. There they were all delayed and checked out and investigated with computers, searched, printed, photographed, frisked, and hassled. Each was made to produce appropriate papers and go through a safety check with his machine. Profiling and harassment at its very best. So I related this story to the radio audience in Oklahoma.

A number of people called in to the show. Turns out OK City is not near as conservative as I thought. Most of the listeners were disgusted and frightened by the current government trend. Many called in with horror stories of their own. Those who were riders agreed we didn't need no helmet laws. They all were in accord that there was no American need for seatbelt laws, or child restraint seat laws, or cameras on the highways, or laws requiring you to watch and tattle on your neighbor.

One of the things I am looking most forward to on my upcoming Summer ride is being able to smoke a cigarette in a restaurant. I've checked; none of the places I'm going has such repressive laws. My intention is to enjoy it while I can. I fear that soon we will be a completely anti-smoking totalitarian police state with laws requiring us to bus our own tables and retrieve our own purchases, maybe on camera.

Much of the fault for all this goes to the business greedheads who run Global Corporate Franchise America. Awhile back I was invited to a relatively small, independent bookstore. This store was located in a neighborhood, in a converted old house. It was a pleasure to not ride into a plazamall on a highway where the bookstore is situated among eleven other franchise operations.

It was a great reading and a fine crowd and a general success. But beyond that, this little independent place had some class and propriety to it. There was an allure that is lacking at the giant huge franchise bookstores in the plazamalls that dominate current America the way chainfood restaurants dominate the food business. This little place smelled like a bookstore.

Now I don't mean to say bad things about the big chain bookstores. They've been real good to me, and I have sold a whole bunch of books and drank a whole lot of complimentary coffee at these places. But they have all the charm of a Mart-Mart Store. And, while the chain stores are all enormous, I swear there was a better selection of books at this little independent outfit. Obviously lacking were the immense displays of Harry Potter books with the obligatory crowd of children, some of them in costume, shrieking and yowling around them. Similarly, there were no massive exhibits of the six best-selling authors who account for about half the book sales in America.

Captain Zero has gone with me to a couple recent readings at the chainstores. On each occasion, he has tried to find several books he has been trying to locate for some time. And every time he has gotten disgusted by the lack of help and the lack of obscure books and the lack of anything but bright lights and best-selling books. Appalled, he has walked out of these chainstores and into the parking lot to wait for me.

At this independent store, he found a half dozen or more of the titles he had been searching for. He spent a lot of money there, and he didn't regret a dime of it. In fact, The Captain commented on how good he felt about contributing money to such a noble effort. There was some mention of that fact that he had found no books entitled, _____For Dummies, and little in the way of motivational, self-help, feel-good, self-esteem publications.

He also commented on how the people there were readers who were looking for books. Often, at the chainstore franchises, you encounter folks on dates, just killing time, or looking for dates, or a place to cut their kids loose, or magazines, or coffee.

As I left the little independent bookstore, the manager thanked me and handed me a twenty-five dollar gift certificate in appreciation for my modest efforts. This has never happened at any of the giant huge chain bookstores I have been to. I am confident that I have sold more books at Barnes and Borderline Books Are Us Amazon A Million Comdot than I ever will at this place. But you can bet I will be back to the little store to cash in my certificate and, as Zero said, to contribute to an admirable endeavor.

But I fear it is a losing endeavor, a lost cause. I suspect it is like trying to support little, local restaurants and hardware stores and scootershops. But it sure was more fun and more satisfying and more interesting than trying to find my way past the Harry Potter exhibit and attendant thrash. And the money everyone spends there will go into the local economy rather than the corporate global economy.

Speaking of which, me and the Tallgirl were settin' on the porch the other night, talking about our upcoming long ride. I said something about avoiding interstate highways for the most part. She inquired about the exceptions. I smiled and told her, "Truckstops." She knows about my miles, and she knows I used to drive for a living. She has been with men who drive most of her life one way or another.

When she looked puzzled, I continued. I told her that in ancient times there were oases and fortresses and strongholds and bastions, often at crossroads where the weary pilgrims could stop and rest. Here the sojourners and pilgrims and wanderers could find a safe place, a fire in the dark night, solace and succor. Here they might get a meal, water, maybe even some provisions to continue their journey. The voyagers could spend time secure from the perils of the road in these places.

These strongholds eventually evolved into safe areas, maybe in churches or other old holy places. Travelers knew they would find shelter and sanctuary in such places. These sites later became stands, stage coach stations, army forts, and trading posts. Like the truckstops of today, these places were peopled by rough, hard men. Some hard women there, too. And, like today, there was a code that permitted families with children to come among them safely.

Today, especially along the interstate highway system, on the American superslabs, there are truckstops. Life can be lived on the highway, and the truckstops can make life pretty easy. An entire subculture exists on the big highways, and the truckstops are their havens.

Truckstops have everything from parts for your car to breakfast. Here you can find first-aid supplies and fuel. The display cases and shelves are stocked with food, from greasy burritos to fresh fruit, soft drinks and beer and ice. You can get tools, clocks, cigarettes, cassette and video tapes and CDs, and books. There are clothes and candy and toiletries and every over-the-counter remedy and pill on the market. Here you can find a great array of magazines and newspapers, provisions of all kinds. You can get a fine meal at some truckstops and something to eat at all of them.

Some of the bigger truckstops have post offices in them; all of them have mailboxes. You can buy and mail greeting cards in case you miss a holiday while you are out there on the road. You can buy and send some postcards back home. There are banks of telephones and video games, fax machines, ATMs, cable and satellite TV, and often Internet computer access. Weather is important to drivers, and truckstops have all the predictions. Some truckstops have lockers you can rent to store your valuables.

Many truckstops have laundry facilities and showers, and an area traffic report service. Truckstops will provide you with repair help and a place to pull off the road and rest awhile. You can get a room if you need one. You can find a place to park in relative safety if you don't.

The interiors of truck stops are always well lighted and warm. Truckstops have waitresses who will smile and call you "Darlin'," even though they don't know you. And the other customers are mostly pretty friendly. They smile and nod at you, for after all, you are sharing the road and the experience of travel.

Most big truckstops have their own regiment of prostitutes, highway hostesses, concrete hookers. Most places, they are pretty discreet about it so as not to piss off the cops or incur the disapproval of the management. And this way, they don't offend the families and church folks. The girls will prowl among the big rigs and crawl up into the sleeper cabs to service the drivers. Sometimes they ride along with the truckers up the road awhile, always to another truckstop. Some of these girls cover the length and breadth of the nation like this. Some of them are well-known and respected members of the highway community. Among them you will find underage girls, little boys, ugly transvestites, dominatrixes, and a few girls who just got too old for the big time. Others are known to be mad or diseased, or both, and to be avoided at all costs. Most truckstops, you can find a Sunday church service. Many have the cheapest gas as well as good deals on diesel fuel.

And there are also the migrant vendors. Some of them set up their fruit stand or souvenir t-shirt booth right in front of the truckstop building. Others conduct their business in a more low-key manner. Often they are selling knock-off watches, jewelry, tools, etc. from the trunks of their cars in the parking lot. These people will work a truckstop for a day, sometimes two or three, until someone, usually a highway cop, takes offense at the fact that they have no license to do business. Lot of cops with knock-off watches around truckstops. Then the nomad vendors will pack up their wares and move their business on down the highway to the next truckstop.

If you ask around, and often this takes several inquiries, you will eventually find someone at a truckstop who can take a bet on an upcoming sporting event. There will be someone who can get you a fake driver's license or a false bill of lading, or even a counterfeit passport. Someone is always around who can locate cheap car parts or a whole car if you need one. These discount salesmen can produce cheap booze or cigarettes or drugs, or maybe a gun. One of the advantages of truckstops is that those who just sort of inhabit them are from the next little town down the road. Between these folks and the employees, you can get all kinds of local wisdom and information and help.

At night, the truckstops are lit up like The Mothership come to Earth. You can see them from miles away. They beckon like the fires in the oases and forts of old. You can drive from one end of this country to the other and never leave the interstate highways. Everything you need, from fuel to food to garbage bags and duct tape, can be found at the Dixie Flyin' Boy J Truckstops of America.

And if you pay cash, you can do it all in absolute anonymity. The long-haul freight drivers know all this. The retired folks out there full-time in their Winnebagos know this. Traveling salesmen and wayfarers know this. And so do scootertrash.

The problem, of course, is that most big truckstops, anymore, like most everything else anymore, are part of the corporate global chain franchise conspiracy.

chapter twenty-one
THE SUMMER'S LONG RIDE
(A Tribute to the Tallgirl
and Some Other Longtime Oldfriends)

Day One: (I have always wanted to start something that way. Either that, or, It was a dark and stormy night). We got one of those classic crack of noon starts. Juanita had spent several many hours packing and sorting and re-packing. I spent near that much time trying to figure out how to get it all on the bike. It was the Saturday of the Fourth of July weekend. My old pardner, Bosco The Bandit, he rode with us up U.S. 301 to the Georgia line just so we'd have some company. Oddly, the traffic was real light for a holiday weekend.

It had been a real long time since me and old Bosco put it down the road together, but we got right back to it as if there hadn't been a lapse. And 'Nita caught on right away as to what we were doing, how we were communicating, the subtleties, how fine we were riding together. It made for an especially good start.

Bosco was pretty skeptical of our load, even with Karl The Kraut's heavy-duty shocks on my ride. Me and old Bosco agreed we had both of us seen more than this on a cycle before. But it was more than either of us had ever piled on our own bike. I had been handling it pretty well the first couple hundred miles. But we had been on easy two- and four-lane roads. Bosco asked what I was going to do. I told him I'd have to peel forty pounds off the load for it to do any real good, so I was just going to keep on with it and hope for the best. Bosco turned it around to home, shaking his head as he rode south.

My main concern was the volume and weight in the saddlebags. I had moved my kitchen from the tailrack into one saddlebag. The other bag had the weight of two rainsuits and a whole bunch of other heavy stuff. They were both jammed so full that I kind of had to jump out of the way every time I opened one. There was probably thirty-five or forty pounds in each bag, about twice what I would have preferred. Then there was around two hundred-eighty pounds of people. And then there were two duffle bags, a big one and a little one, both heavy, strapped too far back and too high on the tailrack. Then there were a pair of leather jackets and my poncho and a denim jacket and the cover for the bike. Juanita the Tallgirl must have had twenty-five pounds of girlstuff: jars and bottles and baggies filled with things that I have no understanding of. The only break I had here was that we had left the tent and sleeping bags to home.

Fortunately, those first couple days were pretty straight, flat, level, and uneventful highways. By the time I had to ride a hard curve or an incline, I had pretty much mastered the art of overloaded riding. And those old BMWs are very forgiving bikes. We got lightly sprinkled on several times the first day, but that was it for rain. And I was already heeding the advice I had gotten from just damn near everyone.

Karl The Kraut had stepped up first. He took the heavy-duty rear shocks off his own ride and swapped them with my old stock ones. Karl likes Juanita, and he knew she was going to overload my ride. Also knowing my propensity for finding bad weather, he sagely advised me, "Don't try to ride through any storms with names."

Then Jimmy G., who also likes 'Nita, he took the harmonic counter-balance handlebar weights out of his bike and put them in mine. Jimmy knows how much my arthritis bothers me here in my old age. He often takes tools away from me just so I won't hurt myself.

Both of them suggested it would be a good idea to take it some easy. I think Jimmy said, "Tiger, don't hurt the Tallgirl with an eight hundred mile day, or a thousand mile night. And don't try to kill her with that damned highway diet of yours." Jimmy knows I tend to live on caffeine, nicotine, sugar, grease, gasoline, and aspirins while I am out on the road.

And then Karl concluded, "Yeah, Tiger, stop once in awhile for her, man. There's nothing wrong with spending two nights in the same state."

Captain Zero, with whom I have traveled some truly fine

miles, and who was remaining at The Redoubt to watch the house and feed the animals, he set me straight about an hour before departure.

He said to me, "Tiger, I really like the Tallgirl. So don't do anything stupid. Slow down, stop often, turn around and go back through it again if you have to. Show it to her, man. And then appreciate the whole thing through her brand new eyes." It seemed like fine advice, so I thanked him and vowed to follow his counsel.

And then he concluded, "And for Chrissakes don't make her spend the night at the Courtyards of Calcutta Motel."

First night out, in South Carolina someplace, I pulled into the Executive Inn. It was the best thing going on in wherever we were, and it was across the road from a Kentucky Chicken place. We had done about four hundred miles, and it was fixin' to rain. The proprietor of the Executive Inn turned out to be a boy named Mike Patel. Honest. I rode the bike up under cover right outside our motel room. It was Mike's idea. Then he sent me down the road to a convenience store his parents ran to get my milk and cookies.

Next day might have been the last time we began the morning without our leathers on. We took a real pretty roundabout upriver ride along beside the Savannah River and then headed north up to Greenville. Rolling along a river with the dappled shadows on the pavement and the big trees on both sides is almost always a fine ride, especially of a Sunday.

I wanted to see if the BMW shop there in Greenville was open on Monday. If they were, I was going to give them a copy of my second book, in which I wrote about them saving me after the tree tried to kill me on The Blue Ridge Parkway a few years back.

This time I drifted in to the giant huge four-story Marriot-8-Day's-Motel-7-Inn on the interstate some ahead of the inevitable thunderstorms. Again, I was following my friends' advice, taking it easy, feeding the girl regular and safely, finding decent motels, stopping often, letting her take pictures. We did several two and three hundred mile days, and I don't think we did five hundred miles but a time or two the entire while we were gone.

Anyway, the proprietor of the giant Hyatt-Econo-Day's-

Motel-6 or 8-Inn there in Greenville, oddly, or so it seemed at the time, turned out to be another boy named Mike Patel. I am not making that up. The Tallgirl collected their business cards as we went. Looked like this Mike had his entire family working there.

Mike's grandfather, the elder Patel, the patriarch, approached me and explained, "You vill please to kindly remain your motorcycle to the front of the building vere it vill be safely out from the veather and velly carefully vatched."

Hard to take any offense when they treat you that way. And I was glad it was under cover when the impending late afternoon thunderstorms came through.

Next day we waited until the Greenville BMW shop would be open before we departed. It was a cool and cloudy morning, and the shop was on our way out of town. But Greenville BMW was closed, it being a Monday and all.

But the Blue Ridge Parkway was open. So that's where we ran to. It was my intention to take 'Nita the whole length of The Parkway and The Skyline Drive. It was still chilly and overcast, and we were in our leathers most of the day.

We got on The Ridge around Asheville and headed south so we could start at the far end of the road. Our intent was to ride it from one end to the other. But it was pretty obviously raining down that way, all over Mt. Pisgah. A couple riders going by northbound in wet raingear confirmed this. So, I turned it around and went north behind the wet riders and ahead of the weather. I hadn't hurt the Tallgirl with hard miles or bad food or bed bugs so far, and I didn't want to do it with mountain weather and a wet road now.

Turned out to be a good move. The next fifty miles north of Asheville, including Mt. Mitchell, were in the clouds. 'Nita just kept looking around and saying, "Oh, wow!" I believe she was quoting John Denver. We rode the several miles up Mt. Mitchell so she could be in the highest place east of The River.

Took her awhile to understand she really was in a cloud. The road was often wet, but if there was any rain, it had fallen ahead of us. It was medium damp and pretty chilly, but we weren't getting rained on. I believe I did go for my gloves for awhile, but that was as cold as it got. In fact, that was the only time I felt the need for gloves the whole trip. And Jimmy's handlebar balancers helped my arthritis, too.

That pattern held up throughout this whole ride. We'd begin the day in our leathers, and then get down to t-shirts and vests by mid- or late afternoon or so. I wasn't over-chilled or bad over-heated, either one, the whole ride. A few days to the north, I read an article in a local newspaper about how the bad rainy weather was ruining North Carolina's tourist season, hurting the economy bad. We sure got lucky in avoiding most of that.

A hundred miles up The Blue Ridge, the weather cleared, and the scenic nature of the eastern mountains became much more visible and spectacular. It was almost as if we came around a curve, and the clouds opened up suddenly and revealed the scenic splendor.

The Tallgirl exclaimed, "Oh Boy!" from behind me. She was surely quoting Buddy Holley that time. Shortly after that, 'Nita expanded her highway vocabulary to include, "Stop here, Tiger!"

A lot of the wildflowers and some of the rhododendrons on the roadside were in bloom. There were a few places that were spectacular and overwhelmingly beautiful. The weather just got better. We rode in our shirtsleeves mostly. The sky was often as beautiful as the mountain scenery. And the wildlife managed to stay out of the road for us.

This was when I truly understood and appreciated the great wisdom my friends had given me about showing it to her and then seeing it fresh again myself. I realized my face had cramped up from all the grinning I was doing. Every time I looked in the mirrors, I had a real happy woman up behind me. And I really was experiencing it all new and different through her eyes. I mean it had me taking a good hard long look at the way I been living my life all my life.

Before we got back home, 'Nita had used up eight of those throw-away cameras. She has a whole lot of pictures of something green at sixty miles an hour. But she also got some truly great photographs of the highway and shadows and the whitelines and deer and turkey and rivers and waterfalls and lakes and sunsets and old barns and flowers and bridges and mountains and valleys and the long vistas, the distance out beyond the handlebars.

The traffic was minimal the whole length of The Blue Ridge

and The Skyline. Oh, there was the occasional idiot, usually in a Winnebago, who couldn't handle the turns and inclines. They were, as usual, intent on going seventeen miles an hour. But their number was minimal this time. Traffic was generally light to sparse, and we often ran for twenty and thirty miles at a time without seeing a vehicle.

We did run into some other BMW riders headed to the national rally. A Canadian couple bought a copy of one of my books. I tried to give it to them, but they insisted on paying me in American money. I thought of the next few hundred miles as their tank of gas. We saw most of these folks again at the rally. Those Canadians said they hadn't stopped laughing since they opened the book. Then they bought the other one. I was real flattered; my vanity knows no boundaries.

Before the rally was done, I had reconfirmed what I had been told about my books being great bathroom books, wonderful airplane books, and fine recovering from a bad wreck books. And I learned that they are also considered terrific books to read while setting out a rainstorm or at the end of the road at the end of the day or during a long Northern Winter.

We stayed one night up on The Ridge at the Doughton Park Inn. There was no TV or radio or telephones. There was a balcony with a fine view of the mountains to the south. There was a damn good ham supper across the road. Juanita said the fried chicken was real tasty, too. I got some gas there so we could just jump on the road the next day. Then we wound up going back there for breakfast the next morning. Great biscuits.

And then that night, there was a spectacular sunset and a kid playing guitar real pretty there at the Inn. We had walked a quarter mile or so away from the Inn after supper. There was a scenic view of the bottom of a valley where some folks had come to a bad end in a flood a couple hundred years back.

And we wound up on a ridge downwind of the Inn itself. The kid was on the balcony there, picking his guitar, and we could hear it from where we were as we watched the mountain sun go down. When we got back, I complimented the boy on his music. He was fifteen and on vacation with his parents. As you might imagine, he was angry about both those things. My comment made his day.

Juanita made two mistakes the whole trip. And I knew it was going to happen. I knew it before we left. And I almost knew where it would happen.

About a hundred miles up the Blue Ridge, she began trying to help me ride. I spoke to her, said, "Baby, let me ride the bike." She hugged me and relaxed. Then again, maybe thirty miles later, there she was leaning into a curve after I had come out of it. And again, I spoke to her.

This time I said "please." And that was the end of that problem.

We managed the whole way up the Blue Ridge and Skyline Drive without getting rained on. Then when we came off the top end of the Skyline, there at Front Royal, the clouds were heavy and ominous in the west. The hard wind was blowing them toward us. I had intended to head over that way and then drop south down through the pretty mountains of West Virginia to get to Charleston and the BMW National Rally. But instead, I turned back south on I-81. And I got into Harrisonburg before the deluge came upon us.

I think this was the only time I ignored all my friends' advice. I tried to get one more exit down the road instead of bailing off when I should have. The storms came at us sideways from the west. Not only did we get wet and slammed around by the wicked wind, but there was nowhere to hide at that exit. I had to turn it around and ride back through the rain the eight miles to the exit I should have taken to begin with. I told the Tallgirl I did it on purpose, so we would be evenly soaked on both sides.

We spent about twenty minutes there under cover with a guy from Texas on a Gold Wing. He told a story about a semi-truck shedding suspension parts in front of him awhile back. Said he didn't drop the cycle, but he flattened both tires and broke both wheels before he got it all back under control. He complimented the AMA Safety Course wisdom about lining the bike up and hitting it straight on. He also praised ABS technology.

The storm decreased a little, and I jumped for the nearest motel. Mike Patel, manager. Again, I ain't making a bit of this up. 'Nita has their business cards to prove it all.

As we were both soaked and cold, I figured an early stop was in order. And it really was an OK place, and this Mike told us about a laundromat a couple miles off. Juanita got her first batch of pictures developed and learned something about high-speed photography with cheap cameras. And the food that evening at a nearby restaurant was especially good.

Next day we rode south and then west and on into Charleston, West Virginia for the BMW National Rally. We rode through White Sulphur Springs and past the Greenbrier along the way. Highway 60 through there is a real fine ride. I had rode this road before, and I wanted to make sure the Tallgirl saw some of it. We rolled into Charleston around mid-day.

The three days after that are a blur. My literary agency/legal staff, Joel, joined us there. I felt like Dr. Hunter S. Thompson, traveling with my attorney. Kept asking Joel if he could try to look a little more Samoan. And the three of us did one eight and two twelve hour days selling my books and tapes and CDs. The rally organizers had the vendors and just about everything else downtown at the Civic Center. So everyone had to park their machines on the fourth level of the nearby inconvenient parking garage. And then walk away from it all a long ways and for a long time.

Most of the riders were camped miles away on the campus of the university there. And they had to park their bikes in the parking lots some distance from their campsites. And the vendors got to stand on indoor concrete.

Logistically, I did real well, though. They put me between the bathroom and the beer there in the Civic Center. I was also between the Corbin and the Mayer motorcycle seat folks. Location, location.

A storm came through the first day. Came right down the Kanawha River Valley and blew the beer tent in the river. Several folks were taken to the hospital, and a dog in one of the other tents was rescued from drowning. In fact, there were quite a few storms. It looked like most of the folks there rode in wet.

I found some old friends among them. Old Harvey had rode in from Pennsylvania. I'd not seen him since he camped in my yard with his dog Mickey awhile back. Sydney had ridden up from Florida. Left Cal to home, but she rode up. I met a boy from Tampa, Aquarium John, who Karl The Kraut had sent to find me at the rally. Turned out John had a pair of heavy-duty shocks like the ones Karl had loaned me. We made arrangements to get together when we got home. Ran into Big Al and some others from the Central Florida Rally. Old Stray Dog was there and came by to say hello. The riders from Canada who had bought my books stopped by to say hello and buy the other one. Muriel from Vermont dropped by and so did some of the Damn Yankees I had met up there a couple years back, including Dana and old El Jefe himself.

And a whole bunch of other riders I didn't know came by to tell me how much they liked my CDs, how much they enjoy my books. Many asked when a third volume would be available. Here you go. Yeah, my vanity knows no limits.

One evening I did a reading from my books for about sixty people. One of the best audiences I've had yet. They laughed at all the right places, they were quiet when they were supposed to be, and a couple of them were near tears at appropriate junctures. Audience. Audience. Audience.

At the end of the exhausting three days, we had sold about a hundred and fifty books and such. More importantly, I had found some old friends and met some new ones. 'Nita had noticed that my thirty year old leather was coming apart. She commented that I had gotten lots more wear out of it than the cow had. Months before, I had given her the one I got myself for Christmas at the Army-Navy surplus store several years ago. And damned if she didn't find one hell of a deal on a new jacket for me and a pair of gloves for herself. Then she made the kid selling the jacket buy one of my books. She also got souvenir t-shirts for Jimmy G. and Karl The Kraut and a rally patch and pin for Bosco The Bandit.

By now, the Tallgirl knew what she was doing, and she packed and sent some unnecessary stuff back home with Joel. She had taken a lesson in that first thousand miles or so. Into an empty book box went a couple extra pair of shoes, my old leather jacket, some books, a pile of clothes she had figured out she wasn't going to get to wear, and a few pounds of girlstuff. We came out of Charleston without twenty of the forty pounds I had been worried about.

We rode out Sunday morning, along with a few thousand other riders, under low cold skies and threatening rain. We scattered like the last buffalo. Me and 'Nita headed north and then west along beside the Ohio River awhile before heading north again. My theory that good roads run along rivers was upheld again. This was a real pretty ride. And the weather cleared ahead of us one more time. There are some fine roads in this part of Ohio.

I had determined before we left home to avoid interstates even more than usual. So I had to navigate and brave several cities on the surface streets. Cities are truly weird places of a Sunday afternoon. I'm talking science fiction strange here.

In Columbus, we were briefly surrounded by children on bicycles. Must have been a hundred of them. And we were part of a religious parade of some sort for about five blocks. Looked to be Santaria or Obeah or something such as that. Winos stumbled into the street to talk to me and ask for donations. I think we were in the middle of two car chases and one drive-by yelling at. Cities.

When we got on the interstate around the Michigan line, the traffic came to a real serious halt within a short mile. A semi driver hollered down to tell me that there was about ten miles of it, that the interstate was closed down up ahead of us. It was a hot day, there was no shade, and this was no place to be with an air-cooled engine. Besides that, I was eager to get in a friendly garage so I could change my oil.

As we slowly moved forward, four feet at a time, in first gear, yet another verse from that old song occurred to me, the one about how, We are driven by the highway and governed by mysterious forces. We are loyal to only the distance and the motion, and we're ridin' stolen horses.

The Tallgirl inquired, "What do we do now?" I told her, quoting briefly from The Blues, "If you got a match, we can watch it burn."

And then for maybe the third or fourth time in my whole life, I dropped over onto the side of the road on the breakdown lane and rode slowly along beside the stopped traffic all the way to the end.

There we were detoured off west down a nasty beat to hell two-lane. With all the detoured traffic, it wasn't a lot better than setting still out on the interstate. Took me awhile to figure out where we were and maneuver my way out of it. That was about the last time I put a tire on an interstate this trip.

This was where 'Nita mentioned that the sky was a different shade of blue up there around the forty-fifth parallel. Her conclusion was that it was a deeper blue than the Southern sky. That night, she commented on the difference between the Northern and Southern skies at night.

After a week in Michigan, we headed back out to home. The big events there in Michigan were my dad's birthday, showing Juanita a Great Lake, and visiting Charlie Syms' widow and giving her a copy of *The Ghost of Scootertrash Past*. We also managed to visit Captain Zero's parents. It's always a joy just to hang out with Mother T. And I got to give her a copy of the new CD.

Also, my dad's neighbor, old A.J., he got to sit on that pretty red bike he had sold to me. I offered to let him ride it when I saw the look of nostalgic rapture on his face as he climbed on it. But he was content to just set there a minute and reflect on the miles.

So the New Full-Time Woman got to experience singing happy birthday to a man on his 82nd birthday, a July day with a high in the fifties, and wading in cold water. And she got to meet my few remaining relatives, including all my pretty nieces. Saw some old friends, too. Some of them old rumors and stories from The Bygone Days of Yore got confirmed for her.

And damned if 'Nita didn't box and send another pile of stuff home. I got my kitchen out of my saddle bag finally. And I came down out of Michigan with a much smaller load than I had left home with a couple weeks before. In fact, she got a little overzealous this time. Figuring we had mostly avoided rain so far, she cut herself down to just a couple changes of clothes.

I also came home with a much more knowledgeable woman. About half-way up The Ridge, she Got It. She understands why I do the things I do. She knows why I took off and left her in charge of my house and animals every Summer for the past twenty years, before we got together. Hell, she even understands why I ride to work every day, why I resent having to get in a vehicle to go anywhere. And she knows that somewhere between the amount she packed in the beginning and the load we got down to in Michigan is the perfect balance.

She understands all about loads and packing now. And she knows more about weather and scooter maintenance than she did. And on two occasions, she saved me. In a steeply inclined parking lot in West Virginia, I got the front wheel crimped too far and was about to just topple over sideways. And damned if the Tallgirl didn't see it coming, and she dropped her foot and held the bike up until I could get under it and hold it up myself. I thanked her. She smiled and said she didn't think I really wanted to lay it down.

And coming down from a scenic pull-over road back down to the Blue Ridge, she saved us both. I came up to the stop sign there at the junction, and, being a literate and law-abiding man, I stopped. As I eased the clutch out to get back to it, she spoke sharply in my ear.

She said, "Stop!"

I could tell by the tone of her voice that this didn't involve halting to photograph a bunny rabbit or some wildwood flowers, or quoting dead singers, so I stopped. And a fool in a station wagon came around the blind curve at about sixty. I believe I had the presence of mind to thank her again. It sure made up for over-packing and leaning into curves trying to help me ride.

Before this ride was over, the Tallgirl had her a three-tank habit and a highway tan. She's lookin' to put it down the road anytime she can. And she also knew most of the other words to the song.

She sure knows the part about, The screaming down the road at midnight, and about the rattle and the roar. She knows enough about it to want to get out there and do it all some more. She understands about the fire and the smoke and the jangle and the clatter and the clash. She knows all about the rumble and the thunder and about rollin' down the road with old lonesome long-gone scootertrash.

So I left Michigan with a fresh oil change, a lighter load, and a much more knowledgeable and experienced companion. In The Ghost of Scootertrash Past, I wrote a page of so of highway advice, sage knowledge and wisdom, truths from my miles and time out on the road.

I came in off this last ride with two more to add to that list of admonitions: Don't never yell "Where the hell are we?" at the driver in the dark. At least not when he doesn't know. And the other one is, Be real careful at the end of the month. Damn road cops are all out there trying to fill their quotas.

The weather was trying hard to make a mess of our departure from Michigan. I had over-tarried, as I often do. It was nearly cold and nearly raining for the first couple hundred miles outbound. I got to Fort Wayne and immediately headed west to try to get away from the southbound weather. That front was bowed into kind of a U-shape with the open end wobbling south. I sort of settled into the clear part and tried to stay inside and ahead of it.

That took us along U.S. 24, a fine two-lane, into Reynolds. There the weather cleared off to our left side, so we dropped south to Lafayette and took U.S. 231 on south from there. I don't recall where we stayed that night, but there was no one named Patel to welcome us, and I kind of felt bad about that.

That 231 was another real good two-lane, and the weather was still off behind of us. It didn't really feel like we were running from it, so we stayed on 231 all the way to the Ohio River there at Owensboro, Kentucky. I was doing something right, as 'Nita took a lot of pictures in which the weather in front of us was clear and fine and that in our mirrors was dark and ominous.

It had been my sort of secret original intention to try to work our way west over to that Land Between The Lakes area in Kentucky. But now the weather was pushing us east away from that region. Years back, me and Bosco The Bandit rode that road, and I still have some fine memories of that ride. But this current weather was still looming and threatening off to the west, so we continued southbound to Nashville.

We had decided to find the north end of the Natchez Trace as kind of a consolation ride. I had never come at Nashville from the north on U.S. 431 before. And I got lost, then I got confused, then I got frustrated, then I got pissed off, and then I got lost again. Then I finally gave up and put us into a motel, Rick Patel, manager, before the evening rains began.

Somehow, 'Nita had collected a bunch of Nashville brochures and maps and such. And she spent some time that evening while it rained figuring it out. The corporate city of Nashville isn't real concerned about folks finding the top end of the Natchez Trace. Apparently there is little corporate profit in history. So it took her awhile. The next morning she navigated us out of town and straight to the northern terminus of the Natchez Trace, where she took a picture.

She was tenacious, and it put me in mind of Captain Zero twenty-some years back when he discovered The Trace from the other end, before it was even finished, during The Perfect Ride. He was similarly determined. And, as I told Juanita about twenty miles down the road, it was a far better ride than the Land Between The Lakes.

The north end of The Trace is higher and hillier than the southern end. Just the opposite of The Blue Ridge. The real problem with The Natchez Trace is that it runs northeast to southwest. And I ain't never going neither of those ways. But, other than a local biker and a couple guys hauling boats, it was stone empty. The speed limit is fifty, but the local rider was doing ninety, and the guys with the boats were going thirty-five, so I didn't spend much time with any of them. No, I just held it around the speed limit and occasionally responded to "Stop here, Tiger!"

One of those stops was at a place called She Boss. Turns out the Indian who owned the trading post there in the early 1800s used to refer his customers to his wife by explaining, "She boss."

The Tallgirl liked that a lot.

We continued on down through the verdant hills to Tupelo, where I parked in some shade at the Visitors' Center. While 'Nita looked for postcards and souvenirs, I started talking to the nice Ranger Lady who was running things there. I reminisced about the sweet old woman who used to be there. And this new girl, she knew my old friend. Told me her name and said she had retired.

I told her I knew that but had no idea how to contact her. She suggested I leave a copy of *The Ghost of Scootertrash Past* with her, and she would deliver it to the sweet old woman if she could find her. I did. I sure hope that happens. But if it doesn't, I suspect my book will get passed around there among the workers at the Visitors' Center. 'Nita found a bunch of things, including a Natchez Trace t-shirt for Captain Zero.

Then, we departed The Trace and headed away from the weather and east into Alabama. Then the weather bent us south to Tuscaloosa. And again, I found a wonderful two-lane, U.S. 43, to do it on. I planned to get back on that road again the next day, but this time the weather turned us east again and then south down

U.S. 331, through Montgomery, and into the Florida Panhandle. And that was another fine ride, in spite of the frequent local road repair and construction projects. Pretty country.

That weather caught up with us around DeFuniak Springs. Actually, I guess we finally caught up with it. The storm was looming huge out over the Gulf twenty or thirty miles in front of us. I stopped in an abandoned plazamall so I could ride up under cover. In retrospect, there was no point in stopping. We could ride either east or west or back north from where we came. The Gulf of Mexico was to the south. And we had to go east, no matter what the rainstorms were fixin' to do.

The weather didn't look like it was going to improve much, so we stayed right there and took a tour of a local winery. Then we settled in for the evening at a motel there, nearby a restaurant with the best hush puppies I've had in years.

Hoping to beat the lingering weather, we got up real early the next morning and got into our leathers. There was a quarter moon hanging low in the dark eastern sky waiting for the dawn to come get it. The highway was waiting for the cycle. And the rain was waiting for us some to the east of Panama City on U.S. 98.

In the next hundred miles, we got to do most of the rain-related things that we hadn't had to do in the previous 3000 miles. We stopped and had some breakfast, hoping the rain would go away. We got into our raingear and faceshields. We stopped under cover of a closed-up fish market to set out some hard rain. We rode through some heavy storms and some steady downpours. We watched the squall lines roll in off the Gulf. We took our rain suits off and made it rain again soon afterward. We watched the lightning flash and burn out over the Gulf.

But, in spite of the weather, I was able to run sixty and sixty-five out there on U.S. 98. There was little traffic along the Gulf as we rode east. When it opened up to four lanes, south of Perry, there was even less. Once again, I was real glad for alternatives to the superslabs.

By now, the New Full-Time Woman, she had some miles on her. Her response to the threatening weather ahead of us was to smile and suggest we just keep right on through it. And damned if she wasn't right. We did have to stop somewhere on 98 at a remote crossroads to get gas. And while 'Nita went in to pay for it, three cops showed up. Actually it was three cop cars with five cops. They didn't quite circle my bike in a predatory manner, but they looked me over closely. Then they gathered in a group and frowned at me and discussed things. And then they walked away.

This was my second encounter with the police on this trip. The first one was when a guy came up to me at the BMW rally. He introduced himself, told me how much he had enjoyed my first book, and bought a copy of the second one. Then he said that he was a cop in a town in Michigan, and he gave me a Get Out of Jail Free card.

He smiled and said, "After reading your first book, I think you might need this." Damn shame it's only good in his personal jurisdiction.

Sometime after the multiple-cop encounter, trying hard to use the good advice I had gotten before departure, I stopped in Perry and fed Juanita a seafood lunch that just couldn't be beat. Then we headed inland some and on to home. There was bad weather in our mirrors the whole time.

We rolled in some ahead of the routine storms. Captain Zero had done an exemplary animal- and house-sitting job. All the dogs and the horse and donkey had gained weight and developed a love and allegiance for The Captain. The house was in fine shape, too.

It took me some time, as it almost always does when I get back in from a long ride, to unload the bike. Somehow the return, the completion of the circle, always makes me sad. It seems the highway call and the roadsongs get stronger as you get nearer to finished.

And I always manage to recall that next to the last verse of The Scootertrash Blues, which address this, It was near day's end when I rolled in. I shut it down with a mournful cry. I had come to the end of my journey, but my soul still longed to fly. And it was with deep regret that I unloaded in the soft sunset. I was glad I was by myself, so no one else could see me cry.

This time, as I unloaded my ride, the rain began to fall. And then, I finished that previous, penultimate verse, Yeah, some of us belong to be nomads. We just need the highway and the motion and a piece of the distance; we don't need to know about the why. We need to ride beside the whitelines and to total up the milepost signs. We need that the way that eagles need the sky.

chapter twenty-two
EPILOGUE

School started back up about a week ago. And, as we have all learned, work is a hindrance. It detracts from things like riding in the Florida Fall, and writing books about it.

Florida Fall fell last Tuesday. Captain Zero is soon to depart on the Amtrak. He is headed to D.C., and then on to New York City, and then New England and Boston. From there, he will probably fly on the airplane back to San Francisco and then back to Detroit for a reunion with old friends in the North. I think his plan from there is to return home to San Francisco to celebrate his 60th birthday. I know he is doing all this just to rub it in, to make me feel even worse about the hindrance that is work.

Anyway, Fall fell a little earlier than usual, or so it seemed. I can feel it in the air late at night. This morning was the first time since before Memorial Day that I had to put a denim jacket on riding to work in the morning. Some real fine riding's coming up here.

Florida Fall means that the temperature no longer goes up to ninety and beyond. No, the Fall highs are mostly in the low eighties. Sometimes it drops to the sixties at night. It's a little drier, less humid. I think there is more wind, and it blows some cooler. I do know that the barometer bounces around and makes a mess of my arthritis.

In the meantime, some real fine things have happened on the highway and in the sky around here. A month ago, the full moon was accompanied by Mars. Paper said it was the closest Mars has been to the Earth in the past 650,000 years or so. That's the kind of statistic that makes me wonder about science. Didn't seem near so close last time.

The Red Ride needed some regular, basic maintenance and a new driveshaft boot and a couple other things after 3500 hard miles. I loaded it on Bosco The Bandit's truck and headed to Dirty Street first chance I got. Karl The Kraut had done some work in my absence, and he was holding my old Black Bike hostage. He also had Bosco's old /7, Donner, holding it for ransom. Captain Zero (ret'd.), he came with us to drive the truck home.

We unloaded my Red Ride there on Dirty Street. Then we set and talked with Karl and Jimmy G. awhile. I told them about the Tallgirl's first long ride. Gave them their souvenir t-shirts and thanked them for their help and advice. Then we took Karl's shocks off The Red Ride, replaced them with the ones I had gotten from Aquarium John, and put Karl's back on his cycle. Then me and Bosco paid our ransons and collected our bikes, and were all set to head home.

Karl The Kraut closed his shop and suggested it would be good if we were to buy him supper. Jimmy G. agreed, so the four of us rode out together in a group with Captain Zero behind us in the truck. As we headed north, the full moon rose nearly red with Mars right behind it. Hell of a sight. We all forgot about supper. Instead, I rode a hundred miles with the moon rising off my right handlegrip and some good friends on the highway with me.

A couple days later, we delivered Captain Zero into the arms of the Amtrak, northbound. The Tallgirl and I talked about how much we already missed him as we drove home that evening.

There was a pretty spectacular full moon rise the next month as well. Mars came up ahead of the moon this time. And me and the Tallgirl were out there on the highway to witness it all. Another fine ride. Moon and Mars came up a bright amber color this time.

In the meantime, I got the Red Ride back from Karl The Kraut. Been alternating between cycles in to work and around local. 'Nita and I were on the Red Ride under that recent moon.

Come the next full moon, I intend to get on that old Black Bike of mine, the one with over a half a million miles, the one I rode to both borders and both oceans. The one I been down with a couple times. Me and that old Black Bike are going out under this next full moon by ourselves.

And the reason for that is, as the very last verse of The

Lonesome Lowdown Long-gone Outbound Scootertrash Blues explains, I don't need a kind word. I ain't lookin' for no sympathy or comfort or a way to lament or atone. I ain't tryin' to find no answers or have no revelations, and I sure as hell ain't hopin' to find no home. I just know that when it gets all the way to beyond the bendin' end, sometimes a man just needs to ride alone.

I was born into a Golden Age in America; I celebrated my 65th birthday a month or so ago. These were the best times this country has ever known for a lot of reasons. I grew up in an era when America had the finest education system the world has ever known.

So, I ride old German iron. When I'm not doing that, I am often afield with a dog and a gun or standing in an incoming tide with my fishing pole or riding my horse. I prefer pale horses and all my good dogs have been black. I like my women laughing, my occasional drink of whiskey is taken neat, and I drink my coffee black. I can't abide a soap opera or a psychodrama. I am better off outdoors, unless it's cold, and then I'm better off farther south and outdoors.

Contact Tiger at:
drmarktigeredmonds.com